Ninnuock

[The People]

D1598663

APR - 2 1996

Ninnuock

[The People]

The Algonkian People of New England

S<small>TEVEN</small> F. J<small>OHNSON</small>

Bliss Publishing Company, Inc.,
P. O. Box 920, Marlborough, Massachusetts 01752

Published 1995. First edition

99 98 97 96 95   5 4 3 2 1

Library of Congress Cataloging-in-Publication Data

Johnson, Steven F., 1954
        Ninnuock (The People): The Algonkian People of New England / by Steven F.
Johnson—1st. edition.

Includes bibliographical references and index.
ISBN 0-9625144-2-X
1. Algonkian Indians—History. 2. Algonkian Indians—Social life and customs. I. Title.
E99.A35J65   1993
974'.004973—dc20

93-34546
CIP

Cover illustration by Antowine Warrior
Illustrations by Christopher Daigneault

PRINTED IN THE UNITED STATES OF AMERICA
BLISS PUBLISHING COMPANY, INC.
P.O.BOX 920, MARLBOROUGH, MASSACHUSETTS 01752

Table of Contents

Maps

Illustrations

Foreword

From a very early age I sat and listened as my grandmother would tell me the stories of our people, the Algonquians of Canada. I started then to desire to know more so that I might be able, one day, to teach others the truth about the people, who before the coming of the French and English, so proudly walked the length and breadth of the land. As the years passed and I no longer had my grandmother to teach me, I was forced to rely on books as my sole source of information. To my great disappointment there was little that could be found on the great tribal peoples of the Northeast. Most of what has been written is on the native peoples to the West and South, while the story of the Algonkians is too often reduced to the persons of Samoset, Squanto and the first Thanksgiving at Plymouth.

This moving book, *Ninnuock: The Algonkian People of New England* is such a blessing to me! It is the story of the people who early on came into contact with European mariners in quest of new horizons to discover. The experience of the Algonkians is told through the use of first hand accounts and original documents from the colonial period. In the ten or so years in which I have travelled the New England and Mid-Atlantic states and three countries to teach others about native peoples, I have never had such a complete tool! Thanks to the work of my friend Mr. Steve Johnson, instead of having to carry several volumes with me, I will now only carry just this one when talking about the tribes of New England.

When I read this work for the first time, I was once again struck with the need to share with people the lessons that can be learned from another culture such as the vast and proud Algonkian people. I have often said to those that I have had the privilege of teaching, "Come and sit straight in the lodge, and you will learn of the people who for generations have hunted and planted in this land. Come and listen at the council and you will learn of truth for your life today. Come and learn my friends, learn for the future from those of the past."

STRAIGHT ARROW
(TIM PATERSON)

Preface

This book is about the Native American experience in New England, from before the Europeans arrived to the American Revolution. It is impossible to write about the Native American history of colonial New England without becoming involved in the controversy that exists today over their past and present treatment. Because the New England Algonkians relied on an oral tradition, much of which went unrecorded, the material used in this book comes primarily from contemporary colonial authors and court records. These sources tell the story of repeated mistreatment of the indigenous people at the hands of European colonists.

Of all the Native American cultures in this country, that of the area we today call New England was the hardest hit by the European invasion. In the South and West the Native Americans today have some traditions and language intact, but in New England very little remains in comparison, largely due to the emphatic efforts of the English colonists. Aspects of the Algonkian culture must be pieced back together using primary historical sources and archaeological findings. For example, the northern Algonkian dialects of Abenaki, Maliseet and Mic Mac are still spoken, but most of the other ten or so dialects of southern New England are gone, and their pronouncions in most cases can only be guessed at.

Most of what we know about traditional Algonkian tribal culture in colonial New England comes from the contemporary writings of English, French and Dutch authors. It has been my intention to show that it is possible to reconstruct a fairly accurate portrayal of Algonkian life in colonial New England using these sources.

The ancestors of the present-day Algonkian tribes in New England left behind a variety of stone implements, pottery fragments and numerous enduring place names. Yet, much has been lost in Algonkian tribal culture. Massachusett, Nipmuck, Pequot-Mohegan and Wampanoag are Algonkian dialects that are no longer spoken, and the fate of the people who spoke them has become somehow muted. I was moved as I wrote this work by the voices of their historic leaders Massasoit, Uncas, Wannalancit, Metacom and Samson Occom. Each of these native leaders sought out different approaches to preserve their people alongside the English. Their attempts at coexistence, military alliance, and assimilation all failed as the initial phase of English colonization rapidly turned into an all-out invasion of their hunting and planting grounds. Ultimately, as an act of self-preservation, some of the Algonkian tribes chose armed force to stem the overseas intrusion, but this only served to accelerate their demise. This book is a recreation of the tragic story of the Algonkian people in colonial New England.

For a Euro-American such as myself it may seem an inappropriate endeavor to tell the story of a people to which I do not belong by right of blood. However, any one who researches the Algonkian culture of colonial New England even briefly, will come to understand that here is a society that was shattered by the ravages of war, social injustice and disease. As a historian and longtime resident of New England, the tragic experience of the Algonkians speaks to a deep sentiment that I have for the native people and their ancestral land.

S. F. J.

Acknowledgements

It is said that there is "wisdom in many counselors." I have gained an even greater appreciation for this proverb during the research and writing of this book. In the completion of the final manuscript, it was my fortune to have the advice of Professor Charles Carroll of the Department of History at the University of Massachusetts at Lowell, Charlene Prince, who serves as the curator and librarian for the Mashantucket Pequot in Ledyard, Connecticut and Brigit Truex of the New England Native American Institute in Worcester, Massachusetts. Their insightful comments were invaluable in finalizing this work. Likewise, I want to extend a thank you to two colleagues: Caren O'Brien, who translated several Jesuit letters from the French, and Mary Egan for helping me out of several word processing jams. And finally, a special thanks goes to Marguerite Howe, who edited the final manuscript, and to my family who were a continual source of encouragement in the completion of this work.

S. F. J.

elakomkwik meaning "they are our relatives." However, the Algonkian nations generally referred to themselves by the collective title *Ninnuock,* a term that means "the people." Some of the New England tribes that belonged to this linguistic family were the Pequots, Narragansetts, Wampanoags, Massachusetts and Pocumtucks, who probably entered New England from the southwest, and the Pennacooks and Abenaki, who may have come into the region from the north. Besides these major confederacies, there existed certain lesser tribes that remained independent of the stronger nations by either paying tribute to them, or having the able strength in warriors to defend themselves. Among these tribes were the Mahican and Mohegan, who occupied southwestern New England, and the several Nipmuck groups of central Massachusetts. In western New England, the Mohawks, a member tribe of the Five Nations of the Iroquois, attempted to expand their political influence eastward. From their homeland in New York state, the Mohawks sent out war parties against the different Algonkian tribes.

Possibly the need for united strength to combat these Mohawk invaders was one of the key reasons confederated Algonkian nations arose in New England, besides the quarrels among the Algonkian tribes themselves. Incursionary strikes by enemy war parties were a fact of tribal life among the seven confederacies, and this led them to erect stockaded villages within their domains. Within these forts they resided during times of war. As the intermittent Mohawk strikes increased, so did the repair and building of new stockades. Such was the case of the Pawtucket people in the lower Merrimac Valley, when confronted with the increased attacks of the Mohawks in the 1660s.

Of the major Algonkian confederations existing in 17th century New England, those of southern New England had the largest populations. The Pequots appear to have been the most expansionistic of the southern New England confederacies. Situated roughly east of the Connecticut River and west of Narragansett Bay, the Pequots and their allies, the Western Niantic, settled along the Thames, Shetucket and Mystic rivers of eastern Connecticut. In his *Historical Collections of the Indians in New England,* Daniel Gookin claims, "the Pequods were a people seated in the most southerly bounds of New England . . . . Their chief sachem held dominion over divers petty sagamores; as over part of Long Island, over the Mohegans, and over the sagamores of Quinapeake, yea over all the people that dwelt upon Connecticut River, and over some of the most southerly inhabitants of Nipmuck country, about Quinnabaag." At the height of its power there were twenty-six sagamores in the Pequot confederation. These people and their Western Niantic allies built at least three stockaded forts in eastern Connecticut. Pequot territory contained areas of fine timber and fertile soil, which brought them into conflict with encroaching English settlers in the 1630s. During his lifetime, Sachem Sassacus and his approximately four thousand men had no intention of surrendering their land to the English, just as they had managed to preserve it from Narragansett encroachment. Sassacus was a diplomatic warrior. Through several secret meetings he attempted to convince the Narragansetts to forget the long-standing feuds between their peoples, and to unite in an offensive against the New England colonies. Though this coalition was never successfully formed, because of Roger Williams' intercession, Sassacus remained opposed to the settlers' presence in Pequot country. Sassacus' deteriorating relations with the New England colonies eventually led the two sides into the destructive destiny of 1637, the year when the Pequots met their unfortunate demise at the hands of the English. During the single most important military campaign of the Pequot War, a combined force of Connecticut and Massachusetts militiamen razed a Pequot fort on the Mystic River, which resulted in the deaths of hundreds of tribespeople.

A powerful nation equal to the Pequots was the Narragansetts. Their territory included land around Narragansett Bay and the majority of the islands in it, now most of present-day Rhode Island. As a confederated nation, the Narragansetts had such tribes as the Cowwesets, Eastern Niantics, Pawtuxets, Shawomets and several of the Nipmuck villages under their jurisdiction. Concerning this nation Gookin states, "The Narragansetts were a great people heretofore; and the territory of their Sachem extended about thirty or forty miles from Sekunk [Seekonk, Massachusetts] and Narragansett bay, including Rhode Island and other islands in that bay, being their east and north bounds or border, and so running westerly unto a place called Wekapage [Weekapaug, Rhode Island], four or five miles to the eastward of Pawcutuk River, which was reckoned for their south and west border, and the easternmost limits of the

Pequots." Narragansett country also included Block Island, located south of present-day Rhode Island.

Of the principal Algonkian nations in New England, the Narragansetts were the most populous. Roger Williams mentions that a traveller might come across numerous tribal villages on a short sojourn through their country. These people were for a time simultaneously governed by two sachems, Canonicus and his nephew, Miantonomo. With a population of over five thousand men, the Narragansetts were able to adequately defend their homeland from enemy encroachment. Their considerable prowess allowed them to maintain possession of a region totally surrounded by equally powerful nations. Holding their own lands, the Narragansetts carried out offensive stikes into the lands of the Pequots, Wampanoags and Massachusetts, and shared Narragansett Bay with their Wampanoag rivals. The struggle for the islands in this bay was probably often a provocation for incursionary strikes of one tribe against another. Verrazzano, an Italian explorer who sailed into Narragansett Bay in 1524, traded with one of these two tribal nations. During his stay his men journeyed into the adjacent woods, which Verrazzano describes as "great and thick." Here they came upon extensive cornfields cultivated by the native people.

It was the Narragansetts' good fortune that they were situated along this bay, for these waters were plentiful in shellfish. From periwinkle shells these people manufactured large stores of white wampum. Black wampum, which was deemed more valuable than the white, was made from the quahog shell. The people of this bay took advantage of their situation. According to William Wood, the Narragansetts became the minters for all the other New England tribes. Of course, this is not to say that the other coastal Algonkian nations of the region were entirely dependent on the Narragansetts, for they, too, were capable of producing shell money. With their large stores of wampum, the Narragansetts were able to ransom captives, purchase assistance from other tribes, and decorate their robes with the most beautiful shell arrangements. The English colonists in New England used wampum as legal tender because of the shortage of coinage, which was continually being drained off to pay debts in England. Corn, furs and tobacco, commonly called "country pay" by the colonists, were also used by them as money substitutes. A stipulation of the treaty between the United Colo-

ALGONKIAN TRIBES OF CONNECTICUT AND RHODE ISLAND

nies of New England and the Narragansetts, in 1645, states in part that the Narragansetts "should pay or cause to be paid at Boston. . . 2000 fathom of good white wampum, or a third part of black wampumpeag . . . the Commissioners accept for satisfaction of former charges expended."

The Narragansetts, in addition to their strength in warriors, and the influence that their large stores of wampum could purchase, also possessed several virtually impregnable fortifications, such as the stockade they built at present-day South Kingstown, Rhode Island. This fort was constructed on a knoll surrounded by swamp, and the Algonkians often used the swamplands after a skirmish, to conceal their escape route. Impenetrable thickets and boggy terrain made pursuit by the colonial militias militarily unwise. For these reasons, the Narragansetts located one of their forts in the swamps at South Kingstown during King Philip's War (1675-1676). With such potentially powerful neighbors at the doorstep of the Plymouth and Massachusetts Bay colonies, the English were usually quite diplomatic in their dealings with them. Providence Plantation, founded in the midst of the Narragansetts by Roger Williams, coexisted in a relatively peaceful manner with the English until King Philip's War, when the Narragansetts were left with no alternative but to unleash their force upon the English in an attempt to reassert their former position of prominence in New England.

Historically, the most famous of the Algonkian nations in New England was the *Wampomaugs*, more commonly known by the tribal name of Wampanoags. This tribal confederation wielded power from the eastern shore of Narragansett Bay to the outer beaches of Cape Cod, although the tribes on the outer Cape were not directly under the influence of the Wampanoags. Nauset sagamores held leadership over this supposed outer Cape confederation. However, the Nausets were generally agreeable to the decisions made by the Wampanoag sachem Massasoit and his sons. Massasoit's nation was exclusively in southeastern Massachusetts, excepting one sagamore at Massachusetts Bay. Also, under the Wampanoags' jurisdiction were the native peoples on Nantucket, Martha's Vineyard and the Elizabeth Islands. The modern historian is more familiar with the Wampanoags than other tribal groups in southern New England, because of the writings left by several of the Plymouth colonists. One of these men, Edward Winslow, wrote several fascinating accounts about the Pilgrims' involvement with the Wampanoags.

In the Algonkian dialect, the word *Wampomaug* means "people of the white wampum" which rightly fit them, for the Wampanoags were able producers of the shell money that passed among the Algonkians in New England. The word *wampom* can also denote "place of the dawn," or "east." Hence, *Wampomaug* may also mean "people of the eastland," which they definitely were, for this nation was the furthest east of the five principal nations in southern New England. Within the domain of these people stood numerous villages, most pledging their allegiance to Massasoit. Under him, naturally, were his own people, the Pokanokets. They had built their wigwams near Mount Hope on the northern shores of Narragansett Bay. The Pokanokets' two principal villages were *Kikemuit* and *Sowams,* which were also the major tribal seats of the Wampanoag nation, and the villages where Sachem Massasoit and his family resided. Near what is now the town of Middleboro, Massachusetts, in the vicinity of Lake Assawompsett, lived the Nemaskets and Munponsets. Sagamore Tuspaquin, or "Black Feather," was the leader of these people. The Pocassets lived to the south from the present-day town of Somerset, Massachusetts to Tiverton, Rhode Island. Their leader, Sagamore Conbitant, early on became distrustful of the Plymouth colonists. He was succeeded by his daughter, Weetamoo, who became the wife of Wamsutta (Alexander), one of Massasoit's sons. The principal village of the Pocassets was *Mattapoisett.* To the south of the Pocassets lived the Sakonnet tribe, whose lands extended along the western shore of Buzzard's Bay over to the Sakonnet River. This group was ruled by Squaw Sachem Awashonks, and their main settlement was near present-day Little Compton, Rhode Island. At what is now Plymouth, Massachusetts resided the Patuxet tribe, whose famous member, Squanto, befriended the Pilgrims. Almost all the Patuxets, with the known exception of Squanto, perished during the years of the plague before the Pilgrims' arrival in New England. To the southeast of Patuxet, along the coast of Cape Cod Bay, lived a small tribe known as the Manamets, whose village was situated near what is now Sandwich, Massachusetts.

Continuing south from Manamet one enters onto Cape Cod, where then, as now, reside the *Masnipi* ("great water") or Mashpee people. This tribe often fished the waters of Santuit and Contuit ponds and adjacent Coatuit Brook. The Mashpee people have a tradition concerning the origins of these waters that involves a giant sea trout. One of these legendary creatures desired to furnish this tribe with a stream of fresh water, so it forced its way inland from the ocean. The stress of this undertaking became so great that the trout died, but it soon was replaced by another that plowed a trench all the way to Santuit Pond. The deceased trout was pushing a sizeable mound of earth when it gave out, and this served to explain the origins of both the brook and this prominent knoll.

Further east towards the outer Cape, the Matachees tribe, whose sagamore was Iyanough, claimed the land. This tribe occupied the land bordering Cape Cod Bay and Nantucket Sound, and their main village was *Matachees*. These people are also sometimes referred to as the Cummaquids, Chawmun or Shaumes. Quite near to the Matachees resided the Nobsquasset tribe, much of whose land also bordered Nantucket Sound. Directly east of the Nobsquassets, facing out into the Atlantic Ocean, was the land of the Monomoys. This tribe occupied the site of the present-day community of Chatham, Massachusetts; and Monomoy Island, south of Chatham, bears the tribe's name. North of the Monomoys were the lands of the Nausets, the most powerful of the outer Cape tribes. Nauset hunting grounds extended northward to the outer tip of Cape Cod at Provincetown. One of their favorite haunts was the Pamet River area, and as a result several early accounts of these people give them the tribal name of Paomet or Pawmet.

Scattered on the islands off Cape Cod were several other tribes that participated in the Wampanoag confederation. The native people around the Elizabeth Islands had a main village which they called *Sokones*. It stood in the vicinity of present-day Falmouth, Massachusetts. Sokones was probably a village belonging to the Mashpees. On *Nauticon* or Nantucket resided the Tomokommoth tribe and their neighbors, the Capawicks, who lived on *Nope* or Martha's Vineyard. The Wampanoag confederation is said even to have had one sagamore under them, known to the Pilgrims as Obbatinewat of *Shawmut*. The village of *Shawmut* was situated in the same general area where today stands the city of Boston, an area deep within the territory of the Massachusetts confederation. Apparently, even a few Nipmuck sagamores paid allegiance to the Wampanoag sachem.

The Wampanog confederation must have been strong, for it was able to maintain itself though entirely closed off by the lands of the Narragansetts and Massachusetts. Gookin claims that the Wampanoags frequently "held war with the Narragansetts; and often joined with the Massachusetts, as friends and confederates against the Narragansetts." During the plague of 1617 in New England, many of Massasoit's subjects perished. The Wampanoags' weakened condition after the plague, along with fear that the Narragansetts would commence a new wave of attacks, were probably the main reasons that Massasoit entered into an alliance with Plymouth Colony. Wampanoag and Englishman lived under this alliance until shortly after Massasoit's death in 1661. After his death, suspicion on both sides increased with each passing year. Metacom (King Philip), the great sachem's second son, became the tribal leader after his elder brother died suddenly, shortly after a visit to Marshfield. Under Metacom Anglo-Algonkian relations became strained, but each side attempted to avoid war. However, in 1675 open conflict broke out between the Plymouth Colony and some of the Wampanoag tribes under Metacom's leadership.

North of the Wampanoags' territory, centered along Massachusetts Bay, were the tribes of the Massachusett confederation. This nation claimed control over a sizeable portion of colonial New England, which is most of present-day Massachusetts, from the Connecticut River to the coast. Some of the older men in the Massachusett nation told Gookin that in the days before the plague, the Nashuas, Nipmucks and Pocumtucks were members of the Massachusett confederation. The confederation derived its name from the hills near the bay, for in this Algonkian dialect, *Massachusett* means "great hill place," a reference perhaps to the Blue Hills. Sachem Nanapashamet, who died around 1619 at the hands of either Mic Mac or Maliseet warriors, presided over this nation. His wife, known to the English as "Squaw Sachem," continued to lead the Massachusett confederation after her husband's death.

This Algonkian confederation owned some of the finest land in New England. The Charles and *Missituck* (Mystic) rivers were some of their favorite fishing and hunting places. All the islands in the bay belonged to them, and according to the Pilgrims, who journeyed to the lands of the Massachusett in l621, most of these islands were cleared end to end and planted in corn. The same plague that killed so many of their Wampanoag allies had an even more devastating impact on the Massachusett. From an approximate population of three thousand warriors before this contagious epidemic, they were afterwards reduced to a fighting force of about one thousand. From the tribal seat of *Winnisemit,* near the marshes of present-day Everett-Malden, Massachusetts, Squaw Sachem and her sons presided over the remnants of the Massachusett nation, which now consisted mainly of the Saugus tribe and other diminished groups near the bay. In 1631, a recurrence of the smallpox epidemic reduced the numbers of the Saugus people. By 1670, their population had decreased even further.

With the great Massachusett confederation waning at its center on Massachusetts Bay, their inland allies were forced to join other tribal nations for their own security. Certain of these allied nations seem to have developed local confederated nations from the remnants of the Massachusett confederation. Such was probably the case with the Connecticut River tribes that participated in the Pocumtuck confederation.

Among the more noteable Massachusett sachems and sagamores were Checkatabutt, his son Josiah, Montowampate, Wonohaquaham, Cutshamequin and Tahattawan. Montowampate acted as a sagamore in the Saugus area, while Wonohaquaham resided at *Winnisemit.* Sagamore Tahattawan and his son John Tahattawan led the Nashobas, who lived along the Concord River and nearby Nagog Pond. The latter area is the site of occasional earth tremors, which led the Nashobas to claim that Nashoba Hill, in the vicinity of Nagog Pond, was hollow. The tribe believed wind sometimes got pent up inside this hill causing a rumbling noise.

At the zenith of its strength, many tribes found protection as members of the Massachusett confederation. The Ponkapoags (Canton, Massachusetts), Neponsets (Milton, Massachusetts), Wessagussets (Weymouth, Massachusetts), Shawmuts (Boston, Massachusetts), Winnisemits (Everett-Malden, Massachusetts), Nahants (Nahant, Massachusetts), Saugus or Saugussets (Saugus, Massachusetts), Nashobas (Concord-Littleton, Massachusetts), Nashuas (Sterling, Massachusetts) and many other tribes among the Nipmuck were among their numbers. The Massachusett, along with their Nipmuck allies, built up considerable experience in warfare, for they were often called upon to assist the Wampanoags in fighting

ALGONKIAN TRIBES OF MASSACHUSETTS

the Narragansetts, or supporting the Pocumtucks and Nipmucks in their struggles with the Mohawks.

The Pocumtuck confederation claimed the middle portion of the Connecticut River Valley, from southeastern Vermont and southwestern New Hampshire to the vicinity of present-day Hartford, Connecticut. At least seven different river tribes participated in this Algonkian nation, namely their main allies, the Norwottucks, the Agawams (Springfield, Massachusetts) and the Squawkheags (Northfield, Massachusetts). The Squawkheags also involved themselves in the Pennacook and Sokoki nations. In 1687, the Squawkheag chieftan, Sagamore Nawelet, along with his tribal subordinates Gongequa, Aspiambemet, Hadarawansett and Meganichcha, signed a land deed granting the town of Northfield a six mile wide tract of land extending on both sides of the Connecticut River. Other active Pocumtuck member tribes were the Tunxis, Wangunk and Podunk peoples of northern Connecticut. Before the smallpox plague of 1634 ravaged the Connecticut River tribes, there were probably never more than one to two thousand warriors in the Pocumtuck confederation. Many of these people resided near the tribal seat of *Pocumtuck,* which was located in the present-day town of Deerfield, Massachusetts.

In New Hampshire the resident tribes of the Pennacook or Pawtucket confederation were sometimes allied with the Massachusett nation. As one of the two great Abenaki nations in northern New England, the Pennacook confederation had its main seats of government at several villages along the Merrimac River. One tribal seat, located near the falls at what is now Lowell, Massachusetts, was called *Pawtucket,* meaning "place of the loud noise or falling water." A sister village at the confluence of the *Musketaquid* (Concord River) and the Merrimac, was called *Wamesit,* meaning "there is enough space for all." Many of the Pennacook people gathered at this site during the annual fishing season. Sachem Passaconaway of the Pennacooks often resided at these villages, as well as two others up river that went by the names of *Naticook* (now Merrimack, New Hampshire) and *Pennacook* (now Concord, New Hampshire). With their famous sachem, who was also one of the most respected medicine men among the New England Algonkians, the Pennacook were able to attract many local tribes to join their confederation, including the Pawtuckets, Pennacooks, Squamscotts

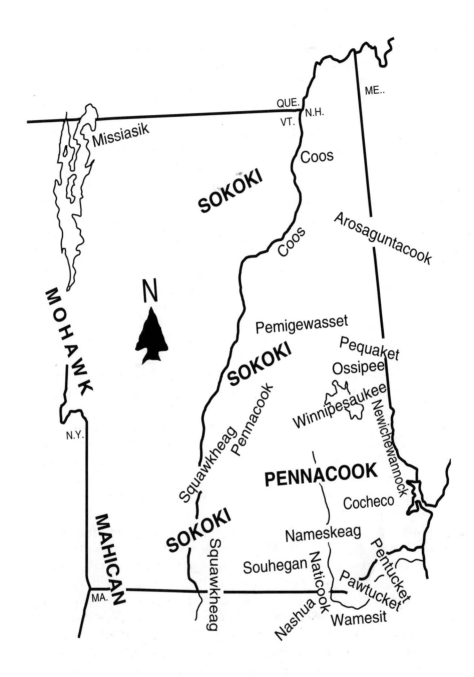

QUE.
VT.   N.H.
ME..

Missiasik

Coos

SOKOKI

Coos

Arosaguntacook

MOHAWK

N

Pemigewasset

Pequaket

Ossipee

SOKOKI

Winnipesaukee

N.Y.

Squawkheag

Pennacook

Newichewannock

PENNACOOK

Cocheco

MAHICAN

SOKOKI

Squawkheag

Nameskeag

Souhegan

Naticook

Pentucket

Pawtucket

MA.

Nashua

Wamesit

**ALGONKIAN TRIBES OF
NEW HAMPSHIRE AND VERMONT**

14

or Cochecos, Wamesits, Nashuas or Nashaways, Naticooks, Souhegans, Nameskeags (of present-day Manchester, New Hampshire), Winnipesaukees, Ossipees, Pemigewassets, Cohas or Coos, Pequakets, Sacos, Agamenticus, Piscataquas or Piscataways, Newichewannocks, Agawams (Ipswich, Massachusetts), Nameskeag or Naumkeag (Salem, Massachusetts), Pentuckets, Wachusetts and Squawkheags. These tribes covered the area of present-day Northfield, the Nashua River Valley and the area around Mount Wachusett in Massachusetts; the entire Merrimac River Valley; almost the totality of New Hampshire, with perhaps the exception of extreme northern Coos County; and extended eastward across the Piscataqua River as far north as the Saco River in Maine. The Pennacook confederation obviously wielded a somewhat nominal control over this extensive region. Even though tribal representation covered a large geographical expanse, the Algonkian tribes of the Pennacook confederation consisted of small populations, with the heaviest concentrations in the lower Merrimac Valley. This nation probably had about three thousand warriors before the plague decimated their numbers.

When the Pennacook suffered from the epidemic of 1617, they were made increasingly vulnerable to the inroads of Mic Mac and Maliseet warriors, whom the colonial English called "Eastern Indians." In colonial times the so-called "Eastern Indians" were sometimes mistakingly identified with the Penobscots, but now it is believed that these eastern raiders were either Mic Mac or Maliseet warriors who originated from the Bay of Fundy area. These "Eastern Indians" made penetrating raids into the lands of both the Pennacook and Massachusett as far south as Agawam and Saugus. According to William Wood, enmity existed between the "Eastern Indians" and the Pennacook and the Massachusetts. He wrote, "Our Indians [area of Lynn-Saugus, Massachusetts] doe feare them [Eastern Indians] as their deadly enemies; for so many of them as they meete they kill. About 2 yeares agoe, our Indians being busie about their accustomed huntings, not suspecting them so neare their own liberties, were on the suddaine surprized by them, some being slaine, the rest escaping to their English Asylum [English settlements], whither they durst not pursue them . . . These Indians are the more insolent, by reason they have guns which they dayly trade for with the French." When Captain John Smith sailed along the New England coast in 1614 he also noted that the Massachusett had intermittent conflict with the tribal nations east of the Penobscot River.

From the west, the Pennacooks also had to contend with the incursions of Mohawk war parties coming across the Connecticut River from Vermont. Warfare between the Mohawks and the New England Algonkians had turned extreme northwestern Vermont into a contested battleground, for both sides used the area of Lake Champlain for hunting and fishing, and as a thoroughfare for war parties. Samuel de Champlain reported in 1609 that he found the area sparsely inhabited, but he may have come at a time when warfare had temporarily disrupted the villages. One of the Algonkian nations occupying northern Vermont was the Sokoki people, a tribal group sometimes confused with the Saco of southern Maine. Sokoki villages often had to defend their hunting grounds from Mohawk attacks. In 1664, the Mohawks sent several emissaries to secure the peace with the Pocumtuck, but after concluding the treaty, the Pocumtuck and their Sokoki allies are believed to have murdered this embassy. This event led to the Mohawk War (1664-1671), in which the Mohawks lost people to Sokoki raids.

The Pennacook confederation was less fortunate than their Sokoki neighbors. Early on the Pennacook were weakened by plague and enemy attack, and consequently declined. Gookin claims that by 1670 only about two hundred and fifty menfolk lived at the twin tribal seats of *Pawtucket* and *Wamesit*. Here the Pennacook confederation managed to survive some of the most challenging times in their tribal history, only to see their fate nearly tied up with some of the other southern New England tribes in King Philip's War. To avoid bloodshed with the English during this conflict, many of the Pennacooks retreated northward, hoping to return to their villages on the lower Merrimac once the conflict was over.

Down east from the Pennacooks, along the coast of Maine, lived the *Wabanaki,* more commonly known as the Abenaki. In their dialect the tribal name means "people of the dawnland," which probably refers to their habitation of the easternmost section of New England. Alternately, it may signify the Northern Lights. Abenaki land ranged from the Maine coast deep into northern New Hampshire and the Northeast Kingdom (Essex County) of Vermont. However, the center of the Abenaki tribal nation was located in the Kennebec and Penobscot river valleys. Among the member tribes of the Abenaki confederation were the Casco and Pejepscot tribes, who lived near the mouth of the Kennebec River; the Canabas, or Kennebec, of the middle portion of that same river; and the Norridgewock tribe, who resided above the Kennebec tribe near the source of the river at Moosehead Lake. The Arosaguntacook or Androscoggin people of the river valley that bears their name, may have been a subtribe of the Norridgewock.

Just to the east of the Kennebec River, in present-day Lincoln and Knox Counties, the Wawenocks occupied the land. Up the Penobscot River lived the Penobscots, who were called the Pentagoets by the French, and the Tarrantines by the English, although Captain John Smith applies the latter term to the tribal groups living east of the Penobscot Valley. From this river valley eastward to the St. Croix River, probably the easternmost boundary of the Abenaki confederation, lived the Passamaquoddy tribe. This tribe, like the other northern Algonkians, moved seasonally between the coast and the interior. A considerable part of their diet consisted of marine mammals. The Maliseet of the St. John River Valley may have been included in the Abenaki confederation, but their wars with the Abenaki suggest that prior to French colonization they were a politically separate nation. Their lands stretched from northeastern Maine well into New Brunswick, where they adjoined the territory of the Mic Mac in Nova Scotia. Later on, during the French and Indian Wars of the 18th century, both the Mic Mac and Maliseet became active member tribes in the Abenaki confederation.

Outside of their nine major tribes, there were other villages that the Abenaki held under a disputed claim, for their Pennacook kindred to the south also looked to them for tribute. Tribes such as the Sacos, Ossipees and Pequakets were all members of the Saco nation, which was situated along the Saco River up into Lake Ossipee. *Almuchicoitt* or "Land of the Little Dog" was the name the Sacos gave to their homeland. Coos County and northeastern Vermont were also favorite hunting grounds for these people, despite Mohawk incursions into the region. Because the Sacos' lands straddled the two Abenaki confederations of northern New England, these people sought an off-and-on membership in both tribal leagues, gaining each nation's friendship for purposes of self-preservation. The fact that an Abenaki tradition told how the Sacos

17

were the parent nation of the eastern and western Abenaki tribes in Maine and New Hampshire must have certainly helped. At times the Abenaki even exacted tribute payments as far south as Cape Ann in Massachusetts.

The majority of the Abenaki people settled near the seacoast, leaving the interior sections of the Maine wilderness less populated. However, the Abenaki tribes of the Sokoki, Norridgewock, Ossipee, Pequaket and Coos (Coosuke) settled along the lakes and in the mountain valleys of the thickly forested interior. Further back in northern Vermont, the Abenaki could claim the allegiance of other Sokokis belonging to the Missiasik, Ammonoosuc, Arosaguntacook, Kikomkwak and Nulheganock tribes. Abenaki tribes in the White Mountains of New Hampshire referred to these timbered slopes as *Waumbec Methna,* or the "white and shining high places." No doubt this name refers to the reflection of the sun's rays off the mineral deposits of mica atop certain of these hills, which later on influenced the English to call them the Crystal or White Mountains. Both the Abenaki and Pennacook people revered the high peaks of Mount Washington in New Hampshire and Mount Katahdin in Maine, which they called *Kadaak-wajo* meaning "hidden high place." The tribes in northern New England believed that at death their souls went to live beyond the White Mountains. According to the late 18th century author James Sullivan, on these mountains lived mysterious, suspect gods, "who troubled the waters and raised a dark mist on the approach of human footsteps, so none would dare enter into the abode of the supernatural." Northern Algonkian tribesmen told both the French trappers and the English colonists that anyone who attempted to ascend Mount Katahdin was struck with delirium, whereupon the spirit forces frustrated the climber's ascent by returning him to the base of the mountain.

For the Abenaki, Pennacook and Sokoki people these mountains were the sacred setting for a tradition that told of their tribal origins. While this account may reveal a certain amount of Christian influence, it nonetheless gives some idea of their original worship of ancestral spirits and nature deities. The Abenaki and Pennacook had it from their tribal elders that in the distant past nearly all their people had been drowned in a great deluge, excepting a powwow (medicine man) and his wife. Having foreseen the impending disaster in a dream, this couple ascended into the White Mountains

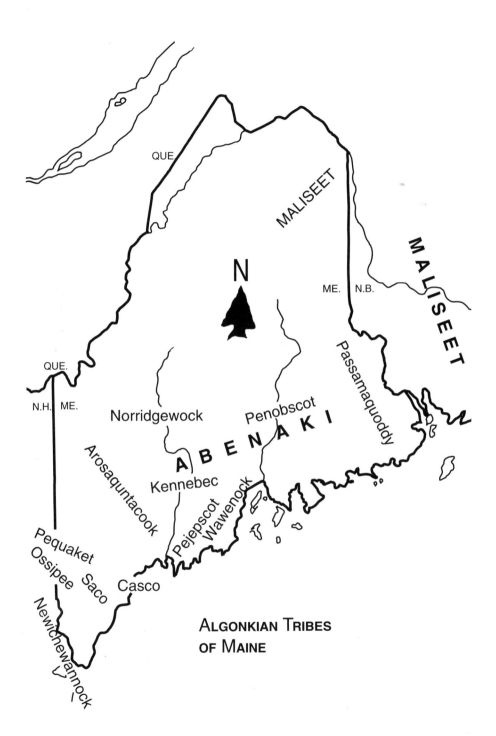

QUE.

MALISEET

N

MALISEET

ME. N.B.

QUE.

Passamaquoddy

N.H. ME.

Norridgewock

Penobscot

A B E N A K I

Arosaquntacook

Kennebec

Pejepscot

Wawenock

Pequaket

Saco

Casco

Ossipee

Newichewannock

ALGONKIAN TRIBES
OF MAINE

19

to find refuge from the flood. They took a snowshoe hare along with them who was called *Wetucks*. This rabbit possessed certain spiritual powers, such as its ability to transform itself into various bodily forms. When days passed into months, the anxious couple finally sent *Wetucks* out. His failure to return emboldened the powwow and his wife to return to the lower elevations, where they lived for many years, and filled the land with many Algonkian descendants. However, the demigod *Wetucks* remained in the land to help the people to survive in their woodland environment.

Before the Pilgrims arrived at Plymouth in 1620, the Abenakis were the New England Algonkians who had the greatest exposure to Europeans. Not surprisingly, from their repeated contact with European fishing captains and traders, the Abenakis also contracted pandemic viruses from the new arrivals. Before the plague thinned their population, the Abenakis were estimated to have ranged from between two to three thousand warriors, as did their Mic Mac neighbors, who seem to have escaped the plague of 1617. Even though the Abenakis proved to be a formidable force during a brief conflict with the English simultaneous with King Philip's War, their desperate struggle with the English in New England came later on, during the years of the early French and Indian Wars (1689-1726). And again, during the American Revolution, the Abenaki, Maliseet and Mic Mac were forces to be reckoned with, when loyalist Nova Scotia and radical Massachusetts waged a diplomatic struggle for their allegiance.

Among the Abenaki, Pennacook and Saco, agriculture never reached any significant degree of importance. The Algonkian peoples of northern New England depended on hunting, fishing and food gathering more than the tribes in southern New England, and as a result the more northerly tribal groups lived in smaller population concentrations in order to ensure yearly survival. The three Algonkian nations of northern New England had closer cultural affiliations with the hunting and gathering lifestyles of the Montagnais (Quebec), Naskapi (Labrador), Ojibwa (Ontario) and Mic Mac (Nova Scotia). However, because the Pennacook and Saco made use of more southerly planting fields in the Saco and lower Merrimac river valleys, these two tribes were more agrarian than their Kennebec and Penobscot kinsmen.

The norm for all the northern Algonkian peoples was a hunting and gathering economy. Throughout most of the spring, summer and autumn, the Abenaki, Pennacook and Saco lived near the sea-shore. In the earliest part of the fishing season they gathered lobsters, clams, fluke and lumpfish. At low tide along the larger bays these people took to their birch bark canoes searching the shallow tidal basins with a sharpened staff about three yards long to jab these bottom feeders. It was not uncommom for a Pennacook youth to take thirty or more lobsters in an hour and a half of spearfishing. Elsewhere along the shoreline the women dug away at the clam banks and cooked their catch by placing the shellfish on hot stones covered over with seaweed. When the alewives made their seasonal run up into the fresh water ponds to spawn, the men took them in abundance using nets fastened on hooped sticks.

As the fishing season progressed, the northern Algonkians caught bass, cod, bluefish, salmon and eel. Generally, they fished for bass and bluefish at the mouths of rivers, using canoes. The fishing equipment consisted of a staff tipped with a jagged bone, the staff fastened to the canoe with a line. Thrusting their javelin darts into these large fish, the fishermen would then haul them ashore. Moving inland for the salmon runs, the northern Algonkian tribes frequented certain falls where they trapped the plentiful salmon and eel in v-shaped fishing weirs that jutted into the rivers.

Throughout the spring and summer months the tribeswomen also spent their days tapping maple sap when in season, picking wild strawberries and blueberries, unearthing tuberous roots, and gathering rushes to weave into matting for the insulation of their winter wigwams. As autumn approached the forest floor was strewn with acorns, beechnuts, chesnuts and hickory nuts, which the women gathered in preparation for the harsh winter season. With the approach of winter the northern Algonkians withdrew from the seacoast into the interior where they settled into their seasonal winter encampments.

When the snowdrifts were able to bear their body weight, the younger men and women would leave the older people and youngsters at the winter campsites. Trekking further into the interior the men hunted moose and deer. Captain John Josselyn, who was familiar with the seasonal, nomadic lifestyle of the Abenaki people, describes a moose hunt:

When the snow will bear them, the young and lusty Indians, (leaving their papooses and old people at home) go forth to hunt moose, deer, bear and beaver, thirty or forty miles up into the country; when they light upon a moose they run him down, which is sometimes in half a day, sometimes a whole day, but never give him over till they have tired him, the snow being usually four foot deep, and the beast very heavy he sinks every step, and as he runs sometimes bears down arms of trees that hang in his way, with his horns as big as a man's thigh; other whiles, if any of their dogs (which are but small) come near, yerking [jerking] out his heels (for he strikes like a horse) if a small tree be in the way he breaks it quite asunder with one stroke, at last they get up to him on each side and transpierce him with their lances, which formerly were no other but a staff of a yard and half pointed with a fishes bone made sharp at the end, but since they put on pieces of sword-blades which they purchase of the French, and having a strap of leather fastened to the but end of the staff which they bring down to the midst of it, they dart it into his sides, the poor creature groans, and walks on heavily, for a space, then sinks and falls down like a ruined building, making the earth to quake; then presently in come the victors, who having cut the throat of the slain take off his skin, their young webs [tribeswomen] by this time are walking towards them with heavy bags and kettles at their backs, who laying down their burdens fall to work upon the carcass, take out the heart, and from that the bone, cut off the left foot behind, draw out the sinews, and cut out his tongue and as much of the venison as will serve to satiate the hungry mouths of the company: meanwhile the men pitch upon a place near some spring, and with their snowshoes shovel the snow away to the bare earth in a circle, making round about a wall of snow; in the midst they make their fire near to a great tree, upon the snags whereof they hang their kettles filled with venison, whilst that boils, the men after they have refreshed themselves with a pipe of tobacco dispose themselves to sleep. The women tend the cookerie, some of them scrape the slime and fat from the skin, cleanse the sinews, and stretch them and the like, when the venison is boiled the men awake, and opening of their bags take out as much Indian [corn] meal as will serve their turns for the present; they eat their broth with spoons, and their flesh they divide into gobbets, eating now and then with it as much meal as they can hold betwixt three fingers . . . . When the Indians have stuffed their paunches, if it be fair weather and about midday they venture forth again . . . they truss up their sardles, and away for another moose, this course they continue for six weeks or two months, making their webbs their mules to carry their luggage.

The moose was important to the northern Algonkian hunting and gathering economy. It supplied a wide range of products, from food and clothing to bowstrings, the latter being made from sinew strands twisted together.

Besides these seven major Algonkian confederacies of the Pequot, Narragansett, Wampanoag, Massachusett, Pocumtuck, Pennacook and Abenaki, four other indigenous populations in New England were powerful enough to be considered separate groups. The Nipmuck nation of central Massachusetts, the widespread Mahican tribes of the Hudson River Valley and western New England, and the Mohegans of Connecticut were large tribal groups. The fourth, the *Canienga* or Mohawk of upper New York State, were actually perennial enemies of most of the Algonkian tribes. As a member of the Five Confederated Nations of the Iroquois, the Mohawks shared with their Iroquoian compatriots a language foreign to their Algonkian neighbors. They spoke a dialect of the Iroquois-Caddoan linguistic family, which was also spoken by the tribes from central Pennsylvania south to the Carolinas. It was a language that only a few of the Algonkians had mastered, mainly those who had been captives among the Mohawks. Of the five tribal nations belonging to the Iroquois confederation, the Mohawks had the greatest impact on the New England Algonkians, because of their geographical proximity in the Mohawk River Valley. The Algonkian word *Mowak* means "eaters of men," since the Mohawk warriors practiced ceremonial cannabilism in times of war. They believed that eating the flesh of a fallen enemy warrior allowed them to share the courage of their foe.

The Five Nation Confederation of the Iroqouis, almost totally surrounded by their Algonkian enemies, was understandably warlike. War could be declared by the confederational council that presided over the entire nation, or by one of the member tribal nations, and the Mohawks often declared war in this way on the New England Algonkians. Springtime usually brought war chiefs dancing the war dance through the Mohawks' villages, to attract volunteers for a strike against their Algonkian enemies. Most of these raids were not open wars, but intermittent ambushes and abductions directed at their enemies. Concerning the nature of the Mohawks' attacks, Gookin says:

The Maquas' [Mohawk] manner is, in the spring of the year, to march forth in parties several ways, under a captain, and not above fifty in a troop. And when they come near the place that they design to spoil, they take up some secret place in the woods for their general rendezvous. Leaving some of their company there, they divide themselves into small parties, three or four, or five in a company; and then go and seek for prey. These small parties repair near to the Indian [Algonkian] habitations, and lie in ambushments by the path sides, in some secure places; and when they see passengers come, they fire upon them with guns; and such as they kill or wound, they seize on and pillage, and strip their bodies; and then with their knives, take off the skin and hair of the scalp of their head drying the inside with hot ashes; and so carry them home as trophies of their valour, for which they are rewarded.

According to William Wood's account of his conversations with the Massachusett tribal people who experienced battle with the Mohawks, these warriors when they assaulted a unsuspecting village would sometimes cry out *"Hadree Hadree Succome Succome,"* meaning " We come, We come, to suck your blood." Mohawk warriors taken prisoner by the New England Algonkians generally faced execution at the hands of their captors, a sentence that was sometimes accompanied with torture.

Wood also relates a story of an Algonkian sagamore who lived near the Mohawks, and continually suffered under their injurious assaults. Deciding to fight for his independence, rather than pay tribute in wampum and other items, this sagamore raised an impressive force of warriors. With his men he marched towards the land of the Mohawks. The Mohawks, having got word of his advance, knew his forces must swim a small river to reach their destination. They concealed themselves near the river crossing, and when the Algonkians began swimming across the river, the Mohawks ambushed them in their vulnerable position. Those who were in the water were shot, except for those who swam downstream to make this story known. Those who managed to get ashore on either side were swiftly struck down. In the end this sagamore suffered a disastrous defeat.

Another battle related to the colonists by the New England Algonkians took place between the Pennacooks and the Mohawks near present-day Concord, New Hampshire. The Pennacooks had built several forts along the Merrimac River as places of refuge from

24

enemy attack. Although the exact date is unknown, according to tradition, the Mohawks had been repulsed by the Pennacooks during one of their raids. Realizing the imminent danger of reprisal, the Pennacooks gathered themselves into the stockaded village where most of their newly harvested corn was stored, thinking they might have to endure a long seige. Sure enough, the embittered Mohawk warriors returned, taking up a defensive position on a small plain across from the fort. Neither side budged for a considerable period of time, so the Mohawks sent out a warrior as a decoy who jauntily walked across the plain in sight of the fort. The Mohawk ruse drew out a number of Pennacook warriors in pursuit, while the main body of Mohawks circumvented the fort and attacked it from the other side. A battle ensued, becoming even more intense when the warriors deceived by the Mohawk decoy returned to find their fort under seige. This brought the conflict to an even match, and the outcome was indecisive, both sides losing warriors.

Warfare between the Mohawks and the New England Algonkians seems to have been intermittent. During the years immediately following the plague of 1617, the Massachusett were more concerned with Mic Mac and Maliseet raids than with Mohawk war parties assailing them from the west. Once English settlement began along Massachusetts Bay, harassment of the coastal Algonkians by these Maritime tribal nations decreased, but the Mohawks continued their occasional attacks. In the 1660s the Algonkians and Mohawks battled each other, from the Abenaki and Sokokis in the north all the way south to the lands of the Mahicans in the Berkshire Hills of western Massachusetts. This conflict came to be known as the Mohawk War (1664-1671), during which the Sokokis and Pennacooks directed a series of strikes against their Mohawk enemies, as did about six hundred Massachusett warriors under Sachem Josiah Checkatabutt. This campaign, which took place in 1669, ended in defeat for these Massachusett tribesmen. During this war Mohawk raids on the New England Algonkians became so numerous that many of these tribal groups either abandoned their villages for areas closer to the English settlements, or held up for long periods in their forts.

Yet despite the long-standing animosity between both sides, the Mohawks sometimes allied themselves with one or more of the Algonkian tribes against another. This happened particularly when an Algonkian nation was willing to pay tribute to them. For instance, when the Mohegans captured the Narragansett sachem Miantonomo in 1643, and turned him over to the English magistrates in Hartford, the Narragansetts called in the Mohawks to assist in their dispute with the Mohegans. According to the Commissioners of the United Colonies at Boston, these Mohawk warriors came within a day's journey of the English plantations to await the judgement on Miantonomo. Again, in 1657, the Narragansetts requested of the Massachusetts court that they be given liberty to aid the Mohawks and Pocumtucks in their incursions against the Mohegans. Even the Pequot sachem Sassacus and the Wampanoag sachem King Philip desperately sought out Mohawk assistance near the ends of their unsuccessful attempts to throw off English colonial domination.

Between the lands of the Mohawks and the Algonkian confederations of coastal southern New England, lay the land of the Nipmuck tribal nation, and it acted as a buffer between the two, making peaceful relations all the more precarious for the Nipmuck people. Such was also the case for the Nipmucks' western neighbors, the Pocumtucks and Mahicans, who were situated even closer to the Mohawks. In order to augment their strength, the Nipmuck relied on alliances with more powerful nations.

The Algonkian word *Nipmaug* means "the freshwater or pond places." This tribal name reflects the fact that these people were an inland population for the most part, living along the lakes, ponds and streams of central Massachusetts, for as William Hubbard states, "the more inland Part of the Country [is owned] by the Nipnets [Nipmucks], a general name for all inland Indians betwixt Massachusetts and Connecticut River." Apparently, the more southerly Nipmuck tribes had close political ties with the Pequot confederacy. Just before the start of the Pequot War (1637), Roger Williams cautioned John Winthrop, the Deputy Governor of the Massachusetts Bay Colony, that it would be a serious misjudgement if the English attacked the Pequots by way of the Connecticut coast. He believed such a strategy would end up forcing the Pequots to retreat north for refuge among their Nipmuck allies, thereby bringing the Pequots even closer to the Bay Colony. For this reason, the English chose to attack them from the direction of Narragansett Bay; a strategy that forced the Pequots to retreat toward the Connecticut River, which in effect cut them off from Nipmuck country.

There were a number of Nipmuck tribes, but the fighting force of the entire nation probably ranged from one to two thousand warriors. Some of the tribes that comprised this nation were the Wachusett, who lived in the area of Mount Wachusett, and the Nashua, or Washacum, who resided not only in the same areas as the Wachusett, but also along the upper course of the Nashua River. Their main seat was called *Washacum*, which was located in present-day Sterling, Massachusetts. To the southwest of this tribe, where Brookfield, Massachusetts is today, the Quabaug tribe occupied the land. The Quabaug and Nashua had close affiliations with one another. Other Nipmuck tribes were the Hassanamissit, Quinebaug, Wabaquasset, Wunnashowatuckoog and Wusquowhannanawkit.

Most of the Nipmuck people were allied with the Massachusett tribal nation, and once the plague weakened this confederation at its seat on Massachusetts Bay, some of the Nipmucks seem to have sought new alliances with other tribal nations. While the more southerly tribes were members in the Pequot confederation before its demise in 1637, others allied themselves with the Narragansetts, Wampanoags, and a few, namely the Nashuas and Wachusetts, were even active participants in the Pennacook confederation.

With several strong Algonkian confederations surrounding central Massachusetts, it becomes obvious that a power vacuum had developed in Nipmuck country. The Nipmucks may have been a strong confederated tribal nation in the time before recorded history, and that nation may have slowly weakened before the English colonists arrived. Gookin, who was familiar with several of the Nipmuck tribes, mentions that "the Nashuas had been a great people in former times; but of late years, have been consumed by the Maquas' [Mohawks'] wars and other ways." No doubt, one of the other ways was through sickness contracted from the white man. Also by Gookin's time, Pennacook influence from the north had penetrated northern Worcester County and adjacent sections of northern Middlesex County in Massachusetts, where certain of the Nipmuck tribes had joined the Pennacook confederation. A semblance of the one-time Nipmuck confederation still existed in the 1670s under the leadership of Sachem Wattasacompanum, for this chief was said to be "ruler of the Nipmuck country . . . ruler of the Nipmuck Indians, a grave and pious man, of the chief sachem's blood of the Nipmuck country." William Hubbard states that the

Nipmucks' principal seat of government was located just outside Brookfield, Massachusetts. The Reverend Fiske, in his account of the settlement of Brookfield, mentions that this Nipmuck village was "called Miminimisset, [located] down a narrow passage between a steep hill and a thick swamp, at the head of Wickaboag Pond." It was a popular place of rendezvous for all the Nipmuck tribes. From this ancient seat, the Nipmucks had spread out in all directions; Nipmuck land reached its northern limits along the upper reaches of the Nashua River, its western extent at today's Quabbin Reservoir, to the south in Windham County, Connecticut, and to the east at Marlborough, Massachusetts, an area that the Christianized Algonkians called *Okommakamesit*.

Whether the Nipmucks were a powerful nation or not, the English settlers described them as having political associations with neighboring Algonkian nations. Apparently, the Nipmucks had lost some of their tribal autonomy when certain of their villages began paying tribute to the Pequot, Narragansett, Massachusett and Pennacook. At the time of King Philip's War, the Nashuas and Wachusetts refused to retreat northward with the remnants of the Pennacook confederation, in order to join up with their companions the Quabaugs, in a conspiracy to attack the frontier towns of Lancaster, Brookfield and Groton, Massachusetts, as well as other outposts. The Nashuas' defection from the Pennacook confederation exposed the entire western frontier of the Massachusetts Bay Colony to attacks by Nashua warriors.

Another tribal group that made its presence felt among the principal New England Algonkian confederations was the Mohegan people of eastern Connecticut, a river tribe possessing land near the lower Connecticut River. According to Gookin, the Mohegans were members of the Pequot confederation until its destruction. Contrary to popular belief, the Pequots did not suddenly vanish in this war, for Hubbard states that "after this Slaughter at the swamp, the Pequods being upon every turn exposed to revenge of the Mohegins on one side, and the Narhagansets on the other, chose rather to submit themselves to the English, by whom they were put some under the Mohegins, and some under the Narhagansets." The Mohegans were eager to adopt some of the surviving Pequots into their tribe, seeing it increased their warrior force from fifty to four hundred men. Of course, such a move promoted conflict later

on between the Mohegans and Narragansetts, as the Pequots under each nation convinced their respective sachems to claim Pequot
country. The Mohegan sachem Uncas weathered several
Narragansett assaults, until the English befriended the Mohegan
people, foiling the Narragansetts' plans to expand into Pequot
country. The English-Mohegan friendship gave the Mohegans a
more favored position among the New England colonies.

Because the Mahican tribes of western New England and New
York state have a tribal name that sounds similar to the word
Mohegan, some New England historians assumed early on that there
must be some cultural connection between these two peoples. Such
an assumption was reinforced by the supposed Mahican and Pequot-
Mohegan connection, which originated from an isolated claim
made by the colonial historian William Hubbard, who wrote that
the Pequot, a nation that the Mohegans were in close association
with, had invaded New England from the west just prior to English
colonization of the region. Upon reaching the Connecticut River,
according to Hubbard, they moved south into eastern Connecticut, where they subjugated the local tribes. However, studies in
comparative linguistics indicate that the Pequot-Mohegan dialect
is more akin to neighboring Narragansett and Massachusetts, than
to the Mahican dialect. Such evidence would indicate that the
Pequot and their Mohegan subjects had been well settled near the
Mystic River and at *Mohegoneak* in eastern Connecticut, long before the beginning of English colonization.

The far ranging Mahican or *Muhhekaneew* established themselves
along the Hudson River. This nation also settled wigwam villages in
the Berkshires and Litchfield Hills of western Massachusetts and
Connecticut. They also moved into southwestern Vermont. For the
most part, the Mahican were a river people, but their tradition as
great wanderers eventually brought the Mahican east of the Hudson
Valley into western New England. Dutch settlers knew them as the
Mahikanders, the English referred to them as the *Muhheckanew* or
Mahiccon and the French spoke of them as the *Manhigan*. Certain
Mahican oral traditions suggest that this nation originally migrated
into the Hudson River Valley, calling this waterway the *Mahicanituck*.
Somewhere in the vicinity of Albany, New York the tribal nation
established a village named *Schodac*. Mahican tribal lore tells of an
arduous journey they undertook from their former homeland west

of the Hudson Valley. During their sojourn to the east they frequently encountered bodies of water (Great Lakes?), but none compared with the beautiful waters of their native lands in Muhhekaneew, until they came upon the Hudson River. After their arrival at the Hudson River, the Mahicans began moving east of the Hudson Valley, overspreading into western New England. They established two principal villages in Massachusetts. One was in what is today the town of Stockbridge, and the other in Sheffield, at a place known as *Skatecook*.

Other local tribes closely associated with the Mahicans ranged along the entire length of the Housatonic River in Connecticut. Some of these were the Housetonucks, Wepawaugs (present-day Milford, Connecticut), Pequannocks (present-day Bridgeport, Connecticut), Paugassets (present-day Derby, Connecticut), Potatucks (present-day Shelton, Connecticut), Cupheags (present-day Stratford, Connecticut), Quinnipiacs (present-day New Haven, Connecticut), and the Wappingers, situated along the Connecticut-New York border. Still other tribes, such as the Pequannocks, Wangunks, Tunxis and Podunks, that may have been Mahican, settled around present-day Hartford, Connecticut. In Vermont, the Mahicans moved up into the lower Green Mountains. Here, the Pocumtucks, Pennacook and Missiasik (Missisquoi) interacted with the Mahican peoples.

As the confederated Mahican nation became established in their new homeland, they also expanded into western Connecticut, and from here crossed over the Sound onto Long Island and the adjacent areas of New York Harbor. Perhaps, with the exception of the Montauk and Shinecook, who had closer political affiliations with the Pequots and Narragansetts, the indigenous people on western Long Island spoke Munsee, a dialect akin to Mahican. When the Dutch arrived in the area of present-day New York City, they encountered the Munsee under the Algonkian name of *Munhattan*. Before the Dutch arrived, a number of Munsee tribes were settled along the lower Hudson River; these were the Esopus, Weckquaesgeeks (present-day Bronx), Canarsees (present-day Brooklyn), Rockaways (present-day Queens) and Hackensacks (present-day Richmond). Mohawk depredations may have been a catalyst in moving some of the Mahican tribes into western New England and onto Long Island, where they settled in among the Munsee. Even tribal groups as far away as the Canarsees were sometimes required to pay tribute to the Mohawks, and when the Canarsee villages failed to do so they suffered the consequences.

However, by the time of the French and Indian Wars of the early 18th century, the Mohawk, Mohegan and Mahican were at peace with one another. Throughout this period these tribes were allied with the English against the French and their northern Algonkian allies. In 1723 delegates from the Mohawk, Mohegan and Mahican at Skatecook journeyed to Boston to reaffirm their long-standing friendship with the English. They were entertained by the Lieutenant Governor of the Massachusetts Bay Colony, who gave each tribal delegation a plate with their tribal totem figures engraved on it. According to Samuel Penhallow, the engravings depicted a turtle, a bear, a hatchet and a wolf.

From this brief overview of the tribes of 17th century New England, certain facts become clear. First of all, the area was dominated by the Algonkian culture. Though very similar from Maine to Connecticut, the New England Algonkians nevertheless developed minor differences in language and lifestyle due to their degree of dependency on agriculture. In southern New England, the coastal Algonkian culture prevailed. Though semi-nomadic hunters and gatherers for the most part, these tribes were more agrarian than the Algonkians of northern New England. The southern coastal Algonkians probably entered into New England from the southwest. Their belief that the souls of the deceased returned to the southwestern sky suggest a possible southerly origin for the tribes in southern New England. From the Merrimac River Valley northward towards the Maritimes, the northern Algonkian culture was dominant. These tribes occupied the Piscataqua, Saco, Kennebec, Penobscot and St.Croix river valleys of Maine. While the southern Abenaki people practiced some agriculture, the more northerly tribes were almost entirely hunting and gathering societies due to the shorter growing season. As their name, "people of the dawn" or "northern lights," suggests, they may have entered into New England from the north. A more northerly origin for these tribes is also suggested by their belief that the souls of the deceased went to live in the north, beyond the White Mountains.

From these two Algonkian groupings evolved seven major confederated tribal nations. Under the coastal Algonkians were the Pequot, Narragansett, Wampanoag, Massachusett and Pocumtuck.

Minor tribal nations under these confederacies were the Nauset, Niantic, Nipmuck and Montauk. The Mahican of western New England, though definitely of the Algonkian linguistic family, seem to have shared more in common with the Algonkian culture in southeastern New York, New Jersey, Delaware and eastern Pennsylvania. In northern New England, the Abenaki had prior to the 17th century separated into the Pennacook confederation of New Hampshire and the Abenaki confederation of Maine. Between these confederations existed minor tribal nations such as the Saco and Sokoki, which were allied with them.

Native peoples hunted and fished most of the areas during their seasonal wanderings in search of food, but only in particularly advantageous places would they erect their villages and plant their gardens. The majority of native peoples lived in southern New England, with the densest populations along coastal Connecticut, Rhode Island and southeastern Massachusetts. Coastal Maine and the lower Connecticut Valley were also well populated. The Champlain Valley was another favorite place for the Algonkians, but warfare probably kept this region in dispute. Interior New England, from the northern extremities of Nipmuck country through the Green and White Mountains on into interior Maine, remained less populated. The severe winters in these regions kept the population low.

Population shifted according to the Algonkians' seasonal movements. During the winter months, families gathered into their winter settlements, while in the warmer season they divided up into smaller familial groups. Roger Williams states that during the winter the Narragansetts settled in wooded valleys, from which they removed to their cornfields during the other seasons. When the salmon, eel and alewives began to run upstream, large numbers of native peoples gathered along the rivers at places such as Pawtucket, Wamesit, Nameskeag and Pennacook to take the fish. However, during the summer, the coastal tribes depended on the seacoast for their main supply of fish, and during the winter went ice fishing on the inland ponds. According to Thomas Lechford, "seldome they are abroad in extremity of Winter, but keep in their wigwams, till necessity drives them forth." This explains why the Pilgrims saw few native people during their first winter at Plymouth.

Any given figure concerning the number of Algonkian people living in New England after the plague of 1617 is obviously a rough estimate. Using colonial sources, the precontact Algonkian population may have been between 100,000 and 150,000 people. According to more recent demographic estimates given by the historian Francis Jennings, the indigenous population had decreased to about 60,600 by the early 1670s. Estimates of native population are likely to have a considerable margin of error, because of the seminomadic Algonkian lifestyle. The Reverend Stephen Badger, who was familiar with the "Praying Indians" of Natick, mentions that in 1759 these people still lived a fairly mobile existence. He observed how they would visit friends, who lived hundreds of miles from them. Travelling on foot, they would sleep in vacant barns, or in the woods, until they reached their destination. Frequently they would stay away from Natick for months, and sometimes even years! Apparently, even as late as the 1830s the Abenaki continued their seasonal life cycle of moving down river from the interior onto the coastal plain. According to the 19th century diarist Mary Hall, who worked as a weaver in the textile mills at Lowell, Massachusetts, these Penobscot families, who numbered about fifty persons, would come down river by canoe each summer and pitch their tents along the river banks behind the Lawrence Corporation near Pawtucket Falls. With seasonal mobility so much a part of the semi-nomadic Algonkian lifestyle, it seems improbable that any of the 17th century colonial authorities could have taken an accurate census of the indigenous populations of New England.

Within the small geographical expanse that is now called New England, the Algonkian people developed a diverse community of confederated tribal nations. These tribal divisions were primarily political, for the Algonkians in New England shared a similar culture in their language, their religious beliefs, their rules of government, and their economic customs. Most European colonial authors described the Algonkian hunting and gathering lifestyle as primitive, but the present ecological crisis facing modern society has proven the wisdom of their ways.

Chapter II
Rooted Like The
Basket Trees.

The hunting and gathering economy of the Algonkian people in New England required that they spend most of their time outdoors. A strong physique was necessary for considerable effort was expended during each season to ensure yearly survival. William Wood describes the Massachusett tribesmen as having black hair, dark eyes, high foreheads and long noses. Atheletic in body proportions, the men were characterized as being upwards of five to six feet in height, with long arms and an erect posture. They tended to have long legs and small feet. William Bradford of Plymouth Colony describes the visiting Samoset as being a tall, straight man wearing his long black hair on his back, with no hair on his face. An apparent skin luster among the Algonkians was due to their practice of rubbing animal grease on their bodies, which protected them from the sun and wind. Continual exposure to the wilderness environment had little effect on the overall hardiness of Algonkian women. Pregnant tribeswomen often worked in the cornfields right up until the time of delivery, and within a day or so after giving birth, a mother was back to her daily activities with the *papoos* strapped in a carrier on her back. Edward Winslow, also of Plymouth Plantation, mentions that he witnessed an Algonkian mother and infant three days after childbirth riding along the seacoast in a canoe during bitter cold weather. Such sights led this author to conclude that the indigenous peoples were of "a more hardy nature" than the English.

As was the case elsewhere in most of the Americas, the New England Algonkians lacked a written language, although ideas were often conveyed through pictographs and porcupine quill designs. The Native Americans passed down their inherited customs, whether religious, political or otherwise, by oral tradition. Even though their Neolithic culture might be termed primitive from a

technological standpoint, it had been proven adequate by generations of trial and error and it functioned sufficiently to meet the
daily needs of their society. A communal lifestyle, reinforced by
the desire to avoid shame, were powerful incentives to respect the
rights of others, and to obey tribal customs set down by the sachem
and sagamores in the tribal councils.

The New England Algonkians were quite hospitable, and would
often go hungry rather than allow a guest to depart unfed. William
Wood experienced their hospitality first hand for he frequently
conversed with the native peoples around present-day Lynn, Massachusetts. He says:

> If a tree may be judged by his fruite, and dispositions calculared
> [calculated] by exterior actions; then may it be concluded, that these
> Indians are of affable, courteous, and well disposed natures, ready
> to communicate the best of their wealth to the mutuall good of one
> another; and the lesse abundance they have, to manifest their en-
> tire friendship; so much the more perspicuous is their love, in that
> they are as willing to part with their Mite in poverty, as treasure in
> plenty. As he that kills a Deere, fends for his friend, and eats it mer-
> rily: So he that receives but a piece of bread from an English hand,
> parts it equally betweene himselfe and his comerades, and eats it
> lovingly.

Such was their practice of generosity. This same author relates
an incident involving an Englishman who, while hunting deer, lost
his way in the woods. Several tribesmen came upon him after this
lost colonist had suffered overexposure to the harsh winter cold.
After nursing him back to health, these tribesmen carried the man
on their shoulders for twelve miles to his place of residence.

The indigenous peoples were generally not overly talkative for it
was frowned upon, but this does not mean that they were without
humor. Roger Williams mentions how every wigwam village had its
own "clowns." An Englishman named John Gyles, who lived as a
captive for six years among the Abenaki and Maliseet, noted that
these people, too, were fond of merry laughter and comic stories.
The stereotype of the dour Native American who was of few words
and excessive hand expressions grew out of the initial language
barrier between the English colonists and the Algonkian peoples,
which impeded the natural flow of conversation on both sides.
Concerning their language, William Wood found the Algonkian

speech to be pleasing to the ear while other colonials describe the native speech as being somewhat nasal in tone.

In everyday life, the Native American had a spiritual respect for his natural surroundings–for the forests and lakes that sustained him. He had a uniquely sensitive understanding of the ecosystem born of continuous observation, which western man is only beginning to rediscover. Native religion can be characterized as nature worship, for the natural environment was a intricate part of their faith, and as is the case with many religions of the past and present, the Algonkians of New England also recognized the power of good and evil forces. These supernatural forces they believed controlled their lives. Native religion involved nature spirits, and of the many forces they believed in, the Algonkians usually favored those spiritual powers that were seen as stronger than the many lesser deities. The Wampanoags and Narragansetts placed their faith in a plurality of thirty-seven deities. *Cautantouwit,* or its variant *Kiehtan,* was one of their most powerful spirit forces. The word Kiehtan refers to antiquity, for the root word, *chise,* denotes an old man, and *kiehchise,* "one who has lived many years." The Wampanoags held this deity to be the ancient one, the creative force behind the primordial matter, that eventually shaped the world for their habitation. Kiehtan gave the corn and bean seeds to them. Such beneficial gifts the Wampanoags could not dismiss lightly, and therefore honored this spirit force with lavish praises.

The Wampanoag people told Edward Winslow that the supreme Kiehtan first created all the other deities, and then fashioned the heavens and the earth. After that he made the ocean and all living things. He created a man and a woman, from which all humanity later came, though the Wampanoag told Winslow they were not sure how mankind had dispersed over such a widespread area. In the Narragansett account of creation, in the beginning there existed no sachem or sagamore; the Narragansett people were nonexistent, and only Kiehtan existed, who lived in the southwestern sky. Everything else was in a chaotic, primordial state. After bringing the land into form, he created a man and woman from a stone. Disliking the outcome of his labor, Kiehtan destroyed this first couple and made a new pair of humans from a tree, which became the progenitors of all humanity. Like the Narragansetts, many tribes in New England believed trees and people had a common origin.

The Passamaquoddy consider themselves to be as deeply rooted to the land as the basket tree (black ash tree) from which they gathered branches to make baskets. A Passamaquoddy legend tells how a mythic giant named Glooskap took his bow and arrows and shot the arrows into the trunks of the basket trees. Wherever the arrows pierced the bark tribespeople emerged. The Cohas tribe of New Hampshire similarly claimed the pine tree as their totem, hence their tribal name *Cohas* or *Coosuke,* meaning pine tree. Algonkian creation myths linking people and trees partly explain why the explorer Giovanni da Verrazzano observed a tribal leader at Narragansett Bay who was curiously cloaked in a deer pelt that had numerous tree branches knotted into it as adornment.

Some Algonkian tribes believed their ancestry was closely related to certain animals, which were part of the tribe's totemic tradition. Mahican tradition apparently held the wolf in high esteem, for in their language *Mahican* means "wolf." The Mahicans' Wappinger neighbors in western Connecticut probably held the oppossum to be their totem, since *wapink* translates "oppossum." Likewise, the Saco of southern Maine called themselves and their land *Almuchicoitt,* which is an English or French mispronunciation of the Algonkian word *Almouchicoisen,* or "Little Dog People."

A Wampanoag tradition tells how upon a person's death, he or she went to dwell with former friends at Kiehtan's abode in the southwestern sky. Here, the deceased enjoyed a new life of pleasures. In order for a person to be with Kiehtan in the hereafter, he had to have conducted his life on earth in an honorable manner. Perverse people were also required to make the same ethereal journey to Kiehtan's home. However, when they arrived at his place Kiehtan would refuse them entrance, bidding them *quatchet,* which in their dialect meant "to walk abroad." Their punishment was to wander restlessly in the spirit world, where Kiehtan gave them endless impossible tasks such as chiseling out a dugout with nothing more than a round stone. William Wood mentions a dog that sat at the entrance to Kiehtan's abode, which snarled and nipped at undesirable people attempting to gain Kiehtan's favor. The dead were buried with their most treasured possessions, in the hopes that these items might win them Kiehtan's approval. These implements were also intended for use by the deceased in their new home in the southwestern sky.

According to tribal traditions Kiehtan communicated with the older men who were wise, but seldom to the young. These tribal elders related their knowledge to the rest of the village population. From the knowledge the old men imparted to the tribe, parents taught their children to respect Kiehtan. Any powers or gifts emanating from this god were generally good. If the New England Algonkians had a good hunting season or plentiful corn harvest, they would gather together in their tribal villages to sing, dance, feast and decorate their wigwams with garlands in memory of this helpful deity. The Wampanoags and Narragansetts called this celebration *Nickommo*. During these occasions as many as a thousand people might congregate at the village.

Precontact Algonkian spiritualism viewed positive and negative forces as aspects of a single reality. Any vague conception of opposing deities in the nature worship of the Algonkians during the Historic period was no doubt due to their exposure to Puritan and Jesuit missionary efforts, for Christian theology is based on a dualistic doctrine of God versus Satan. The Algonkian spiritual realm was seen as a balance of good and evil forces, and life as a natural admixture of both joy and pain. The New England Algonkians also paid homage to the mischevious spirit force known as *Hobbamock* or *Hobbamoqui*. The Wampanoags as well as others appealed to Hobbamock to cure their sick and wounded. Hobbamock was rarely sympathetic unless he was appeased by material sacrifices. When angered by a negligent devotee, Hobbamock sent injury, sickness, remorse, death, defeat in battle, or natural catastrophe. If an accident befell any Narragansett tribesman, the tribe might assume this deity was angry with that person, which in their dialect translates *Nummusquaunamuckqun manit*, or "god is angry with me." The Wampanoags told Winslow that they were often in doubt about Hobbamock's intentions, for he sometimes deceived them. Those who had seen Hobbamock claimed he had the power to transform into several animals, his favorites being a deer, fawn, eagle and snake, as well as a man. Only the shamans witnessed most of these apparitions, even though others in the tribe desired the honor of seeing him.

The northern Algonkian tribes of the Abenaki and Pennacook also worshipped Hobbamock, whom they called *Abbamocho* or *Chepe*. "Chepe" comes from the Algonkian word *chepewessin* meaning "northeast wind," and suggests that Hobbamock's spiritual abode was the cold northern skies. Captain John Josselyn relates how the northern Algonkian people claimed that Hobbamock sometimes deliberately frightened them by taking on the appearance of a Mohawk warrior. On other occasions he would glide on the wind over their wigwams which they took to be a warning of impending death at the hands of their enemies. The Abenaki were so respectful of Hobbamock's power that they had a sacred site at Hobbamock Point on the Kennebec River. According to Samuel de Champlain, whenever these tribesmen passed this place they would paddle ashore to leave an arrow out of fear misfortune might befall them if they failed to do so.

Frequently Hobbamock appeared to the *powwows* (medicine men) and *pnieses* (braves) in the tribe in order to reveal his future designs. Algonkian tribesmen believed these *powwows* knew many of the mysteries of the supernatural and they could propitiate the spirit forces to raise storms and tempests against enemy tribes. To facilitate communication with the spirit world, *powwows* often slept on a sacred animal pelt which induced dreaming. The *powwow's* responsibility was to use his knowledge of herbal medicines, excorcism and sacred chants to win Hobbamock's favor in curing diseases and wounds, which were believed to be evil spirits in the infirmed person's body. *Powwows* cast spells and went into trance like states. From the forest they gathered herbs and plant oils to use in healing. Native plants such as the pipsissewa, wild mint and alder were given for burns, blisters and vomiting, while tobacco was used for toothache pain. Burdock leaf, well pounded and mixed with fat, reduced swelling. To heal severe frostbite the Algonkians used a salve made from fir balsam. Of course, the effectiveness of these herbal remedies was quite limited when it came to life threatening illnesses. Franciscan missionaries living among the Mic Mac mention how the *powwows* were often unable to save people from gangrenous wood and fish bone splinter wounds. In the 18th century, the Mohegan missionary Samson Occom, knowing of Montauk reliance on the *powwow* as healer, incorporated the role of the medicine man into his Christian missionary strategy. Occom's familiarity with herbal remedies is apparent in his "Ten Indian Remedies from Manuscript Notes on Herbs and Roots," which he wrote in 1754.

Apparently, the *powwows* gathered other plants for their halluci-nogenic properties. In Occom's "An Account of the Montauk Indi-ans on Long Island," he observes:

> As for the Powaws, they say they get their art from dreams; and one has told me they get their art from the devil, but then partly by dreams or night visions, and partly by the devil's immediate appear-ance to them by various shapes; sometimes in the shape of one crea-ture, sometimes in another, sometimes by a voice, & c. and their poisoning one another, and taking out poison, they say is no imagi-nary thing, but real. I have heard some say, that have been poi-soned, it puts them into great pain, and when a powaw takes out the poison they have found immediate relief; at other times they feel no manner of pain, but feel strangely by degrees, till they are sense-less, and then they will run mad. Sometimes they would run into the water; sometimes into the fire; and at other times run up to the top of high trees and tumble down headlong to the ground, yet receive no hurt by all these. And I don't see for my part, why it is not as true, as the English or other nation's witchcraft, but is a great mystery of darkness.

Tribal members believed the *powwow* held the power of life and death in his hands. Some *powwows,* besides being medicine men, also held the title of sachem. One of the most famous *powwows* was Passaconaway, who was also sachem of the Pennacook nation dur-ing the first half of the 17th century. This sachem-powwow became famous among the New England Algonkians for the many magical feats he was reported to have performed, and tradition has it that Passaconaway once dove off the bank of the Merrimac River and swam halfway across its turbulent waters before a mist shrouded him from sight. When the mist cleared away Passaconaway was stand-ing on the opposite bank. Another story tells how he was able to place a dead leaf in his hand and turn it green upon opening his fist. He also was said to command the rocks to sway and dance, and make ice appear in the heat of a summer afternoon. On certain occasions, when the *powwow* sang a sacred chant coupled with hand gestures over an ill person, the members of the village were allowed to chant along. If the individual was wounded the *powwow* might appear to suck on the lesion. When the wound was curable he would not touch it, because *askooke* the snake, or *wobsacuck,* the eagle, sat on the patient's shoulder licking the wound. Apparently, this was

Hobbamock in one of his several forms. Few besides the *powwows* saw supernatural phenomena, and they took them as signs of the person's recovery. The *powwow,* while reciting sacred incantations, Thomas Lechford says often worked himself into "extreame sweating and wearinesse, even to extasie." While he chanted to Hobbamock he usually promised to sacrifice skins, bowls, baskets, wampum and stone tools in his name if he would come to the aid of the sick or maimed. Annually, some of the Pennacook tribes journeyed down east to a sacred outcropping of stone along the Maine seashore where they sacrificed strings of wampum and fur pelts to Hobbamock by dropping them into a deep crevasse.

One Narragansett ceremony to Hobbamock exceeded mere devotion. When the time came the tribe built large spacious longhouses in the village which only the *powwows* were permitted to enter. On a given day the villagers were required to bring sacrifical gifts such as arrowheads, flint knives, copper trinkets, pelts and other prized possessions to the *powwows,* who waited at the doors of the longhouses. The *powwows* tossed the gifts into the fires inside the houses as an offering to Hobbamock. Each individual brought something to this offering, and the more personal items a person surrendered, the higher his prestige in the tribe. Indirectly, this ceremony was a way to equalize the material possessions of a tribal village by disposing of some items to this spiritual force. The Wampanoags assumed they suffered from the plague of 1617 because they failed to practice the Narragansetts' sacrifical custom. The proof of this they believed to be self-evident for the plague afflicted few losses among their enemies across the bay.

Among the New England Algonkians, the common terminology for anything that was extraordinary or defied explanation was called *Manitoo.* "Manitoo" means "that which is more than," or " something that surpasses." Roger Williams defines the word as simply meaning "god." The Algonkians sometimes applied the term to what they considered unusual because it did not appear in their culture. For example, the Narragansetts called the English sailing ships and the skill of writing, "Manitoo." Today, the term survives as the place name of Lake Manitook (Manitick) in Granby, Connecticut, which means "the Manitoo place." Here, the local Algonkian river tribes probably witnessed what to them seemed to be an unexplainable incident, and they gave this lake and the adjacent hills this special name.

The spirit of Manitoo, which was present in their many deities, often communed with the Algonkian mind through dreams. Through the medium of dreams the *powwows* often had deeply insightful spiritual journeys into the realms of their nature deities who gave them information about people, places and events. Roger Williams relates how he knew of a Narragansett tribesman who had an ominous dream one night. He dreamed he encountered the sun god, *Keesuckquand*, who darted a fiery ray at him, piercing his chest. When he awoke, the man became convinced *Keesuckquand* had served as a messenger to communicate his impending death. He hastily gathered family and friends and told them his Manitoo experience. Then he gave gifts and entertainment and kept awake for ten days and nights invoking certain spirit powers for protection.

Even though colonial authors make only a few cursory references to the Thunderbird deity, it was one of the more popular themes in Algonkian stories about their lesser nature spirits. Archaeologists and relic hunters have found stone, and some copper images of an eagle-like bird in excavations across New England. When the Algonkians heard thunder, they said it was the Thunderbird flying high in the storm clouds, where the flapping wings caused the wind and echoing rumbles. When they saw a streak of lightning slice the sky, they said the Thunderbird was blinking its eyes. Obviously, this bird was revered as the deity of thunder and lightning.

The Abenaki and Pennacook people called the Thunderbird *Pamola*, or *Gulloua*, and believed it nested atop the higher mountain peaks of New England. When a tribal youth suddenly vanished due to accident or abduction by an enemy tribe, the *Gulloua* was sometimes accused of having snatched him away as food for its nestlings. An Abenaki tradition tells how a boy went out hunting one day at the base of a mountain when he was seen by a thunderbird soaring high above on the thermal air currents. The bird dived on the youngster, seized him in its talons, and carried him back to the nest as food for its young. At first the child remained motionless to avoid attracting the attention of the two large eaglets, but then he saw they had recently gorged themselves on fish. Because her young seemed disinterested in the human prey, the *Gulloua* returned the

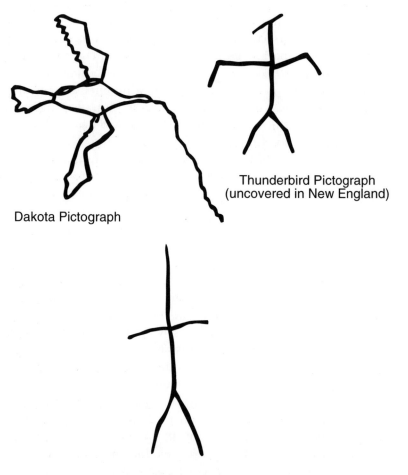

Dakota Pictograph

Thunderbird Pictograph
(uncovered in New England)

Thunderbird Pictograph
(uncovered in New England)

PICTOGRAPHS OF THE THUNDERBIRD DEITY.

boy to the spot where she found him. Similarly, a Wampanoag story tells of a youngster snatched from a beach in the full view of his parents. The frantic couple attempted to follow the Thunderbird in their canoe as she soared higher and higher out over the ocean. Eventually they lost sight of the bird and when they tried to turn back got lost at sea. The ocean currents finally brought them ashore on Nantucket where they made the tragic discovery of their child's remains.

Other supernatural powers of the Narragansett spirit realm were *Wompanand,* the Eastern God; *Checkesuwand,* the Western God; *Wunnanameanit,* the Northern God; *Sowwanand,* the Southern God, and the domestic deity, *Wetuomanit,* who guarded the household. Some of their nature spirits were *Nanepaushat,* the Moon God; *Paumpagussit,* the Sea God, and *Yotaanit,* the Fire God. One Narragansett tribesman, trying to prove the existence of *Yotaanit* to Roger Williams said, " fire must be a God, or Divine power, that out of a stone will arise in a Sparke, and when a poore naked Indian is ready to starve with cold in the House, and especially in the Woods, often saves his life, doth dresse all our Food for us, and if it be angry will burne the House about us, yea if a sparke fall into drie wood, burnes up the Country." *Yotaanit* may also have been a harbinger of death among the northern Algonkians, for the Pennacook believed in a flame that would appear in the night over a person's wigwam just prior to his dying. The Maliseet claimed this light was a supernatural fireball that left the body during dreams, and could travel for great distances.

Another nature deity worshipped by the New England Algonkians was *Muinwa,* the Rain God who lived along a lake in the sky. The Algonkians looked to *Muinwa* for relief from seasonal droughts that threatened their cornfields. If the growing season was dry, the native people called solemn gatherings atop certain hills, from where they would call upon *Muinwa* and other deities to bring rain. Sometimes these tribal hilltop appeals would last upwards of three weeks. Another spirit force involved with water was *Manibozho,* the deity of the flood story, an oral tradition now viewed as nearly universal by cultural anthropologists.

The Algonkians also had patron deities that protected them from harm. *Squauanit,* or its variants pronounced *Squant* or *Squantam,* was the patron spirit of the tribal women. The Algonkians seldom sought to appease this spirit force, for like the benevolent Kiehtan, she did them no harm. Another patron spirit called *Muckquachuckquand* watched over children. About this latter force Roger Williams states, " I was once with a Native dying of a wound, given him by some murtherous English[man] . . . this Native dying called much upon Muckquachuckquand, who of other Natives I understood (as they believed) had appeared to the dying young man, many years before, and bid him whenever he was in distresse call upon him."

Religion in Algonkian society was a way of life, and not limited to propitiating their many deities. The *manittowock*, or pantheon of deities, penetrated every aspect of life. "They imagined a great number of Gods," writes Samson Occom, such as "the gods of the four corners of the earth; the god of the east, the god of the west, the god of the north, the god of the south; and there was a god over their corn, another over their beans, another over their pumpkin, and squashes . . . one god of the day, another of the night; and there were four gods over the four parts of the year." Supernatural forces existed everywhere and were directly responsible for a person's health as well as illness and eventual death in old age. Captain John Josselyn reports the Algonkian people faced death "patiently," as a deeper communion with the spiritual realm, for they had no knowledge "of a Hell to scare them." The spirit forces were as distant as the southwestern sky, and as near as one's body wherein dwelled divine powers that attended to the heart, lungs and pulse.

In an attempt to appease these forces, the native peoples performed certain ceremonies to obtain supernatural favor. In illness, for example, when a member of the tribe fell sick his friends gathered at his wigwam until he either recovered or died. If the person managed to throw off his illness, then all his friends gave him presents, and then feasted and danced to their friend's health. However, if the person died, then all who knew him remained for a while and mourned knowing the deceased person's *michachunck*, or soul, must make the long journey to Kiehtan's home. They lamented from dawn to dusk for many days after the burial, chanting sorrowfully for the one who had passed away. When a family member died, the relatives painted a paste of soot mixed with water on their face and bodies. The mourners rubbed these masks on themselves for days and even months if the person who died was of high status. Out of respect for the deceased the family members avoided all expressions of joy. The dead person's name could not be mentioned until one of their relatives was given that name. To console the bereaved, friends would often say, "*Kutchimmoke, Kutchimmoke*," which means, "Be of good cheer," while tenderly stroking their cheek. The end of the mourning period was marked by a great dance that lasted all night.

Involving their mortuary ceremonies, the New England Algonkians followed certain customs. When they prepared to bury a deceased tribal member, the *Mockuttasuit*, or person in charge of the burial ceremony, wrapped the corpse in mats. Samson Occom states that before wrapping the body in mats, the Montauk people first "wash their dead clean, and adorn them with all manner of ornaments, and paint the face of them with divers colours, and make a great lamentation over their dead." From the village the body was then taken to the sacred burial grounds, where it was temporarily laid next to the grave, while everyone continued in great lamentation over the deceased. A short time after the burial there was another period of mourning. During this ceremony the family and friends spread the mat that the person died on over the grave along with the dish he or she ate from. On a nearby tree they hung the deceased person's favorite furs, which, once placed there, were not to be removed. If a sachem was being buried, they covered the corpse with elaborately designed mats along with many of the deceased sachem's possessions. When a child was buried, the father placed some of his most precious possessions in the grave, along with those of his son. According to Roger Williams, when Canonicus, sachem of the Narragansetts, lost his son he " burned his own Palace, and all his goods in it, (amongst them to a great value) in a sollemne remembrance of his sonne, and in a kind of humble Expiation to the Gods, who (as they believe) had taken his sonne from him." In such cases where the man or woman of the house died, the wigwam was stripped of its bark walls and the stick frame was left standing, then in or near their dwelling place they were buried. Sometimes the body was buried in a squatting position, or bound up into a bundle with strings and buried facing toward the southwest. Children were usually buried in the latter manner. Red ocher, an aromatic iron oxide powder, was ceremoniously sprinkled over the body before burial in the sacred grounds.

During their wanderings on the outer Cape, the Pilgrims came upon what they thought to be a Nauset graveyard, which they described as "a great burying place, one part whereof was incompassed with a large Palazado, like a Churchyard, with young saplings four or five yards long, set as close one by another . . . within it was full of graves, some bigger, and some less, some were also paled about, and others had like an Indian house made over them, but not matted . . . without [outside] the Palazado were graves also." Probably, from the Pilgrims' description, this place was formerly a stockaded village that succumbed to the plague. Its deceased residents were buried there and the place was then abandoned. Those burial plots that were palisaded were probably the graves of sagamores and powwows.

Besides the influential medicine men who attended to the spiritual affairs of the tribe, there were the *pnieses* (warriors) who had considerable authority in government and warring activities. The *pnieses* were seasoned fighters to whom Hobbamock appeared on occasion. The New England Algonkians believed these *pnieses* or braves had made a covenant with the spirit force, Hobbamock, which made them immune to death. Before going to meet the enemy in combat, the *pnieses* painted their faces with vegetable dyes from such native plants as pokeweed. *Pnieses* were so feared for their courage and supposed indestructibility that sometimes one alone chased a hundred enemy warriors from the battlefield, for it was said that whoever stood in their way would surely die. A tribesman named Hobbamock, who was a Wampanoag *pniese,* accompanied Captain Miles Standish and his militia on an expedition against the Wessagusset people. Edward Winslow relates that during a brief skirmish "Hobbamock cast off his coat, and being a distinguished pniese chased them [Wessagusset warriors] so fast, their [pniese] now having been killed, that the [militia] were not able to hold sway with him." The *pnieses* were often members of the sachem's council, and the sachem seldom acted on important matters without their advice.

The animistic religion of the precontact Algonkians expressed a harmony with nature that allowed for the development of a unique concept of land ownership. Their concept of possession was a right of usage, which was the privilege to hunt, fish, plant, gather food and whatever else allowed survival. These rights were shared with everything else on the land, animate and inanimate alike, including their many nature spirits, for their deities were not inaccessible forces residing in some distant place. According to Thomas Cooper, a Christianized Capawick tribesman, "whenever the Indians worshipped, they always sang and danced, and then begged of the sun and moon, as they thought most likely to hear them, to send them the desired favour; most generally rain or fair weather, or freedom from their enemies or sickness." Spirit forces even dwelled in the wind that blew across the lake, and the waters that rippled in response. On the highest peaks lived *Pamola*, the thunderbird deity. The Narragansetts revered the silver fox because this animal possessed the sacred power of *Manitoo*. These same people hunted the *"waatuckques,"* or rabbit which they believed to be the physical embodiment of one of their nature deities.

The Algonkian believed each part of the natural world, including the inanimate objects such as mountains and rivers, had its own spirit force, which presided over its own realm and rebuked the negligent individual who disturbed the harmonious relationship between a nature deity and its domain. The native people took from the land only to fulfill their seasonal needs. This relationship to their ancestral lands, inherited from their fathers, was very different from the English concept of land ownership, and the differences later became a source of contention between the Algonkian peoples and the English colonists. When the indigenous population invited the English to settle on their tribal lands, did they knowingly offer a share in their usage rights, or did they relinquish their rights to the physical land itself? Possibly both types of transactions occurred. For example, in establishing the boundary markers between the town of Yarmouth, Massachusetts and the local sachem's lands in 1641, the English claimed the adjacent lands "excepting and reserving unto Massatanpaine, the sachem, the land from Nobscussetpann westerly, from a marked tree there unto another marked tree at a swamp extending westerly." Again, involving the concerns of real estate in 1648, Captain Miles Standish, acting on behalf of the settlers at Barnstable, Massachusetts, purchased from a local tribesman named Paupmunnuck "with free and full conssent of his said brother and associats, freely, fully and absolutely barganed and sold unto the Captain Miles Standish, in the behalfe and for the use of the inhabytants of Barnstable aforsaid, all his and thayer right, title and interest in all his and thayer lands lying and being within the precints of Barnstable." Usually these transactions stipulated that the native people were selling their land to the English, but preserving the right to hunt, fish and plant on it. Of course, we must remember the English drew up these contractual agreements and expected the local tribal leaders to comprehend the white man's definition of a legal title, a concept totally alien to the Algonkian notion of a usage right to the land.

The viewpoint of the English concerning Algonkian land use is clearly expressed by Robert Cushman, who early on made a brief visit to Plymouth Colony. In his Eurocentric assessment of Wampanoag use of the land, Cushman states, " The country is yet raw; the land is untilled; the cities not builded; the cattle not settled. We are compassed about with a helpless and idle people, the natives of the country, which cannot, in any comely or comfortable manner, help themselves much less us." Algonkian mores had no such concept as possessing a title, for the land they occupied was also used by the animals and plants that sustained them. The ambiguous force of *Manitoo* resided in the land. When *Yotaanit*, the fire god became angry, he made his power known by engulfing their forests and villages in flames. The Algonkian mind thought it was illogical to own the land in the way that the English conceived of possession, for the Algonkian man and woman saw themselves as an equal part of the great circle of life that shared the land with them. The land was therefore not theirs to sell in the English sense of the word, but their hospitable customs allowed them the right to invite others to participate in the land's usage. The English could indiscriminantly exploit the land for their Judeo-Christian god was the Creator, and nature was his undeified creation; but the animistic worship of the indigenous people required that they appease the appropriate spirit powers living in the land, before exploiting any part of the natural environment.

The English sometimes recognized the Native American concept of a usage right, for in the sale between Captain Standish and Paupmunnuck, the latter preserved a tract of land for himself and his associates, so they could hunt and trap on the land. The English permitted this activity as long as "they gave notice to the said inhabitants before they set any trappes," and diligently checked them everyday because the settlers' livestock often got caught in

"This may inform the honorable court, that I, Philip, am willing to sell the land within this draught, but the Indians that are upon it may live upon it still; but the land that is mine may be sold, and Watashpoo is of the same mind. I have put down all the principal names of the land we are now willing should be sold."

From Pacanauket (Pokanoket),
the 24th of the month, 1668.

Philip: P: his mark.

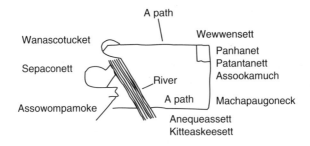

"Know all men by these presents, that Philip has given power unto Watashpoo, and Sampson and their brethren, to hold and to make sale of to whom they will, by my consent, & C. C. Witness my hand that I give it to them."

The mark P: of Philip, 1668

"John Sassamon is a witness."

A Land Sale Involving King Philip
From the records of Plymouth colony. The land described seems to be the present area of Rochester, Massachusetts.

them. For the tribal groups who remained in the midst of their English neighbors, unfenced cattle and swine became a serious problem when they trampled down their cornfields. As a result, in the land transaction with the residents of Barnstable, Paupmunnuck requested that part of his land be fenced off. The fact that the New England Algonkians often preserved their usage right to specific areas, and occasionally proceeded to have these remaining areas fenced off from their English neighbors, also suggests that some of them understood their right of usage had been restricted in certain property transactions with the colonists. Metacom (King Philip) seems to have made such a distinction in a land sale to the Plymouth colonists in 1668 for he states, "This may inform the honorable court, that I Philip, am willing to sell the land within this draught, but the Indians that are upon it may live upon it still; but the land that is mine may be sold, and Watashpoo is of the same mind. I have put down all the principal names of the land we are now willing should be sold." When the process of acculturation became more rapid in the late 17th century, the Christianized "Praying Indians" lived on reservations set aside for them by the Massachusetts Bay Colony. Even though these Christianized Algonkians claimed ancestral usage rights to these reserves, they often came into conflict with encroaching colonial farmers who challenged their usage rights with pretended titles to reservation land.

A sachem was quite familiar with the lands occupied by his people. He travelled annually through the principal villages of each member tribe to reaffirm old alliances and to initiate new member tribes into the confederation. During this yearly procession the sachem took the opportunity to view tribal areas in the domain of the confederation. The sachem's arrival at a distant village was cause for celebration but it was also a time of great solemnity. The sagamores of each tribe could request personal counsel with the sachem. Algonkian tribal government allowed the sagamores to freely voice their opinions. About this, Roger Williams says, "the sachims have an absolute Monarchy over the people; yet they will not conclude of ought that concerns all, either laws or subsidies, or warres, unto which the people are averse, and by gentle perswasion cannot be brought."

The positions of sachem and sagamore seem to have been interchangeable, depending on the status of the tribe and its chieftan.

If a tribe was a member of a confederated nation, then the leader of that tribe was a sagamore or subchief under the sachem of that confederation. On the other hand, if his tribe remained unaligned, then the sagamore of that tribe would automatically be the sachem, for he was the embodiment of the highest office within that particular tribe. Thus, when a sachem submitted his people to a stronger nation, he in effect demoted himself to a sagamore, which was politically the second most influential position after the sachem of the confederation. As both positions were practically one and the same depending on tribal political affiliations, they naturally functioned in a similar manner.

The New England Algonkians esteemed hereditary descent lines in their governments to a limited extent, particularly when it involved the position of sachem or sagamore. If a sachem proved to be a charismatic leader, then his son was often invited by the tribal council to assume his father's position on his death. However, if the sachem's son proved ineffectual, then he could be challenged by more dynamic sagamores, who were often only too eager to draw the allegiance of the people to themselves. This was the apparent situation during the earlier years of Massasoit's sachemship, for one of his most obvious challengers was Conbitant, sagamore of the Pocassets. Likewise, Squanto attempted to use his close association with Plymouth to advance his own desire for leadership among the Wampanoags.

After being made sachem, the new chief lived in the *Sachimmaacomack*, or sachem's house. This longhouse was much larger than the other structures in the village, and decorated with the finest mats. Sachems and sagamores were generally wed to women of like status, who were known as *saunks*. While Passaconaway presided over the Pennacook people from the tribal seat of Pawtucket, his daughter married Numphow, sagamore of the Wamesits. Of his several sons, Nanamocomuck became sagamore over the Wachusett people through marriage. The sachem Massasoit also had several children, and according to custom, and to reaffirm intertribal solidarity among the Wampanoag people, his son Wamsutta (Alexander) married Weetamoo, daughter of the Pocasset sagamore. His daughter Amie married Tuspaquin, sagamore and powwow of the Nemasket tribe.

Algonkian society was in some cases matrilineal, descent being traced through the mother's side of the family. The lineage of certain sachems, such as the Narragansett sachem Canonicus, was glorified by tribal traditions, which must have heightened respect for this leader. It is said that Canonicus was a direct descendant of the venerable Tashtassuck, one of the wisest of sachems to ever preside over the Narragansett people. If this legendary figure ever actually held the Narragansett sachemship, it was some time prior to the arrival of the English in Rhode Island. During his lifetime, Tashtassuck became the father of two children, a son and a daughter, but unable to find any Narragansett sagamore or *saunk* worthy of them, Tashtassuck married them to each other. Four sons were supposedly born from this union, Sachem Canonicus being the eldest.

If a sachem had more than one son, then the sachemship was usually bestowed on the eldest son. For example, when Massasoit passed away in the winter of 1661, his eldest son Wamsutta, became sachem of the Wampanoag nation. Similarly, when the Pennacook sachem Passaconaway died around 1665, Wannalancit, his oldest surviving son, became the new sachem. In cases where the oldest son prematurely died while serving as sachem, the next brother, or in certain situations sister, became head of the nation. Such was the case when Metacom (King Philip) succeeded his older brother Wamsutta to the sachemship.

A woman leader was called a *sauncksquuaog,* which the English referred to as a "squa-sachem." Several famous *sauncksquuaog* of New England were Weetamoo of the Pocassets, Awasaunks (Awashonks) of the Sakonnet tribe, and Squa-Sachem, as the English referred to this *sauncksquuaog,* of the Massachusett confederation after her husband's death. If a sachem died before his son or daughter was old enough to be sachem, then the child had a person of great esteem in the tribe, such as a *wauontam,* or wiseman, as a protector. The protector became the overseer of the youngster and sometimes was considered the acting sachem until the child was old enough to assume the position, at which time the youth's guardian stepped down. The position of overseer was not very secure, for William Wood claims the Algonkians only tolerated the individual, "and if his faire carriage beare him not out the better, they will soon unscepter him."

The federal council, representing all the member tribes in a tribal confederation, was made up of sachems, sagamores, powwows and prominent pnieses. A sachem rarely took any major action concerning the nation without first calling a council, which the Narragansetts termed a *miawene*. At this meeting the council members voiced their opinions to each other concerning the issue at hand. Roger Williams sometimes attended these meetings, and he observes that "their wise men and old men (of which number the Priests are also,) whom they call Taupowauog (powwows) they make solemne speeches and Orations, or Lectures to them, concerning Religion, Peace, or Warre and all things." Occasionally, one of them would speak for two and three hours on a certain issue, while the audience, which often numbered in the hundreds, attentively listened. One time Roger Williams sat as a member of the audience while Sachem Canonicus gave an oration on his distrust of the *Wunnaumwayean* (Englishmen). After he expressed his apprehension about the white man, he took a stick, and broke it into ten pieces, and as he related ten reasons that caused him to fear the colonists, he laid down each piece of the stick.

It was common for a sagamore to publicly charge his sachem with neglecting his duties, particularly during times of war. When a sagamore felt he was not receiving adequate protection against his enemies, he had the right to withdraw from the confederation. "Their sachems have not their men in such subjection," Gookin writes, "but that frequently their men will leave them upon distaste or harsh dealing, and go and live under other sachems that can protect them." This was not always a judicious move on the sagamore's part, for if the sachem was insulted the sagamore might suddenly find himself an enemy of his former chief. When Obbatinewat, sagamore of the Shawmuts, placed himself under the Wampanoags to receive greater protection from the ransacking Mic Mac and Maliseets, he made enemies with Squa-Sachem of the Massachusett, who was angry when he deserted her confederation.

Yet some sachems were so benevolent that they won the admiration and affection of their people. Massasoit was highly esteemed by many of his fellow Wampanoags. Edward Winslow relates how his Wampanoag guide, named Hobbamock, became deeply saddened while they were enroute to Pokanoket country, because word came that Massasoit had died from a prolonged illness. When he heard this news Hobbamock became so grieved that he cried out *"Neen womasu sagimus, neen womasu sagimus,"* or "My loving sachem, my loving sachem. Many have I known, but never any like thee." At times Hobbamock's grief became so intense, according to Winslow, "it would have made the hardest heart relent."

Among the New England Algonkians the term "sachem" was the more commonly used word, but the Abenaki also called their chieftans *bashabas.* James Rosier, who participated in the Waymouth expedition of 1605, records how the Abenaki used the title of *bashaba* even when referring to the English ship captains. When Samuel de Champlain voyaged along the Maine coastline he recorded the personal names of the sachems of the Penobscots and Kennebecs as "Bessabez and Cahabis." In all likelihood these are probably not the personal names of these two sachems, but a corrupted pronounciation of the Abenaki word *bashaba.* Among the Mohegans these positions may have also been referred to as *wauyauwaghou,* a word that translates "chieftan."

Any person acquiring the sachemship took on considerable responsibility. The duties of the sachem and sagamore went beyond political matters, to the welfare of the people. Sachems and sagamores were responsible for the widows, orphans, aged and maimed, if their relatives were unable to provide for them. However, relatives seldom allowed the less fortunate to fall into this predicament because it was seen as a disgraceful situation by their peers. The sachem and sagamores also oversaw the allocation of planting fields when a family in the village desired more garden space. Tribal customs generally prohibited a sachem from relinquishing the usage rights to tribal land without the local sagamore's consent. In 1638 Sachem Passaconaway had to receive joint approval from his sagamores Runnaawitt of Pentucket, Wahangnonawit of Squamscott and Rowle of Newichewannock, before he could allow the English to settle in the Merrimac and Piscataqua river valleys. Likewise, the Abenaki bitterly protested against the encroachment of the English into the Kennebec River Valley during the early 18th century because the usage rights to this land had been extended to the English by individual tribesmen apart from the consent of the *bashaba* and all his sagamores.

Algonkian custom required that when an embassy came into a tribal village, they generally lodged at the sachem's dwelling. Tribal ambassadors were required to announce the purpose of their journey and the duration of their visit. The visitors were the sachem's personal guests while they remained at the village and received entertainment according to their status. Edward Winslow was dispatched from Plymouth on a diplomatic mission to Sachem Massasoit, in Pokanoket country. Winslow and his companions were cordially invited to sleep in Massasoit's bed. Winslow later recalled, "He laid us on the bed with himself and his wife, they at the one end and we at the other, it being only planks laid a foot from the ground and a thin mat upon them. Two more of his chief men, for want of room, pressed by and upon us; so that we were worse weary of our lodging than of our journey." Likewise, the Massachusetts Bay Colony sent an embassy to the Narragansett leaders, Canonicus and Miantonomo, to dissuade them from joining forces with the Pequots, who the English considered a threat to their security. Edward Johnson, who may have accompanied Edward Gibbons, John Higginson and Cutshamequin on this embassy, gives a detailed account of their Narragansett hosts. Johnson writes:

> The Indian King [Canonicus] hearing of their coming, gathered together his chiefe Counsellors, and a great number of his Subjects to give them entertainment, resolving as then that the young King [Miantonomo] should receive their message, yet in his hearing. They arriving, were entertained royally, with respect to the Indian manner. Boiled Chesnuts is their White- bread, which are very sweet, as if they were mixt with Sugar; and because they would be extraordinary in their feasting, they strive for variety after the English manner, boiling Puddings made of beaten corne, putting therein great store of black berryes, somewhat like Currants. They having thus nobly feasted them, afterward give them Audience, in a State-house . . . . In this place sat their Sachim, with very great attendance; the English coming to deliver their Message, to manifest the greater state, the Indian sachim lay along upon the ground, on a Mat, and his Nobility sat on the ground, with their legs doubled up, their knees touching their chin; with much sober gravity they attend the Interpreters speech. It was a matter of much wonderment to the English, to see how solidly and wisely these savage people did consider of the weighty undertaking of a War; especially old Canonicus, who was very discreet in his answers.

The sachem and sagamores' control of food stockpiles reinforced the social bonds between tribespeople in the villages. Each year the pnieses of the Wampanoags required that the people bring baskets of corn to their sachem and sagamores, and they appointed a certain time and place near the sachem's dwelling where the people were to deposit their baskets of grain. The pnieses stood by thanking the people on the sachem's behalf, and the following year the sachem bestowed gifts on those families that had generously given a portion of their harvest. Cultural anthropologists refer to this practice as redistribution, a custom whereby the food given to the sachem was stored as a safeguard for the tribe against poor harvest seasons. During hard times the sachem and sagamores ordered the grain deposits to be redistributed among the villages. These grain stores also fed the sachem's dependents who were unable to provide for themselves. The village also stockpiled food for annual celebrations. At a certain time each year the Narragansett sachem and sagamores hosted a solemn celebration involving the entire nation, where the people feasted most of the day while the sachems and sagamores ate nothing until evening. Even though redistribution can be found in most cultures, it is vital in Neolithic societies such as the New England Algonkians. The sachem, sagamores and powwows were held in such high esteem that even though they willingly labored for their own food, they probably had regular access to the food stores, and consequently the custom of redistribution allowed the whole village to benefit.

Tribal law was usually meted out by the sachem and sagamores who consulted with the tribal council. In cases of theft, these men decided the appropriate punishment. Under the Wampanoag code of law, which was unwritten, a person found guilty of thievery had three chances to cease his criminal activities. For the first infraction, the convicted person was humiliatingly rebuked in the presence of his peers. If he committed the same offense a second time, he was beaten on the back with a cudgel by the tribal chief. With the third offense, the obstinant culprit was physically disfigured by having his nose split upwards, so he would be permanently disgraced among his neighbors. When a village member was found guilty of murder, the victim's relatives were generally compensated by one of two means: large payments in either wampum or some other items sometimes sufficed, but if the family considered this payment not sufficiently just, then the other alternative was death.

Executions for murder appear to have been the duty of the sachem and sagamores, for they usually carried out the death sentence. The malefactor was brought before a council of the tribe's key officials who sat in judgement. Here the accused was permitted to plead his case. If he was found guilty, the council would announce the sentence, "*Nippitch ewo*," or "let him die," and they set the appropriate mode of execution. According to Edward Winslow, the sachem saw to the execution personally, but when the guilty party lived at a distance, the sachem sent a representative to see that the law was upheld. Most death sentences given to persons in distant villages were carried out with the sachem's personal knife, which he sent with his replacement. Under a death sentence the manner of execution apparently varied from one nation to the next; the Massachusett and Narragansett struck the criminal in the back of the head with a tomahawk. Algonkian punishment for homicide seems to have been enforced equally regardless of status. William Bradford describes a council discussion he witnessed, where a certain Wampanoag powwow was condemned to be executed for murder.

The social hierarchy among the New England Algonkians was loosely drawn. Each village had three main groupings: the sachem or sagamore and their relatives were at the top, with the *sannup,* or the tribal people in general under them. In the Massachusett dialect *sannup* means "men." The *sannup* were the largest social group within a tribal village, and they possessed the right to use the tribal lands. The Abenaki told Captain Levett that the *sannup* were not permitted to speak freely with the sachem's family. In the Algonkian village, the third segment of the population was captives from other tribal nations who had not been formally adopted by any of the *sannup* families in the village. As the lowest group, they lacked rights to the land and generally functioned as servants to the other two social groups. A number of French sailors for example, who had been captured by a force of Massachusett warriors, were distributed among five Massachusett sagamores to be their servants. These sailors were forced to fetch wood and water for their Algonkian lords, due to their rank as unadopted outsiders. Likewise, John Gyles, a young Englishman from Fort Charles (Pemaquid, Maine), lived for six years as a captive among the Abenaki and

Maliseet during the early French and Indian Wars, spending much of his time in service to his Algonkian masters.

Among the sachem, sagamores and sannup families, the all-important social institution of the clan persisted. People in a village who belonged to the same totemic clan were spiritually related to others of their clan. A clan was represented by animal emblems such as a hawk, wolf, turtle or bear, and anyone claiming association in one of these clans also recognized the animal emblem as his totem or legendary ancestral helper. For this reason, many of the Algonkian peoples painted the appropriate animal emblems on their apparel, or proudly wore a specific pelt, feather arrangement or pendant signifying their clan. The term "totem" is derived from the Algonkian word *ototeman*, meaning a person's brother-sister kinship.

In the Algonkian community a man's principal task was to help provide for his entire village, and particularly his extended family. He lived a communal lifestyle and was generous to his extended family and friends, as they were to him. Tribal survival depended on communal cooperation, and generosity was expected. However, each tribesman had the direct responsibility to care for his immediate family. Hunting and fishing occupied a certain part of his time, but he also made canoes, weapons, tools, tobacco pipes and various ornamentations. Men also cleared the woodlands for new planting fields, cultivated the tobacco gardens, and cut the bark shingles and support poles for the wigwams. Young boys were raised by the women until they reached puberty, at which time they were initiated into manhood. From this age on a boy was allowed to wear his hair long.

As a young boy approached adolescence, he increasingly joined the company of the men. Under the men's tutelage, tribal sons were taught to hunt, track, fish, canoe, make stone implements and memorize tribal oral traditions. The latter often emphasized tribal history and the importance of being a member of the family clan. Once initiated, adolescent boys were encouraged to participate in the campfire conversations of the pnieses and the tribal elders, where they heard the stories of the feats of tribal members past and present, which taught them to respect their ancestors. During his initiation ceremony a youth's bravery was put to the test. He might have to drink the juice of a pungent herb until he

ANIMAL FIGURES DRAWN BY THE ABENAKI
AND THEIR ALLIES.

vomited, or be required to travel into the wilderness. During this quest the adolescent and his peers had to accomplish certain tasks. Young men who successfully passed the initiation rites aspired to be future pnieses, powwows and sagamores. The tribal youth during their adolescent years were usually given another name, which they used interchangeably with their birth name.

Each Algonkian child between infancy and adulthood acquired two names, and as Edward Winslow points out, "all their names are significant and variable; for when they come to the state of men and women, they alter them according to their deeds and dispositions." The naming of a child was a joyous occasion that usually involved the entire village. Algonkian parents invited family and friends to a celebration of gift giving and dance, during which guests suggested names for the child. Birth names were sometimes associated with the circumstances surrounding the birth. Daniel Gookin tells how a Christianized Capawick tribesman named Hiacoomes nearly lost his wife and newborn child due to complications during delivery. Because both mother and daughter survived the ordeal, he gave his little girl an Algonkian name, which translates "Return." The father later explained that this name had been given because God had "returned to them with mercies, in his wife's safe deliverance."

As male children matured they were given a second name that might at times signify a dominant characteristic of their personality. Such was the case with Passaconaway's son Wannalancit, whose calm disposition earned him the name *wunnennashanat*, an Algonkian word that means "breathing pleasantly." Young women also acquired a second name, which often related to their domestic roles in Algonkian society. The Pocasset squa-sachem's name, Weetamoo, has its origins in the Algonkian word *wetu*, which refers to the wigwam, and the domestic spirit force of the wigwam. Occom tells how elderly men and women often gave themselves a third name to mark their entry into old age.

Women had an equally important role alongside the men for they did most of the domestic work such as building and repairing of the wigwams. Whenever a family moved, the tribeswomen of the household dismantled the wigwam and lugged it to the new site. The woman's job was also to make clay vessels; she also did all the farming, from planting corn to harvesting it. Along the seashore in the summer, women spent their time digging for clams and searching out crabs in the rock crevices. Often they dove head first into the waters to retrieve a lobster from the shallows along the shore. William Wood observed women who trudged two and three miles carrying a hundred lobsters on their backs. Algonkian women also gathered acorns, chesnuts, edible roots and herbs while in the woods and along the lakes, to supplement the meat in their diet. In the village they wove baskets, mats, and they prepared various foods, such as deer, moose, bear, wolf, dog, raccoon and other animals. Most cooking was done in the open, but Algonkian women prepared food indoors, too. Gookin notes,

> Their food is generally boiled maize, or Indian corn, mixed with kidney-beans or without. Also they frequently boil in this pottage fish and flesh of all sorts, either new taken or dried, as shads, eels, alewives or a kind of herring, or any sort of fish. These they cut in pieces bones and all, and boil them in this furmenty all sorts of flesh, they take in hunting: as venison, beaver, bear's flesh, moose, otter, or any kind they take in hunting; cutting this flesh in small pieces, and boiling it as aforesaid. Also they mix with the said pottage several sorts of roots; as Jerusalem artichokes and ground nuts, and other roots, squashes, and also several sorts of nuts or masts, as oak acorns, chestnuts, walnuts; these husked and dried, and powdered, they thicken their pottage therewith. Also sometimes they beat their maize into meal, and sift it through a basket, made for that purpose. With this meal they make bread, baking it in the ashes, covering the dough with leaves. Sometimes they make of their meal a small sort of cakes, and boil them. They make also a certain sort of meal of parched maize. This meal they call nokake. It is so sweet, toothsome, and hearty, that an Indian will travel many days with no other food but this meal, which he eateth as he needs, and after it drinketh water. And for this end, when they travel a journey, or go hunting, they carry this nokake in a basket, or bag, for their use.

The tribal women also beat raspberries, blackberries and strawberries into a powder which they used to sweeten their corn meal used for breads. They gathered foodstuffs into root cellars for storage when winter arrived, and here also they preserved corn, bean and squash seeds. They used specially designed smokehouses to cure meats, which they later hung from the ceilings of their wigwams along with ears of corn braided together.

Most of the everyday domestic products such as utensils and baskets were made by the women in the village, who artfully worked them into expressions of beauty. Josselyn writes how they made "delicate sweet dishes of Birch-Bark sewed with threads from Spruce or white Cedar-Roots, and garnished on the outside with flourished works, and on the brims with glittering quills taken from the Porcupine, dyed some black, others red, likewise Buckets to carry water, large boxes too of the same material, dishes, spoons, and trayes wrought very smooth and neatly out of the knots of wood."

A young girl was expected to acquire all this domestic knowledge by working alongside the women. When she reached the age of menstruation, a ceremony ushered her into womanhood, and at this stage in her life a young tribeswoman had acquired all the essential knowledge concerning the female role in Algonkian society.

Marriage between young people was sometimes prearranged by their parents, but it did not preclude a son or daughter from marrying someone of their own preference. According to a few cursory remarks made by several colonial authors in their writings Algonkian marriage customs permitted polygamy. Roger Williams observed that although the Narragansetts approved of having many wives, in practice the men usually had one spouse. Thomas Lechford noted that the Algonkian men had numerous wives. Conbitant, sagamore of the Pocasset tribe, told Edward Winslow that he thought there "were many inconveniences in it, that a man should be tied to one woman." Apparently, the men preferred this polygamous lifestyle, because more than one wife increased the work force in the family's cornfields, and allowed them continued sexual interaction, since their wives were disallowed this during the first year of rearing an infant. Children were not weaned until they were about two years of age. Because the squa-sachem's family was held in higher esteem by the tribe, her infant children were often tended by nursemaids.

Most early New England authors who wrote about native culture agree the New England Algonkians loved their children and held an undying respect for their parents. Thomas Morton was so impressed with their respect for the aged that he writes, "It is a thing to be admired, and indeede made a precedent, that a Nation yet uncivilized should more respect age then some nations civilized, since there are so many precepts both of divine and humane writers to instruct more Civil Nations." James Sullivan, who wrote the *History of the District of Maine*, gives a fine example of this deep respect.

> Some years ago I was on the banks of the Kennebeck and saw an [Abenaki] who I supposed was of the Norridgewoock tribe. His name was Quenockross. He had in his family, his mother and his wife. He had been wounded in the war, and was lame in one of his feet. His mother was very aged; he had her in a canoe, with a blanket carefully spread over her: and when he came ashore he kindled his fire, took her out in his arms, and laid her tenderly down by it. When he had cooked his food, he gave it to her, and he and his wife waited until she had done eating. Upon seeing me notice it, he exulting pointed to her, and said, 'She is my mother.'

Most of the men, women and children who made up the social structure of each village community were related to one another by blood and clan membership. Even unmarried adults seldom found themselves isolated from the tribal community, for Algonkian lifestyle encouraged single people to live with their relatives until marriage, and single persons in an Algonkian village did not have their own wigwams. A village of a hundred people might have as few as seven extended families. Labor was divided, the man being the hunter-warrior, while the women and children cultivated the family gardens. Such social divisions and familial relationships made for a truly communal lifestyle.

Agriculture never reached any high degree of sophistication among the natives of New England, when compared with the agrarian achievements of indigenous peoples elsewhere in the Americas. The New England Algonkians, particularly those tribes situated in northern New England, relied on hunting and food gathering for the major part of their sustenance. However, among the Algonkian tribes of southern New England it was agriculture that provided between 65 and 85 percent of a person's daily food. From May to September, these tribes settled in the midst of their planting fields, which were annually assigned to village families by their sachem and sagamores.

Using slash-and-burn agriculture, the New England Algonkians cleared away sections of forest. Twice a year, generally in the early spring and autumn, the native peoples set fire to the woodlands, which sometimes burned for days, consuming miles of undergrowth. This cleared the forest floor to make travel easier, opened new land for farming, and indirectly improved grazing land for deer. In the burnt areas selected to make garden plots, the Algonkians cut down the timber still standing and then turned over the soil. Tilling was generally a communal effort. Verrazzano saw extensive cornfields that ranged over a mile in length, but generally fields were smaller and scattered on the most productive soil. Islands were ideal garden sites, for during the harvest season their grain was less accessible to being confiscated by enemy tribes. For this reason, the Massachusett and Narragansett farmed the islands in their bays, while the Pennacook cultivated Wickasauke (Tyng's) Island, along with other islets in the Merrimac River. In many of their gardens the Algonkians built small watch-houses where the older children lodged during planting season and harvest, to scare off the blackbirds and crows from the corn sprouts, and later, ripening ears. Algonkian women planted corn kernels deep to prevent the birds from pulling the seedlings out of the soil.

The Algonkians sometimes rotated their garden plots, but often cultivated the same planting fields year after year by fertilizing them with fish. Gardens contained corn, squash, beans, tobacco and probably certain herbs, and they were cultivated with a stone hoe lashed to a wooden handle. Sometimes these hoes were made entirely of wood. At other times the Algonkian farmer used a simple hand spade, which, lacking a handle, was held directly in the hand. They planted corn with a corn kernel planter, a slender pointed stone tied to a pole which poked holes in the soil.

The Algonkian mind was a storehouse of information on the proper care of native plants. The Pilgrims received their first lessons in cultivating corn from the Wampanoag tribes, who lived near Plymouth. The Pennacook cautioned the first English settlers in New Hampshire not to plant their corn until the spring leaves of the native White Oak were as large as a mouse ear. Some New England Algonkians in the north even possessed rights to certain maple groves, and in early spring when the sap was running, it was the women's chore to tap these trees and boil the sap down into syrup.

The only domesticated animals in the Algonkian villages were dogs, and in certain circumstances, hawks. In times of scarcity dogs were a convenient food source, and they may have been used in the hunt. Tamed hawks, raised as fledglings, were sometimes perched in the family cornfields to scare off blackbird flocks. During the Historic period, Christianized "Praying Indians" obtained livestock and domestic fowl from the English.

Since the native people depended on hunting for a large part of their food supply, they lived close to nature, and acutely observed the habits of their quarry. Seldom did hunters take game without first appeasing the spirit forces through many prescribed ceremonies. Besides tracking animals on the run, the Algonkian hunter used snares and a hedge-like structure that funnelled deer herds through a narrow passage. "They have other devices to kill their game," William Wood remarks, "as sometimes hedges a mile or two miles long, being a mile wide at one end, and made narrower by degrees, leaving only a gap of sixe foot long, over against which, in the day time they lye lurking to shoot the Deere which come through that narrow gut." Hunters sometimes entrapped deer by driving them onto small peninsulas along the seashore. A snared deer might remain trapped for a day before a tribesman checked his trap lines. In the meantime, the deer might be devoured by wolves, so "the Indian made a falling trap," Williams says, "called Sunnuckhig, (with a great weight of stones) and so sometimes knocked the Wolfe on the head, with a gainefull Revenge, especially if it bee a blacke Wolfe, whose Skins they greatly prize." During a communal hunt, the Algonkians gathered into groups of thirty to forty men who ranged the woods, and drove the deer towards a designated spot, where other hunters, concealed in thickets, shot at the animals as they passed. In areas where the deer herds congregated the hunters built camouflaged hunting houses in which the men stored their snare lines, spears, knives and other implements to catch, kill and skin the deer on the spot. Customs among the Algonkian nations controlled deer hunting, and each Algonkian confederation had a rule that required hunters to use their own tribal grounds when pursuing deer. If a deer was shot in another tribe's hunting territory, then the forepart of the animal was given to that village. On the other hand, if the deer was brought down in water, then the skin went to the sagamore of the tribe where the deer was taken.

Black bears were usually hunted during the winter season while still in a state of hibernation, for only then did an Algonkian hunting party have the advantage. To kill a hibernating bear, one member of the hunting party would crouch down into the den and attempt to drag the animal out into the open, while the other tribesmen waited nearby to strike the bewildered creature as soon as its head was exposed. John Josselyn relates how sometimes the tribesmen were not quick enough, which resulted in a hunter being seriously mauled. The Algonkian people so admired the bear's strength, that they often named their children in honor of this totem animal. The name of the Pennacook sachem, Passaconaway, translates "Child of the Bear," being derived from *Papoeis* (a child) and *Ogawinno* (the one who likes to sleep so well).

The Algonkians also hunted birds for food. Every year during the first two weeks of April expansive flocks of passenger pigeons returned to their nesting colonies across New England. The Narragansett called these areas *wuskowhannanaukit,* or "pigeon countries." Some of the breeding grounds covered extensive areas of timbered land, and the Algonkian people converged in these places to take both parent birds, and squabs when they were about to leave the nest. Hunters also took pigeons at the old planting fields, where huge flocks frequently fed on wild strawberries. Precontact Algonkians took enough pigeons to meet their needs, but did not jeopardize the future existence of these remarkable birds; as when the colonials started hunting them excessively. The Algonkians smoked pigeon breast for future consumption, and rendered fat from the squabs.

Each year during the salmon runs, the native people flocked to their specially constructed fishing weirs to catch the fish as they passed upstream to spawn. In the smaller brooks fishermen tapped the annual eel and alewife migrations, sometimes using just their bare hands. The Algonkian was an expert fishermen who knew the appropriate bait for each season. He made his line from hemp and his hooks from bone. His fishing nets were anywhere from fourteen to eighteen feet long weighed down with stone weights, generally of two designs. One was a simple disk with notches carved out on each side. The other was more ornate, resembling a surveyor's plummet. During summer evenings, the Algonkian fishermen often took to their canoes with a torch in hand, and waved it over the surface of the water to bring up bass and other fish. When the larger fish appeared the fishermen jabbed them with a short spear. The coastal tribes, as the warmer months approached, took to the ocean to do their fishing, and often scanned the shore-line for sleeping seals and beached whales. At night they captured cormorants asleep on island rookeries. In winter, the Algonkians cut holes in the freshwater ponds, fishing out pike, pickerel, bass, perch and breem.

For hunting and fishing the Algonkians used many tools. Some were multi-purpose that they also used in warfare. "Their weapons were bows and arrows," Gookin says, "clubs and tomahawks, made of wood like a pole axe, with a sharpened stone fastened therein; and for defence, they had targets [shields] made of barks of trees." And William Wood observes, "their bowes they make of a handsome shape, strung commonly with the sinnews of Moose; their arrowes are made of young Elder, feathered with feathers of Eagles wings and tailes, headed with brasse in the shape of a heart or triangle, fastened in a slender peece of wood six or eight inches long, which is framed to put loose in the pithie Elder, that is bound fast for riving: their arrowes be made in this manner because the arrow might shake from his head and be left behind for their finding, and the pile only remaine to gaule the wounded beast." Algonkian tribes-men made eagle claws, bone and the pointed tail of the horseshoe crab into arrowheads. To shoot his arrows a tribesman held his bow horizontally. These tools, weapons and trapping devices allowed them to find enough game to supplement their starchy corn diet.

The indigenous peoples travelled great distances on foot paths because they had to hunt as well as gather a considerable quantity of their food from the forest. The New England Algonkians often walked ten to twenty miles in a day. They wore light-weight mocca-sins in summer, and during the winter they used snowshoes made from the upper branches of sapling trees. The forest floor was a network of paths which followed the contours of the land, con-necting one village to another. Roger Williams, who traversed many a footpath in Narragansett country, notes, "it is admirable to see, what paths their naked feet have made in the wildernesse in most stony and rockie places." Using these trails the native people had access to most areas. One of the most famous trails in New En-gland led south from the St. Francis River past Lake Memph-remagog to the Passumpsic River in Vermont. From here it fol-lowed the Connecticut River Valley, bringing war parties within strik-ing distance of the New Hampshire, Massachusetts and Connecticut frontiers during the French and Indian Wars. Other trails that became warpaths during this protracted conflict led out from interior New Hampshire and Maine. These routes jeopardized the entire "Eastern frontier" of Maine (then part of Massachusetts) and New Hampshire, along with the Massachusetts Bay frontier from Amesbury to Marlborough, leaving villages open to assault by the "Indian enemy."

The Algonkians like most people living close to nature knew the movements of the heavenly bodies, which they used to give them a keen sense of direction. Even the children knew most of the constellations by name. The sun and moon were called by several names, but generally were known by the collective term *munnanock*. The name of Mount Monadnock in New Hampshire is an anglicized version of "the place of the sun," probably referring to the fact that the sun's morning light touches this peak before it shines on the surrounding thick forest. The Narragansett people called the Morning Star (Venus) *Mishannock*, and they called the constellation of the Great Bear (Big Dipper) *Moske*, the word for the native black bear.

In their travels, the Algonkians generally used overland trails or waterways interchangeably, depending on the direction of their journey. They were ingenious in using the rivers as highways, and concealed their dugouts at various places along a river, so that when a member of their tribe was going down river, he knew where to find them; if he needed to cross overland to another tributary, he would have a dugout available. Dugouts required large pine trees, which were felled and burned out at the center. The canoe makers chipped the charcoal with clam shell tools and stone adzes. Some of these dugouts weighed two hundred and fifty to three hundred and fifty pounds, and were between forty and fifty feet long.

Where birch trees were plentiful, the indigenous people preferred to build birch bark canoes. Contrary to popular belief, these canoes were used in southern New England, as well as in the north, although they were in most cases probably acquired from the Abenaki and Pennacook through trade. Martin Pring, an English explorer who spent the summer of 1603 along the southeastern coast of Massachusetts, describes these canoes as made of bark and tough twigs sewn together, with an exterior and interior shellacking of turpentine derived from pine pitch. Some of the larger birch bark canoes were upwards of seventeen feet long and four feet broad. Both the larger birch bark canoes and dugouts were used for travel along the seacoast. In Maine, English coastal settlements were sometimes attacked by Abenakis travelling by canoe, who paddled down to the colonial outposts from their villages up river. Besides canoes, the Algonkians also built rafts, generally used to cross rivers, although English colonials report that native families also used them on the coastal bays and sounds.

When the Algonkians were not at war, their land and water routes became thoroughfares of communication and trade. A tribe with a commodity to offer distant villages bartered it as a valuable item. "Salvages that live by the seaside," Thomas Morton observes, "trade with the inlanders for chesnuts and such like useful things as one place affordeth, are sold to the inhabitants of another, where they are novelty amongst the natives of that land." The Narragansetts traded with tribes who lived near to the Mohawks (and possibly with the Mohawks themselves) as well as other coastal Algonkians, and received ornately carved pipes made by their mortal enemies. Carved from wood and chipped from stone into beautifully designed animal shapes, some of these Mohawk pipes were up to two feet in length. The Mohawks also manufactured ceramic pipes, designed with a coiled snake, the head of a wolf or the face of a woman. The New England Algonkians copied these skillfully done Iroquoian products, such as pipes and collared pottery, which diffused into their culture through trade. Likewise, the Mohawks indirectly acquired items from the neighboring Algonkian tribes. Because the coastal Algonkians were seminomadic farmers, they had plenty of time to make specialized goods. Certain families in an Algonkian village might produce all the wooden dishes, others make bows and arrows, others weave, and others make ceramics. The seaside-dwelling Wampanoag, Narragansett, Pequot and Quinnipiac supplied the inland tribes, the Nipmuck, Pocumtuck and Sokoki, with wampum in exchange for superior furs.

The New England Algonkians of the Historic period (1600-1726) used wampum and corn as commodities of exchange, and these were also recognized as legal tender by the English colonists. "The Indians bring downe all their sorts of Furs," Roger Williams says, "which they take in the Countrey, both to the [other] Indians and to the English for this Indian money: this money the English, French and Dutch, trade to the Indians, six hundred miles in several parts [North and South from New England] for their Furres, and whatsoever they stand in need of from them: as Corn, Venison, etc." The colonists in New England established a coin value for this wampum, at six beads of white wampum for one English penny, and three of the black wampum for the same price. These beads were usually strung on strings, which the Narragansetts called *enomphosachick*. Often the Algonkians used wampum to make caps, aprons and belts, as these shells also had ceremonial meaning. The Wampanoag sachem Metacom (King Philip) visited Boston at one time wearing a cloak "set thick with these beads in pleasant wild works" and a broad wampum belt.

Since the New England Algonkians mainly lived out-of-doors in the changeable New England climate, clothing and shelter were extremely important. They made most of their apparel from plant materials and animal hides; in summer the men wore a hide around their groin, while the women wore skirts made from hides or plant fibers, which they sometimes wore in combination with cloaks. Algonkian women also wore leather leggings decorated with hide strings. As winter approached, the native people dressed in a combination of hides and furs. They wrapped the bottoms of their leggings inside their deerskin moccasins, and fastened these breeches around their waist with buttons. Deerskin cloaks were commonly worn, which style dictated must have the deer tail undamaged. They could turn the cloaks to the windward side for greater warmth, and often painted colorful animal designs on them, and embroidered them with wampum.

Travelling to a distant village, the native wore an otter, beaver, fox, wolf or lynx skin on one shoulder, to signify his rank and the animal emblem of his clan. Besides the usual feather placements to dress up the hair, the tribesmen sometimes placed a stuffed sparrow hawk with outstretched wings on top of their heads. "They take a great pride in the wearing of such an ornament," writes Thomas Morton "and give to one of us [English], that shall kill them one for that purpose, so much beaver as is worth three pounds sterling, very willingly." These kestrels were so valued as ornaments, that sometimes they were given as ransom for a captured sagamore. Algonkian parents also used turkey feathers to make colorful cloaks for their children.

The New England Algonkians built their lodges according to two structural styles: the *puttuckakaun* (wigwam) and the *qunnekamuck* (longhouse). The wigwam was a circular structure about fourteen feet high and ten to fifteen feet wide. Wigwams built to hold more than one family were larger. Reinforced with strong frames made from sapling trees, the wigwam was covered with bark shingles, rushes, corn husks and woven mats. The women hung artfully designed mats on the inner walls for decoration. In summer, the walls of the wigwams were covered with chesnut and birch bark; in winter the mats were much thicker. An opening in the center of the roof allowed smoke to escape from the cooking fires. In the autumn of 1620, when the Pilgrims were wandering on the outer Cape, they came upon two wigwams near the Pamet River, which they describe "as a crude affair being made of sapling trees which were bent and stuck in the ground at both ends." Both circular structures were covered to the ground with mats, and had a doorway on one side which was less than a yard high. Inside the wigwams were four slender poles hammered into the ground, and on these poles were small sticks used as hangers for their pots. Mats and furs to sleep on were arranged around the fireplace. The Pilgrims observed that the walls of both structures had double siding for greater warmth. On the dirt floor inside, the occupants kept wooden bowls, trays, dishes, earthenware and an unusual basket constructed of crabshells. Outside, near the wigwams, lay bundles of rush.

Possibly the dome-shaped design of the Algonkian wigwam was a deliberate attempt to imitate the structure of the beaver lodge. According to one Algonkian tribal tradition, the beaver was one of their tribal forefathers, and hence a totem animal. A Maliseet tradition tells how one tribesman lost his way while he was hunting and wandered into a large structure of piled wood, where he found some dried eels. His curiousity about who had built such a fine shelter was soon satisfied when a family of beavers arrived: he realized he was inside a huge beaver lodge. According to the story, winter was fast approaching so the beavers allowed the tribesman to stay with them, but when spring came they turned him out of the lodge, and he found his way back to his own people, praising the beavers' kindness. The design of the Algonkian wigwam may have been their way of commemorating the hospitality of the beaver.

The long house, the other structure commonly built by the New England natives, was a much larger affair. Gookin claims he saw long houses that were a hundred feet in length and thirty feet wide. Many families lived in these large, rectangular buildings. The number of fireplaces inside depended on the number of occupants. Each family used a section of the house, where they set up their beds of mats on wooden planks. Long houses were probably most common in villages that were also tribal seats, because sachems were required to entertain many guests. Both the wigwam and the long house were said to be much warmer than the English houses.

In addition to the wigwam and long house, the Algonkians had other smaller structures, for special purposes. In the *wetuomemese,* or "little house," an Algonkian woman customarily spent her monthly menstruation period, as tribal mores required. Roger Williams, who noted this practice among the Narragansetts, says, "their women and maids live apart in, foure, five, or six dayes, in the time of their monethly sicknesse, custome in all parts of the Countrey they strictly observe, and no Male may come into that house." Other specially designed structures were the sachem's residence, and a house specifically for gambling. The Algonkians also had saunas, which were usually about eight feet high, and held about fifteen people at a time. In these saunas the tribesmen sat around for an hour or more, smoking and chatting. According to the Narragansetts, the sauna cleaned a person's skin and purged his body of sickness. After the occupants had perspired enough, they took a quick dip in a nearby stream or pond, and these social steam baths kept the indigenous people relatively clean during the winter months.

Because they were seminomadic, the New England Algonkians built temporary villages to suit their mobile lifestyle. When the soil became unproductive, or the supply of firewood ran low, they moved to a new spot within their tribal lands. Roger Williams recalled, "I once in travell lodged at a house, at which in my returne I hoped to have lodged againe there the next night, but the house was gone in that interim, and I was glad to lodge under a tree. They are quicke; in halfe a day, yea, sometimes at few houres warning to be gone and the house up elsewhere; especially, if they have stakes readie pitcht for their Mats." The Nipmucks were just as quick at erecting a wigwam as they were in dismantling it. In Mary Rowlandson's account of her captivity among the Nashuas and Quabaugs during King Philip's War, she writes, "When night came on we sat down. It rained but they quickly got up a bark wigwam where I lay dry that night." Apparently, when the tribeswomen carried the dismantled wigwams with them, they were capable of establishing camp in a matter of hours.

All the Algonkian nations, from the Penobscots to the Pequots, built forts to protect their people in the event of war. These palisaded structures generally had two entrances that were closed up with brush during times of intertribal conflict. In 1621, when the Pilgrims journeyed to the lands of the Massachusett nation, they came across a fort that these people had constructed to defend themselves from Mic Mac and Maliseet warriors. The walls of the fortress were made of forty-foot poles set close to each other; around the outside and inside of this stockade was a ditch four to five feet deep, with a bridge leading over it to the only entrance into the fort. William Wood writes,

> They make themselves Forts to flie into, if the enemies should unexpectedly assaile them. These Forts some be fortie or fiftie foote square, erected of young timber trees, ten or twelve foot high, rammed into the ground, with undermining within, the earth being cast up for their shelter against the dischargements of their enemies, having loopholes to send out their winged messengers, which often deliver their sharp and bloody embassies in the tawnie sides of their naked assailants, who wanting butting Rammes and battering Ordinances to command at distance, lose their lives by their too neare approachments.

Warfare among the seven major Algonkian confederacies was ongoing. Since most of the native population lived along the narrow New England coastal plain, territorial disputes often escalated into hostilities. Except for the Pequot expansion over the lower Connecticut River tribes at the beginning of the Historic period, wars among the New England Algonkians generally consisted of sporadic strikes. Roger Williams states;

> Their Warres are farre lesse bloudy and devouring then the cruell Warres of Europe; and seldome twenty slaine in a pitch field: partly because when they fight in a wood every tree is a Bucklar. When they fight in a plaine, they fight with leaping and dancing, that

seldome an Arrow hits, and when a man is wounded, unlesse he that shot followes upon the wounded, they soon retire, and save the wounded: and yet having no Swords, nor Guns, all that are slaine are commonly slaine with great Valour and Courage: for the Conquerer ventures into the thickest, and brings away the Head of his Enemy. They are much delighted after battell to hang up the hands and heads of their enemies.

Generally sachems went into battle with their warriors. Each side tried to capture or kill the enemy sachem, which was sometimes accomplished through treachery. When the Saco and Kennebec tribes went to war in 1607, each side tried to murder the other's sachem and their sons in line of succession. Either Mic Mac or Maliseet warriors killed Sachem Nanapashemet of the Massachusett in their war of 1619. Conbitant, sagamore of the Pocassets, spread the rumor that Massasoit, sachem of the Wampanoags, had been kidnapped by the Narragansetts, in his attempt to terminate Massasoit's alliance with the Pilgrims at Plymouth. The loss of a sachem during wartime was a devastating blow for a tribe, and they usually retaliated against their enemies.

When a tribe declared war, the men prepared for battle, while the women and children took refuge in the strongest forts, or in seemingly impenetrable swamps, for safekeeping. Tribes usually fought on land, but Roger Williams claims that the Narragansetts sometimes engaged their enemies in sea battles.

If a tribal nation abused a deceased sachem's name it was reason enough for a tribe to begin hostilities against the insulting tribe. This was one of the reasons Narragansett warriors pillaged the Nipmuck village of Quatisicke in 1667. If an Algonkian tribe wanted to declare hostilities they sent a certain symbolic object to their enemies. In 1621, either the Narragansetts or a group of conspiratorial Wampanoag sagamores sent such a threat to the Plymouth colonists. "That great people of the Narragansetts," William Bradford writes, "in a braving manner, sent a messenger unto them [Pilgrims] with a bundle of arrows tied about with a great snakeskin, which their interpreters told them was a threatening and a challenge." The Narragansetts also sent messengers into their tribal villages in times of war to announce the declaration of hostilities. "He that is a Messenger," Roger Williams writes, "runs swiftly, and at every towne the Messenger comes, a fresh Messenger is sent, he hollowes often, and they that heare answer him, until by mutuall hollowing and answering hee is brought to the place of audience, where by this means is gathered a great confluence of people to entertaine the newes." During her captivity in King Philip's War, Mary Rowlandson noticed how war parties returning from raids on the English settlements shouted out their coup counts. She writes:

> The next day, viz. to this, the Indians returned from Medfield; (all the company, for those that belonged to the other small company came through the town that now we were at.) But before they came to us, oh the outrageous roaring and whooping that there was! They began their din about a mile before they came to us. By their noise and whooping, they signified how many they had destroyed, (which was at that time twenty- three.) Those that were with us at home were gathered together as soon as they heard the whooping, and every time that the other went over their number, these at home gave a shout, that the very earth rang again. And thus they contin-ued till those that had been upon the expedition were come up to the Sagamore's wigwam; and then, oh the hideous insulting and triumphing that there was over some Englishmen's scalps that they had taken and brought with them.

Quintin Stockwell of Deerfield, taken captive a year later, reports that when his captors dispersed into the woods they "made strange noises, as of wolves and owls, and other wild beasts, to the end that they might not be discovered by the English." These customs iden-tified the returning war parties after a raid. By shouting the success of their mission or using familiar calls one to another, these war-riors could not be mistaken for an enemy force as they approached.

The New England Algonkian language expresses relationships using compounds. Recognizing this characteristic in their speech, William Wood states, "our Southerne Indians use seldome any short Colloquiums, but speake their minds at large, without any inter-jected interruptions from any." In place names, for example, cer-tain words that produce compounds are important. *Msqui*, is the Algonkian word for the color red, and *naumas* the word for fish. These terms are evident in such place names as Nameskeag (Amoskeag) in present-day Manchester, New Hampshire, which means the "fishing place," and Misquamicut, Rhode Island, the "red fish" or "salmon fishing place." Other common Algonkian place name words are *achu,* denoting hilly ground, as in Massachusetts and Mount Wachusett; and *cook* or *ock* also a term denoting a "place," "ground" or "soil." Hence the place names of Suncook, New Hampshire, the Squannacook River in Massachusetts and Millinocket, Maine. The Algonkian word *keag* also denotes a "place" or "area," as in Mattawamkeag and Passadumkeag, Maine. Connecticut is an anglicized pronounciation of the Algonkian term *kweni-tegu; tegu* meaning river, which was applied to the river of that same name. *Massa* was used to describe anything that was large or great, as in Massabesic Lake in New Hampshire and Massapoag Pond in Tyngsborough, Massachusetts. An Algonkian word frequently used for ponds and lakes is *nipi* meaning water. Names such as Lake Sunapee and Lake Winnipesaukee in New Hampshire, Nipmuck Pond in Massachusetts and Nepaug Reservoir in Nepaug, Connecticut contain this word.

The native people attached descriptive words to these and other place names, to distinguish the uniqueness of one locality from another. For example, they used the Algonkian term *Wachusett,* for the area around Mount Wachusett in present-day Princeton, Massachusetts. The word ending *sett* is the anglicized pronounciation of the Algonkian word *ock* or *auk,* which means a "ground," "place," or "area." *Achu* is the Algonkian word for hill. When these two words are brought together in the compound term *Wachusett,* it means "hill-place," or "high-place." In the place name *Cohasset* as in Cohasset, Massachusetts, *set* means place, while *cohas* is the word for pine tree. When joined these two words make the compound word *Cohasset,* which means the "pine-tree-place." A similar compound word is *Coheassuck,* a Narragansett place name in Kent County, Rhode Island that again refers to the presence of pines in that area. Still, one final example is the word *Winnipesaukee.* An Abenaki place name, *winni* means "in or about the area," while *nipi* denotes water and *aukee* is a generally used term for land. Translated, *Winnipesaukee* means "the land or grounds about the lake place."

The New England Algonkians, because of the prevalence of compound words in their language, were able to give elaborate descriptive names to areas by simply adding words, as in Lake Memphremagog in Vermont, Chemquassabamticook Lake in northwestern Maine, or Lake *Chargoggagogmanchaugagogchaubunagungamaug,* a name well-known for its length, the Nipmuck name for Lake Webster in Webster, Massachusetts. In this last, the name is translated roughly "the place wherein we both fish on opposite shores," indicating that the Nipmuck people had an agreement on shared usage rights with either their Narragansett or Pequot-Mohegan neighbors. The ancestral usage rights of these three tribal nations converged in the general area of Lake Webster, and no doubt the tribes disputed who could use this fishing ground.

Algonkian language evolved minor dialectic variations from one nation to the next, even though the New England Algonkians shared a relatively small area. Differences in pronounciation, however, were so small that a Pennacook tribesman could understand a Wampanoag, and a Narragansett a Pequot. The native dialects of New England were linguistic subdivisions of the widespread Algonkian language, which was spoken by the majority of the indigenous peoples from the Carolinas to Nova Scotia. The Wampanoag language, according to Edward Winslow, was "very copious, large and difficult." Within a hundred-mile radius of Plymouth, he adds, there were minor variations in speech, but they did not inhibit communication among the New England tribal nations. "Every Countrey," William Wood points out, "doe something differ in their Speech, even as our Northern people [Pennacook] doe from the Southerne [Narragansett] and westerne [Nipmuck] from them; especially the Tarrenteens [Mic Mac], whose tongues runne much upon R, that they drawl much in pronounciation." Certain tribes lacked the "l" and "r" sounds, according to Roger Williams, while others had these sounds in their speech. Sachem Massasoit is said to have pronounced Edward Winslow's surname as "Winsnow." The Reverend John Eliot, who mastered the Massachusett language so he could preach them the gospel, also observed minor variations in tribal dialects. The New England Algonkian word for dog, for example, illustrates the minor differences between the dialects:

> Cowweset - *Anum*
> Massachusett - *Anum*
> Narragansett - *Ayim*
> Nipmuck - *Alum*
> Pennacook - *Arum*
> Quinnipiac - *Arum*
> Saco - *Alum*

Daniel Gookin, who assisted Eliot in his missionary efforts among the Massachusett, states that the Algonkian tribes along the seacoast differed little in their dialects. According to his observations, "the Indians of the parts of New England, especially upon the seacoasts, use the same sort of speech and language, only with some differences in the expressions, as they differ in several counties in England, yet so they can well understand one another." Thomas Hutchinson elaborates on Gookin's statement, for he claims, "the language of the Indians, from Piscataqua to Connecticut, was so nearly the same, that they could tolerably well converse together. Labials they used with freedom. It is observed of the western Indians, particularly the six nations [League of the Iroquois], that they have no labials in all their language, and they and the Nipmucks, who lived little more than 100 miles from them, could not better understand one another than the English and Chinese."

There were three main dialectic divisions of the Algonkian language in colonial New England: first the Abenaki and Pennacook; second, the Massachusett, Narragansett, Pequot-Mohegan, Wampanoag, Nipmuck and Montauk; and third, the Mahican and Wappinger. The Maliseet, whose name means "broken talkers" or "garbled talk," spoke a dialect similar to the Passamaquoddy, but different from the Mic Mac, who labelled the Maliseet "broken talkers" because they had difficulty understanding them. Little is known about the Pocumtuck language, but it was probably akin to one of the two linguistic subgroups in southern New England.

Linguistic variations remain in Algonkian place names across New England. A map of the six-state region shows the indigenous term -*cook*, or its frequent anglicized version -*scot*, and the term -*keag* are more often found as place names in northeastern New England. In Maine, for example, are found Chementicook, Chesuncook, Kenduskeag, Menduxnekeag, Montsweag, Musquacook, Naskeag, Pemadumcook, Penobscot, Pejepscot, Sheepscott, Winnecook and many others. In New Hampshire, Contoocook, Naticook, Penacook, and others appear. In the northern border towns of Massachusetts, fewer are seen: Naumkeag and Winnekeag Lakes in Ashburnham, the Squannacook River in Townsend and Baddacook Pond in Groton. And beyond Nobscot, Skatecook, Swampscott and a few other places in southern New England, this name diminishes. The anglicized Algonkian word *sett* (meaning place, ground or soil), and its variants of *et* and *it*, appear more frequently in Massachusetts and Rhode Island than in northern New England. In Massachusetts, *et* and *it* appear in the Algonkian place names Acoaxet, Acushnet, Apponagansett, Assabet, Cohasset, Madaket, Manomet, Mattapoisett, Megansett, Miacomet, Monponsett, Nabnasset, Nantasket, Nantucket, Nauset, Nissittissit, Onset, Pocasset, Segregansett, Siasconset, Snipatuit, Squibnocket, Wamesit, Wauwinett and Winnetuxet, just to name a few. *Sett* is also common in Rhode Island, found in Canonchet, Chepachet, Cowesett, Narragansett, Pawtucket, Ponaganset, Sakonnet, Touisset and Woonsocket. To the west, in Connecticut, *sett* appears in Cockaponset, Hammonasset, Pataganset and Shetucket. In Connecticut, the word *sett* is also commonly pronounced *ic*, as in Meshomasic, Housatonic, Tagonic and Scantic. *Sett* is less frequent in northern New England, but can still be found in Carrabasset, Millinocket, Nubanasit, Pequaket, and Wiscasset. The anglicized Algonkian word *sett*, as mentioned previously, was originally pronounced *auk* by the indigenous peoples. The correct pronunciation of Massachusett therefore is *Massachusauk*, and Narragansett becomes *Narragansauk*, translated "at the point of land jutting between waters."

The New England Algonkian nations often named their places for some features of the terrain. A particular word for a recurring characteristic of their land often reappears in the surviving place names. The Nipmuck tribes formerly occupied lands that contained numerous ponds. One Algonkian word associated with fresh water areas is *paug*, which the Nipmucks used for the many lakes and ponds in their territory. To this day Nipmuck place names survive in their homeland of south central New England, as Muschopaug, Mashapaug, Nepaug, Pistapaug and Quonnipaug. Almost all are associated with lakes, ponds and rivers in that area.

Many Native American words that have entered into English are Algonkian, because Algonkian was the first major indigenous North American language group with which the English had long-term contact. Borrowed words used in politics, transportation, clothing, diet, and science, come from the Algonkian. In the American presidental campaign of 1884, a Republican faction that refused to support the party nominee James G. Blaine was dubbed the "Mugwumps;" a Massachusett term that translates as "big man." Today, "mugwump" is applied to a person who is neutral on a controversial political issue. "Toboggan" and "moccasin" are Algonkian words. "Succotash" is a derivation of the Narragansett word *msiquatash.* English colonists adopted both the word and this Algonkian dish of corn and beans. The word "monadnock," an Algonkian place name for a mountain in the southwestern corner of New Hampshire, has become a geological term for a residual postglacial mountain elevated above the surface of an eroded plain. Many Algonkian names for native flora and fauna entered the English vocabulary, particularly when the colonists lacked equivalent words for the new plants and animals. Squash, pipsissewa, chinquapin, quahog, tautog, chipmunk, musquash (muskrat), skunk, raccoon and moose, are just a few of the native names for wildlife.

The New England Algonkians often had leisure time because agriculture allowed them a seminomadic lifestyle; they did not need to put all their efforts into survival. They had spare time to play numerous games, some of which were for pleasure, and others to improve their physical skill. Coastal tribes frequently met along the seashore to play their football games, which the Narragansetts called *pasuckquakohowaug* [they meet to foot the ball]. These football games sometimes lasted for several days. "Their Goales be a mile long placed on the sands," William Wood reports, "which are as even as a board; their ball is no bigger than a hand-ball, which sometimes they mount in the Aire with their naked feete, sometimes it is swayed by the multitude; sometimes also it is two dayes before they get a Goale, then they marke the ground they winne, and beginne there the next day." The players usually painted themselves before the contest began, to create a striking effect during the game. Customarily, the players laid their weapons at a distance before any game began. The women cheered their husbands on, as young boys piped away on reed flutes. Usually, anywhere from forty to eighty men competed on opposing teams, and when rival tribes played, there were sometimes four hundred participants in the game.

The indigenous people of New England occasionally played a sport called chunkey. The players started out by running abreast, one of the competitors threw a disk-shaped stone in as straight a line as possible, and the others hurled poles towards the place where they thought it would stop. Whoever threw his pole closest to the stone scored points. Chunkey was more common in the southeastern United States, but some stone balls which are gaming stones similar to the disk-shaped chunkey stones have been unearthed in a number of archaeological sites in New England, although little is known about how these were used. Their shape suggests that they were rolled along the ground. Other Algonkian sports were archery, running and swimming. Native people, according to William Wood, used the side stroke.

The New England Algonkians enjoyed gambling, and played many games of chance. One game of chance was similar to dice, where they tossed painted bones or plum stones into a tray. William Wood writes that the native people called this game *Hubbub*. The game consisted of five small bones in a wooden tray. The dice were jostled about by thumping the tray against the ground, which continually changed the color ratio. Wagers of wampum were placed on the chances of a certain color combination appearing in the tray. Contestants often expressed their excitement for the game by "smiting themselves in the breast and thighs," says Wood, "crying out Hub, Hub, Hub; they may be heard play at this game a quarter of a mile off." Even though the game is no longer played, the Algonkian word "Hubbub" passed into English usage to denote a confused noise of many voices. The Narragansetts built specially-designed houses sixteen to twenty feet high to gamble in, and inside they strung their wampum that was to be gambled away. Gambling was not only popular, some Algonkian men were obsessed with it. They gambled off their wampum and all their possessions, according to Edward Winslow, even the skins on their backs and those of their wives, even though their wives might be miles away at the time. Apparently, the stakes were unlimited, for a player could even bet himself and if he lost, had to spend so many days in servitude to the winner. Another popular game was called *puims*, played with short sticks called *puims*. A skilled gamester proudly wore these sticks in one of his pierced earlobes for all to see.

Sometimes emotions became so intense during a game that murders were committed, which could place strains on tribal relations within a confederation. Governor Bradford and his Wampanoag guide Hobbamock, while visiting Sagamore Coneconam of Manamet, heard about an incident when two Monomoy tribesmen came to seek counsel from this sagamore on a bitterly cold winter night. The two visitors entered the village, laid aside their bows and quivers according to custom, and sat down in the presence of Coneconam. After sharing some tobacco, one of the Monomoy men explained how their powwow and a member of a neighboring tribe had begun to argue during a gambling contest. As their tempers flared they came to blows, and the powwow killed the tribesman. Now the neighboring tribe threatened to retaliate if the Monomoy sagamore did not execute the powwow. The sagamore of Monomoy, knowing Coneconam was greatly respected among the Wampanoag people for his wisdom, put off his decision until he had Coneconam's advice. After Coneconam, the two Monomoy tribesmen and Hobbamock deliberated at length, the sagamore of Manamet advised that the Monomoy powwow be executed.

Public gatherings for gaming and atheletic contests were largely entertainment, but the Algonkians also had games and dances that were more solemn public events. In the Narragansett ceremony called *Keesaqunnamun*, the players sat under a tree and practiced a combination of sports and religious ceremony. *Qunnekamuck* was another Narragansett celebration, named for the long house near which this ceremony took place. Many thousands of men and women met on the grounds around this long house, according to Roger Williams, and were entertained by fellow tribesmen who danced before them. Generally, the more generous would seek the honor of being dancers, for the ceremony required that each dancer give away wampum, deer cloaks, hide leggings, knives, and any other possessions they were willing to part with. Recipients begged dancers for gifts, saying *Cowequetummous*, meaning "I beseech you." This ceremony also redistributed material possessions within the tribe.

Stomp or ring dancing, a common form of Algonkian entertainment, was witnessed by a number of colonial authors. The explorer Martin Pring, Owen Griffin of the Waymouth expedition, Mary Rowlandson and Captain Benjamin Church in King Philip's War, and John Gyles during the French and Indian conflict witnessed this ceremony. In preparation for the dance tribal audiences gathered into several concentric rings around a fire; the tribal elders generally seated in the circle nearest the center. To start the dance an elder usually stood up and acted out through both word and deed a tribal story, the role of the hunter, or a call for warrior volunteers to go into battle. Once the elder tribesmen had made his initial appeal, others in the tribe were invited to continue the dance by imitating the elder, thereby showing their approval. The dancers would chant tribal songs and stamp their feet as they moved in a circular pattern around the fire. Some ring dances lasted for hours, provided periodic intervals of rest were allowed each circle of dancers.

To mark the passage of time, the New England Algonkians reckoned by the daily sunset, the movement of the constellations, and the monthly phases of the moon. The Massachusett tribal nation counted the passage of time by nights instead of days. Five days' time, in a European time frame, the Algonkians called *abonetta ta sucqunnocquock*, or "five sleeps." *Nequitta ta sucqunnocquock* meant "six sleeps," *enotta ta sucqunnocquock* was "seven sleeps " and so on, until the moon went through its phases to complete the passage of a month or *aquit-appause*, which contained a specific number of "sleeps."

The Abenaki gave the moon of each month a special name associated with the changing seasons. The Hunger Moon (January), occurred when their food reserves had run low and animals were scarce. The Ice Crusted Snow Moon (February) reflected the changing texture of snow in late winter. The Egg Laying Moon (March) is the season when Great Horned Owls build their nests. The Smelt Moon (April) drew the Abenaki to their seasonal fishing sites. The Corn Planting Moon (May) found the Abenaki sowing their corn, and during The Hoeing Moon (June) the women spent much of their time cultivating the family gardens. The Moon of Ripening Corn (July), soon gave way to The Moon of White Chubs (August) and The Moon of Eels (September). The annual cycle ended with The Moon of Hazelnuts (October), The Moon of Shoreline Ice (November) and The Old Moon (December).

Similarly, the present-day Mic Mac still refer to the monthly phases of the moon in terms of seasonal changes. January is Frost-fish or tomcod; February is Snow-blinding or sore eyes; March is Spring; April is Egg-laying; May is Young Seals or get herring; June is Summer or leaf-opening; July is Sea-fowl shed feathers; August is Young birds are full-fledged; September is Moose-calling; October is Fat, tame animals; November is All Saints' Day moon and December is the chief moon.

The Algonkians often entertained each other by telling the history and legends of their people. Without written language, they passed on their history almost entirely in stories. The past was also kept alive through songs, dances and the use of special art designs. Wampum and dyed porcupine quill designs often served as mnemonics for the storytellers. The Wampanoags dug holes to mark where any incident of historical importance occurred. Edward Winslow writes:

> Instead of records and chronicles, they take this course. Where any remarkable act is done, in memory of it, either in the place, or by some pathway near adjoining, they make a round hole in the ground, about a foot deep, and as much over; which when others passing by behold, they inquire the cause and occasion of the same, which being once known, they are careful to acquaint to all men, as occasion serveth, the therewith; and lest such holes should be filled or grown up by accident, as men pass by, they will oft renew the same; by which means many things of great antiquity are fresh in memory. So that as a man travelleth, if he can understand his guide, his journey will be the less tedious, by reason of the many historical discourses which will be related unto him.

Ever conscious of their historical landmarks, the New England Algonkians shrouded them in legendary traditions that involved the tribe and its deities. Some oral traditions told how certain animals came to exist; others explained the origins of the tribe. A legend of the people of Capawick (Martha's Vineyard) contains both these themes. It was told by Thomas Cooper, a half-blooded Algonkian of Gay Head, to Benjamin Basset of Chilmark, Massachusetts in the mid-18th century. Cooper originally heard the tale from his grandmother.

> The first Indian who came to the Vineyard, was brought there with his dog on a cake of ice. When he came to Gay Head, he found a very large man, whose name was Moshup. He had a wife and five children, four sons and one daughter; and lived in the Den. He used to catch whales, and then pluck up trees, and make a fire, and roast them. The coals of the trees, and the bones of the whales, are now to be seen. After he was tired of staying here, he told his children to go and play ball on a beach that joined Noman's Land [island south of Martha's Vineyard] to Gay Head. He then made a mark with his toe across the beach at each end, and so deep, that

the water followed, and cut away the beach; so that his children were in fear of drowning. They took their sister up, and held her out of the water. He told them to act as if they were going to kill whales; and they were all turned into killers, [that is Killer Whales] the sister was dressed in large stripes. He gave them a strict charge always to be kind to her. His wife mourned the loss of her children so exceedingly, that he threw her away. She fell upon Seconet [Sakonnet, Rhode Island], near the rocks, where she lived some time, exacting contribution [tribute] of all who passed by the waters. After a while she was changed into a stone. The entire shape remained for many years. But after the English came, some of them broke off the arms, head, but most of the body remains to this day. Moshup went away nobody knows where. He had no conversation with the Indians, but was kind to them, by sending whales ashore for them to eat.

Another Wampanoag account that involved this legendary giant tells how one time Moshup used Cape Cod as his bed, but unable to sleep he turned to and fro till his moccasins filled with sand. This so angered Moshup, that when he awoke the next morning he flung his moccasins into the ocean, one landing to form Martha's Vineyard, while the other fell nearby to become Nantucket. Whenever fog banks enveloped Cape Cod and the islands the Wampanoag claimed it was "old Moshup's smoke," an allusion to his pipe smoke.

Moshup, the legendary Algonkian giant, was called *Glooskap* among the Abenaki people. Like his Wampanoag equivalent, *Glooskap* is described as a tribal hero, who helped the Abenaki and the animals they hunted. One story involving *Glooskap* tells how he at first created a moose that was too large and powerful, making it impossible for the Abenaki to hunt them. To resolve the problem, *Glooskap* downsized the moose by squeezing it in his mighty hands. In a similar story Glooskap subdued a giant Bullfrog by compressing the creature in his hands; the characteristic wrinkles on the lower back of the Bullfrog are said to still show the imprint of Glooskap's awful grip.

Tribal legends also concern several of the highest mountain peaks in New England. An Abenaki tale speaks of a powerful god that lived atop *No-tar-dn*, or Mount Katahdin in Maine. In 1804, a surveyor named Charles Turner, climbed Mount Katahdin with two Abenaki guides, who told him the legend of the supernatural force that resided there. Turner describes the story in a letter to a friend:

The Indians have a superstition respecting this mountain, that an evil spirit, whom they call ' Pamola,' inhabits it, at least in the winter, and flies off in the spring with tremendous rumbling noises. They have a tradition, that no person, i.e. native, who has attempted to ascend it, has lived to return. They allege, that many moons ago, seven Indians resolutely ascended the mountain, and they were never heard of afterwards, having been undoubtedly killed by Pamola in the mountain. The two Indians, whom we hired to pilot and assist us in ascending the mountain, cautioned us not to proceed ahead - however, when they found that we were determined to proceed, even without them, they again went foward courageously, and seemed ambitious to be first on the summit. On our return to Indian Old Town [Old Town, Maine], it was with difficulty that we could convince the natives that we had been upon the top of Mount Catardin, nor should we have been able to satisfy them of the fact, so superstitious were they, had it not been for the Indians who had accompanied us.

Another Abenaki tradition involving nature spirits is associated with the headwaters of the Penobscot River. A Penobscot couple and their beautiful daughter, the legend goes, camped together at the headwaters of the Penobscot under the shadow of mysterious *No-tar-dn*. One morning the parents became frantic because their daughter was missing. After many days of searching they sighted her near the river bank, where she seemed to be wading with a young man. The youth's hair flowed into and with the rapids of the river, so that he seemed to be one with the water. When the parents approached the two young people, both the young man and their daughter vanished. The parents understood that their daughter had been lured away by a nature spirit in the river, and thereafter the river spirit often showed his gratefulness to the Penobscot people, for whenever they called on him, he sent them moose, deer and bear, which seemed to emerge from the very waters of the river.

Favorite legends and stories among the Algonkians in southern New England concerned agriculture, since farming was more crucial to their seminomadic existence than the hunter tribesmen in the North. The Narragansetts respected the crow, even though this bird frequently devoured their corn seedlings. According to one of their legends, in old times, the god Kiehtan, who cultivated extensive bean and cornfields in the southwestern sky, decided to send some of these seeds to the Narragansetts as a gift. Placing a corn and a bean seed in the ears of a crow, he commanded the bird to fly from the southwestern sky to the earth, where it delivered the seeds to the Narragansetts. This tale apparently attempts to explain the origins of planting corn and beans.

Narragansett folklore also tells of a heroic figure named *Wetucks*, who according to Roger Williams, "wrought great miracles amongst them and walked upon the waters," as a demonstration of his supernatural powers. The name *Wetucks* is derived from the Algonkian word *wautuckques* (rabbit), hence *Wetucks* is "Great Hare" or "Rabbit Man." This mythological figure went back to Algonkian dawn-time, and the Narragansetts believed he taught the Algonkian tribes the skills that allowed them to survive in the eastern woodlands. The Algonkians saw *Wetucks* as having supernatural qualities, yet they did not generally worship him as a deity. He can perhaps be better described as a demigod.

Vestiges of legends that have spiritual significance can still be found in some of the many enduring Algonkian geographic place names across New England. Mount Watatic, a sizeable hill situated in both Ashby and Ashburnham, Massachusetts, is named after the Algonkian word *witeo* (*wetu*) which means "wigwam " and *auk* a word that translates as "at the land or place." Hence, *Witeoauk* (Watatic) means "at the wigwam place." Anyone who has viewed this hill from the east will understand why the Algonkians gave it this name, for it resembles a dome-shaped wigwam. A colonial folktale tells how area tribes used to climb to the top of this hill with a stone in hand to leave as an offering to the deity residing on the mount in order to ward off misfortune. The hill was probably considered by the Nashua and Souhegan people to be a spiritual abode of *Wetuomanit*, the spirit power that guarded every wigwam household from mishap. Mount Watatic was probably the site of tribal pilgrimages to gain the favor of the wigwam god.

Traces of other Algonkian legends remain in certain colonial folktales. The story of Chief Chocorua is a fragmentary account of the last Ossipees and Pequakets, who had retreated into the White Mountains because of English encroachment upon their lands. Before his death the legendary chief supposedly cursed the area surrounding Mount Chocorua. Another colonial folktale involves a Christian tribesman named Saint Aspenquid, who is said to have preached the gospel to the Abenaki people at the base of Mount

Agamenticus in southern Maine. Legend has it that he was buried on this mountain. The authenticity of most of these supposed Algonkian legends that survive as New England folktales is questionable. At best, they bear only slight resemblance to the oral traditions that disappeared with the tribes that may have told them.

The New England Algonkians, from what colonial authors have written about them, had a culture consisting of tribal government, tribal law, religion, language, art, and a communal lifestyle based on the extended family. These were ancient customs that the indigenous peoples had lived by for centuries before the white man arrived. European influence during the 16th and 17th centuries placed a new stress on the New England Algonkians, for it brought on a cultural collision between a technically advanced society and a seminomadic Neolithic people. With the arrival of explorers, profiteers, fishermen and colonists along their shores, the unsuspecting Algonkians were shaken from their isolation, and gradually made subject to the European colonies that supplanted them.

Chapter III
Appearance Of The
"Walking Islands"

Before 1500, the New England Algonkian culture was isolated from contact outside the North American continent. The Algonkians knew their own tribal domains well, but only vaguely comprehended the topography and people beyond New England. Though they were aware of the Iroquoian political confederation of the eastern Great Lakes area, their knowledge of the land and people living south of Long Island was quite limited. "Though Virginia be not above a hundred and fifty leagues from us [at Plymouth]," writes Edward Winslow, "yet they have never heard of Powhatan [a chieftan of Virginia, c. 1550-1618] because the water is not passable for them, who are very adventurous in their boats." Some of the Wampanoags also told these same colonists that the Hudson River was an extended inlet from the ocean, that somehow interconnected with the St. Lawrence River to the north, a misconception which led them to believe they lived on an island.

As more and more European explorers, traders, fishermen and colonists arrived along their shores in the 17th century, the coastal Algonkians tried to piece together from their own cultural viewpoint why these strangers had appeared. The Narragansetts told Roger Williams that when the English first arrived in their bay, they thought it was because these colonists had run low on firewood in their previous homeland, just as tribal groups were forced to relocate when they exhausted the available firewood in an area. One wonders what the Algonkian tribal peoples thought when they saw a European sailing ship for the first time. Some Massachusett tribal people thought these majestic vessels were "walking islands." "They took the first ship they saw for a walking island," says William Wood, "the mast to be a tree, the saile white clouds, and the discharging of ordnance for lightning and thunder, which did much trouble them, but this thunder being over, and this moving island steadied . . . they manned their canoes to go there. Being saluted by broadside, they cried out . . so bigge walk, and so bigge speak, and by and by kill; which caused them to turne back, not daring to approach till they were sent for."

Most of the North American coastline remained unexplored by Europeans until 1524, when Giovanni da Verrazzano sailed along the North Atlantic shore under the authority of "the most Christian King of France, Francis I." Verrazzano explored the New England coastline, and during part of this voyage traded with the Algonkian tribes along Narragansett Bay. According to Verrazzano's account, he and his crew set an easterly course from present-day New York Harbor until they arrived off Block Island, where they saw smoke rising from encampments on shore. These fires may have been deliberate, for later English and French expeditions reported how the northern Algonkians lit fires near the shore to attract attention for trade. From Block Island, Verrazzano and his crew set their course towards the mainland for ten leagues, which brought them to the entrance of Narragansett Bay. There they encountered about twenty canoes manned by tribesmen, who had paddled out to greet the ship entering their bay. Surrounding the vessel, they yelled and made hand gestures that they wanted to trade with the crew. At one point these native people all shouted in unison, as if in approval of their unexpected guests. Either because of inexperience or curiousity, the tribesmen about Verrazzano's ship were fearless in their approach, and when the crew imitated the Algonkian gestures, the natives came even closer to retrieve the azure glass beads, bells and other trinkets cast overboard for trade. Of the many gifts these people received, they treasured the glass beads and bells the most, which they hung on their ears and around their necks. This tribal people had numerous pieces of worked copper, which suggests trade contact with the Great Lakes region, the nearest source for copper nuggets.

Among those who came aboard were "two kings" who, since they were in excellent physical condition, led Verrazzano to believe the eldest was less than forty years old, and the younger in his twenties. The elder sachem wore a deer pelt with branches fastened on it, and except for a long strand of hair tied up in knots on his head, was entirely bald. The younger chief, who was probably the sachem's son, was dressed the same way. The crew showed the sachems a piece of armor and several glass objects, which made them curious as to how such things were made. For most of Verrazzano's visit, he anchored his ship, the "Dauphine," a league off at sea to avoid being grounded on the shoals by a passing storm. When the weather improved, several tribesmen paddled out to the vessel in their canoes. They directed the crew using hand motions, to where they might safest sail the vessel further into the bay; and here the ship dropped anchor, remaining guests of these tribal people for another fifteen days while they replenished their depleted supplies. Because the ship was closer to their wigwam villages, the native people came in great numbers to see this phenomenon anchored in their bay. A considerable number of tribeswomen also came, but the Algonkian men would not permit them to board the ship, instead making them view it from a nearby island. These women wore their hair long, tied into knotted designs to decorate their heads, some of them had lynx skins draped on their shoulders.

On May 5th, Verrazzano and his crew weighed anchor and sailed eastward from Narragansett Bay, through Nantucket Sound, and around the outer tip of Cape Cod. Travelling north-northwest, the ship arrived off the Maine coast near Casco Bay, where the crew encountered some of the Abenaki people. According to Verrazzano, these natives differed greatly from those of Narragansett Bay, for they were hostile. When his men came ashore, the Abenaki shot at them with arrows and then slipped back into the woodlands along the beach. Several of the crew in one brief, friendly encounter managed to trade with some of these wary people from a cliff. The Abenaki lowered a basket attached to a line which was filled with what they chose to give to the men, and in return, the tribesmen received tools, fishhooks and other implements. When the ship left the area the Abenaki acted in such an insulting manner toward the crew that Verrazzano noted he felt unwelcome to come again and trade with these ungrateful natives. Some of the tribesmen demonstrated their disdain for the French sailors by exposing "their bare buttocks and laughing immoderately." "We did not find anything of great value in this land," Verrazzano writes of the Maine coast, "except for the vast forests and some hills which could contain some metal: for we saw many natives with pasternostri beads of copper in their ears."

Most historians believe that these native people acted in such a hostile manner because of earlier mistreatment by other European visitors, who may have cheated, abused or captured some of the Abenaki and sold them into the Spanish slave market. As more vessels frequented the New England coast, incidents of hostility became more prevalent. Because of the Abenakis' behavior, Verrazzano named this land "Terra Onde di Mala Gente" or "Land of the Bad People." He continued his voyage northeastward toward the Maritimes, before setting his course east into the open sea for France. Information from his voyage gave European cartographers a more accurate picture of the geographical shape of the eastern shoreline of North America.

For nearly a century after 1524, no earnest attempts to explore New England were made, even though ships of various European flags continued to sail off the coasts of Virginia and the Maritimes. Fishermen were attracted to the Maritimes in ever increasing numbers by stories of abundant fishing along the Newfoundland coast. They built fisheries in Newfoundland quite early, so that ship captains were able to extend their fishing season. Crews could dry much of the cod in fisheries on shore before shipping it overseas. As a result, a captain needed to make fewer transatlantic voyages during the fishing season. A greater catch also increased profits at season's end.

In 1578, at least three hundred and fifty fishing vessels were off the Newfoundland coast. The majority were French vessels, fifty were Portuguese, and a hundred boats were under the Spanish flag. Undoubtedly some of these ships sailed south along the New England coastline to fish and occasionally traffic with the indigenous people. Those tribes that lost some of their people to distant slave markets quickly learned to greet the next visit with flying arrows.

At the end of the 16th century, the English became interested in the unexplored territory they called Northern Virginia (New England), to distinguish it from the original Virginia, further south. In 1602, Bartholomew Gosnold, an English navigator, ventured down the New England coast from Maine to Massachusetts, accompanied by John Brereton, a crew member, who later wrote a descriptive account of this voyage. When they arrived at the Maine coast, six Abenaki men in a masted shallop sailed out to greet them. "About twelve o'clock the same day," Brereton relates, "we came to an anchor, where six Indians, in a Basque shallop with mast and

94

sail, an iron grapple, and a kettle of copper, came boldly aboard us, one of them apparelled with a waistcoat and breeches of black serdge . . . hose and shoes upon his feet; all the rest (saving one that had a paire of breeches of blue cloth) were all naked. These people were of tall stature, broad and grim visage, of a blacke swarthy complexion, their eyebrows painted white." Brereton concluded these tribesmen received the shallop and clothing during an earlier bartering transaction with Basque fishermen.

Towards evening, Gosnold sailed south from Maine and his ship arrived the next morning off a "mightie headland," which was undoubtedly Cape Cod. Here, Gosnold, Brereton and several other crew members sighted an Algonkian man and went ashore to meet him. After attempting to talk with him they returned to the ship. Still anchored there, the crew caught so many cod they were forced to dump the excess back into the bay. Making their way around the outer Cape they entered Nantucket Sound, and when they passed the outer islands they observed several bark wigwams and "manie Indians." From here, they sailed in a westerly direction, dropping anchor off the Elizabeth Islands where they began to build a small fortified shelter. Within a short time, about fifty natives paddled out to the island in canoes to visit the crew. They came ashore to sit on the rocks and call out to the men who were busily constructing their dwelling. Once the crew made their acquaintance, they spent the rest of the day bartering. Brereton mentions how these people, besides having furs, decked themselves out in copper jewelry. The Algonkians stayed with the sailors for three days, and shouted happily when they left the English, which the crew acknowledged by tossing their caps into the air to the sound of a trumpet. Six of the natives stayed on to help the sailors cut sassafras from the nearby woods.

While Gosnold and some of the crew cut cedar wood elsewhere on the Elizabeth Islands, Gabriel Archer was put in charge of nine sailors onshore at Cuttyhunk Island. Archer relates that one day he sent four of the crewmen to search out crabs among the rocks. Two of the sailors had lost their way in the woods, when they encountered a small Algonkian hunting party. The startled tribesmen shot arrows at the two men wounding one of them in the side. The other sailor, who Archer describes as a "lusty and nimble fellow" rushed upon the natives before they had time to rearm. In the scuffle that ensued, he managed to cut several of their bowstrings with his knife before the tribesmen fled into the woods. The next day the two sailors happily found their way back to the fortified shelter. Though Gosnold hoped some of his crew would stay behind to establish a permanent trading station at Cuttyhunk Island, all were eager to make for home. After their vessel "had taken in so much Sassafras, Cedar, Furres, Skinnes and other commodities," they set their course for England.

In the year following Gosnold's visit to New England, Martin Pring made a summer voyage to the region. Landing either at Patuxet (present-day Plymouth) or on the north side of Martha's Vineyard, the crew constructed a "small barricado" for their own protection while they collected sassafras from the local woods. The Algonkian people who lived in the area visited the fortified shelter in large numbers. "Sometimes ten, twentie, fortie and at one time one hundred and twentie [came] at once," Pring mentions. At the shelter, the tribal people traded, danced and on occasion, at Captain Pring's invitation, ate with the crew. Whenever one of the sailors played his cittern they would dance "twentie in a Ring . . . using many Savage gestures, singing lo, la, lo, la, la, lo: him that first break the ring, the rest would knock and cry out upon." Pring observed that some natives wore brass chest plates a foot long, and carried bows made from witch hazel that were painted black and yellow. Their bow strings were made of three strands of animal sinew twisted together. Over their shoulders they strapped reed quivers painted with red and yellow designs. One sailor brought two large mastiffs named " Foole and Gallant," which he let loose on the visiting tribesmen whenever the crew felt these people had overstayed their welcome.

By late July the crew had gathered enough sassafras to leave. Apparently, the native people in the area had come to a similar conclusion, and decided their unexpected visitors had worn out their welcome. About a hundred Algonkian warriors waited until the heat of the afternoon when most of the crew were gathering sassafras from the woods and only a handful maintained watch at the shelter. Armed with bows and arrows, the tribesmen encircled the fort and asked its defenders to speak with them. Captain Pring, who was on board the ship with several crew members, ordered one of the cannons to be discharged, which momentarily frightened the warriors off and warned the men deep in the forest. At a second cannon shot, sailors at a distance gathered their weapons, called for the two mastiffs, and beat a hasty return to the shelter. As they approached the fort, the Algonkian warriors quickly fled into the woods. Aware of the Algonkians' increasing hostility, Captain Pring and his crew left a few days later with a large store of sassa-fras, and six months after leaving England they arrived back safely. Again, in 1606, Martin Pring sailed along Northern Virginia and gave such a favorable report of the Maine coast that English inves-tors started laying plans to found a colony there, namely, the Sagadahoc Colony of 1607.

Meanwhile, Captain George Waymouth in 1605 explored Monhegan Island and nearby areas of the Maine coast. On board his ship he entertained some Abenaki tribesmen who wore red paint on their faces with blue stripes on chin, nose and upper lip. Their heads were crowned with striking coronets of stiff hair dyed red, and the white breast feathers of a seabird. From the natives he learned about the region with an eye to colonizing it, and also learned something of their culture, such as the Abenakis' practice of hunting for whales on the open sea. Whenever they sighted a *powdawe*, or whale, they would chase after it in their canoes, using a bone harpoon attached to a line to spear it. If the communal hunt was a success they brought the whale ashore, sang a song of thanks, and divided up their catch. Whale meat was considered a delicacy by the New England Algonkians, when they had it they gave it as a special dish to their closest friends.

Before Captain Waymouth returned to England, he decided to abduct several Abenaki men to bring back as living specimens of the "wild salvages" of New England. He ordered two unsuspecting tribes-men to be seized during a bartering transaction. It took six men to hold these two Abenaki men down until they were imprisoned on board the ship. Waymouth also kidnapped several others elsewhere along the coast. Sir Ferdinando Gorges refers to one of these natives as Squanto. Gorges tells how Waymouth came into the port of Ply-mouth, England, where Gorges was then commander. Waymouth was returning from his voyage of 1605 along the Maine coast, and on board his ship, Gorges claims, were five natives taken captive. Three were named Nahanda, Sketwarroes and Tisquantum (Squanto). Gorges took these captives into custody and taught them

English so he could learn first-hand about New England because he planned to establish a colony there. Apparently, Gorges was confused for James Rosier participated in the Waymouth expedition, and wrote an account of the voyage that same year entitled *A True Relation of the Most Prosperous Voyage Made this Present Year 1605*. Rosier states the names of the Algonkian captives on board Waymouth's ship were Tahanedo (Nahanda), Amoret, Skicowaros (Sketwarroes), Maneddo and Sassacomoit. There is no mention of Squanto.

Another account given by the Governor and Council for New England claims Squanto was captured by Captain Thomas Hunt off of Cape Cod in 1614, and he somehow ended up in Newfoundland, where a Captain Dermer informed the Governor and Council for New England of the invaluable service Squanto could render the Council. Dermer took Squanto on his voyage back to England, and for the next several years Squanto lived in England under the custody of Gorges who taught him English.

In the spring of 1619, Captain Dermer says, he returned Squanto to his homeland. In a letter dated December 27, 1619, he mentions that when they arrived at Patuxet they found all the members of Squanto's tribe had died from a contagious sickness. From Patuxet, Dermer and Squanto went west to Nemasket where they found villagers. From there they sent an Algonkian messenger a day's journey further west to Pokanoket. In short order, there "came to see him two kings attended with a guard of fifty armed men." These two kings were undoubtedly the sachem Massasoit and his brother Quadequina. Eventually Captain Dermer was allowed to depart safely from Nemasket. However Squanto arrived in England, its importance is in the fact that he learned how to speak English there, and his facility with the language allowed him to speak often to the Wampanoag people on the Pilgrims' behalf.

Even though the English were actively exploring New England, this did not deter the French from sending two exploratory expeditions along the New England coastline. Between 1604 and 1607, a French expedition under Sieur Pierre Du Gua DeMonts, and a second under Sieur de Poutrincourt, ranged the coast from the St. Croix River to Cape Cod in search of a site to colonize. Samuel de Champlain went on both voyages, and wrote a fascinating account entitled *Les Voyages Du Sieur De Champlain,* which gives considerable insight into the life of the New England Algonkians.

On Champlain's voyage out of France with DeMonts and a crew of seventy-nine men, the group constructed a small settlement on an island in the St. Croix River as a rendezvous before they began to explore the New England coast. They left the St. Croix River for their first anchorage, the Penobscot River, where they met the *bashabas* (sachems) of the Penobscot and Kennebec tribes. These tribes were joined in a defensive alliance to protect their villages from Mic Mac and Maliseet war parties. Bessabez, chief of the Penobscots, and Cahabis, chief of the Kennebecs, met with Champlain at the mouth of the Penobscot River, and they and some of their people received "hatchets, paternosters, caps, knives and other little knick knacks" in return for beaver pelts. The French sailed further down the coast to the mouth of the Kennebec River, but when Champlain's Maliseet guides realized he intended to visit their Kennebec enemies, they deserted the expedition out of fear. With winter fast approaching, the expedition was forced to return to St. Croix. All winter the men were trapped on the island outpost because ice floes passing down river kept them from going ashore. Champlain's crew was plagued by a fatal outbreak of scurvy which reduced them from seventy-nine to forty-four men by the following April. The Maine winter was too severe for DeMonts, who wisely decided to spend the coming summer in search of a milder climate.

On June 8, 1605, DeMonts sailed from St. Croix with twenty sailors bound for the Kennebec River. There some coastal Abenaki tribesmen told them the Kennebec and Mic Mac hostilities had unsettled their villages so much they no longer planted cornfields on the coast because their grain stores were continually stolen by enemy warriors. DeMonts left these coastal tribespeople, who were probably Pejepscots, and sailed southwest for Almuchicoitt, the homeland of the Saco nation. The Saco were the most successful farmers of all the Abenaki. "The savages," Champlain writes, "dwell permanently in this place, and have a large cabin surrounded by palisades made of rather large trees placed by the side of each other, in which they take refuge when their enemies make war upon them. They cover their cabins with oak bark." The Saco planted gardens around their fortified village and cultivated them with wooden spades and the shells of horseshoe crabs. They planted their corn in hills three feet apart, and sowed several bean seeds in them that interlaced with the maturing corn stalks. They also grew squash, pumpkins and tobacco, planting their fields in May and harvesting them in September.

DeMonts and Champlain spent three days at Almuchicoitt and set sail for Cape Ann, arriving on July 16. Several Agawam tribesmen came near the ship and eventually DeMonts sent Champlain ashore to meet with them. He gave them a knife and a portion of biscuit, and inquired into the contour of the coast by making a crayon drawing of Cape Ann. The Agawams, knowing the shape of the coast much better than he, took the crayon and sketched "the outline of another bay [Massachusetts Bay], which they represented as very large; here they placed six pebbles at equal distances apart, giving [Champlain] to understand by this that these signs represented as many chiefs and tribes. Then they drew a river [the Merrimac River] which he had passed, which has shoals and is very long."

From Cape Ann, DeMonts sailed into present-day Salem Harbor, where he made a brief stop among the natives of Naumkeag, before arriving in Massachusetts Bay. All along the shore from Cape Ann to Massachusetts Bay the crew sighted cornfields and many wigwams, suggesting the area was well populated. While Champlain and his group visited the Massachusett people, he saw them building a dugout canoe. "After cutting down," he observes, "at a cost of much labor and time, the largest and tallest tree they can find, by means of stone hatchets, they remove the bark, and round off the tree except on one side, where they apply fire gradually along its entire length; and sometimes they put red-hot pebble-stones on top. When the fire is too fierce, they extinguish it with a little water, not entirely, but so that the edge of the boat may not be burnt. It being hollowed out as much as they wish, they scrape it all over with stones, which they use instead of knives."

DeMonts and Champlain traded with Honabetha, a chief who lived near the present-day Mystic River. They crossed from Boston Harbor south to Hingham Bay, and when they arrived, the local natives, probably Wessagussets, came to the shore to trade. DeMonts bartered with them, and then continued his search for a more promising site for settlement. They reached Cape Cod Bay, and eventually the outer Cape, where DeMonts visited a Nauset village. He asked the people about their land and the severity of the winters on Cape Cod. Once the Nausets understood DeMonts' question, "they made an attempt to inform him by signs, by taking some sand in their hands, spreading it out over the ground, and indicating that it was of the color of DeMonts' collar, and that it reached the depth of a foot. Others made signs that there was less, and gave him to understand also that the harbor never froze; but DeMonts was unable to ascertain whether the snow lasted long." The sailors, on this visit with the Nausets, started to argue with them over a stolen kettle, and a brief skirmish ensued resulting in the death of one sailor. Later the same day, several Nauset tribesmen returned to trade, claiming that the hostilities had been instigated by a tribe that lived further inland.

After about a week on the outer Cape, DeMonts returned to St. Croix, sailing to Cape Ann and from there up the Maine coast to St. Croix. It was now the first week of August and DeMonts, who was determined not to spend another winter at St. Croix, decided to resettle across the Bay of Fundy at Port Royal, Nova Scotia. By December 20, 1605, when the first snow fell, the crew was securely established at the new outpost, and the winter that year was milder. Nevertheless, they suffered the agony of scurvy a second time, which took the lives of twelve men, and reduced the crew to thirty-one. Meanwhile, DeMonts returned to France to petition the French crown for more money to support his expeditions to New England.

The following summer Sieur de Poutrincourt, a new commander, arrived at Port Royal in a hundred-and-twenty-ton vessel manned by fifty sailors. Poutrincourt had been commissioned by DeMonts to act as Lieutenant-General at Port Royal. To Champlain's delight, Poutrincourt set out on a second voyage along the New England coast on September 5. Two Maliseet sagamores, Secondon and Messamouet, who lived on the St. John River in present-day New Brunswick, went with the expedition as far as Almuchicoitt, where they wanted to make an alliance with Onemechin, sachem of the Saco nation. On September 21, the expedition anchored at the mouth of the Saco River. It was the height of the harvest season in the Saco Valley, and the Saco people were busily laboring in their fields. Messamouet gave presents of kettles, knives and hatchets to Sachem Onemechin, who insulted Messamouet in return by giving him an inferior gift of vegetables. Angrily Messamouet left Almuchicoitt, intending to make war on the Saco people in the spring. Secondon remained with the expedition, which continued on to Cape Ann.

Champlain noted at least two hundred Agawam natives while the ship was anchored off Cape Ann. They had just finished harvesting, and their food stores were pumpkins, squash, artichokes, corn and beans. The sachem Onemechin, surprisingly, reappeared here during the crews' stay. They gave him a coat, but he handed along the gift to someone else because he found it uncomfortable. Champlain mentions that besides harvesting their crops, the Agawams were clearing new land for the next year's planting. "Some of the land was already cleared up," he says, "and they were constantly making [new] clearings. Their mode of doing it is as follows: After cutting down the trees at the distance of three feet from the ground, they burn the branches upon the trunk, and then plant their corn between these stumps, in course of time tearing up also the roots." The Agawams promised Champlain that at least two thousand natives were coming to join them in welcoming Poutrincourt's arrival, but the crew had already finished caulking the ship and Poutrincourt was unwilling to stay any longer.

Leaving Cape Ann, they sailed into Cape Cod Bay, anchored temporarily in Barnstable Harbor and then sailed northward around the outer Cape and sailed down the coast to Mallebarre [Nauset Harbor], which had been named Mallebarre by DeMonts on the previous voyage, for the shoals. They sailed south to Monomoy [Chatham], an area inhabited by the Nauset and Monomoy tribes. Cultivated fields lay all along the hillocks surrounding Monomoy. When the French expedition arrived the harvest season was also underway at Monomoy, and the natives were building underground granaries. "They make trenches in the sand on the slopes of the hills," Champlain writes, "some five or six feet deep, more or less. Putting their corn and other grains into large grass sacks, they throw them into these trenches and cover them with sand three or four feet above the surface of the earth, taking it out as their needs require. In this way, it is preserved as well as it would be possible to do in any granaries." To keep the grain dry the granaries were often lined with either bark or woven mats.

The French, during their anchorage at Monomoy, estimated the indigenous population to be about six hundred. Because Monomoy seemed very promising as a site for settlement, Poutrincourt and several of his crew scouted the entire region, to the amazement of the Nausets, who often encountered the sailors deep inside their territory. Back at the harbor, the crew established a temporary camp onshore. Eventually the Nausets and Monomoys grew suspicious of the crew's expeditions into their land. With each passing day they grew more alarmed, and soon ordered the wigwams closest to the harbor be dismantled and their women and children moved to a more distant village. As Champlain watched the activity onshore, he realized these tribal people probably intended a surprise attack on the camp. Poutrincourt ordered all his men off the beach until the following morning but five obstinant sailors refused to obey orders and slept at the campsite overnight. As dawn broke on the horizon, a force of four hundred Nauset and Monomoy warriors attacked the camp. The startled sailors, fleeing the best they could, made for the ship in the harbor but fell dying on the beach from arrows. As they struggled to reach the shore they shouted "Help, they are killing us" to the watchman on board the ship, who immediately sounded the call to arms. Some of the crew made for the camp in a shallop but they ran aground on a sandbar, so the men abandoned the boat and waded ashore. The warriors showered the rescuers with arrows before retreating into the nearby woods. The sailors, knowing they would be ambushed if they followed, stayed at the shore to bury the five dead men.

Later that day, several warriors returned to the beach; the crew, who were all now back on board, discharged several cannon shots at them. The warriors, hearing this thunderous noise, momentarily crouched on the beach. Once they discovered where the bodies were buried, they disinterred them and threw the corpses on the beach as an insult to the crew. Towards evening several Frenchmen went ashore to rebury the bodies.

Poutrincourt, leaving the harbor in a revengeful frame of mind, ordered a southwest course. The ship travelled along Nantucket as far as Vineyard Sound before doubling back to Monomoy. Here, according to a vindictive scheme concocted by Champlain, the crew planned to capture several braves and force them to labor at a handmill grinding corn as punishment for the murder of the five dead crewmen. If the crew could not hold their captives down, they were ordered to stab them to death. Beyond Champlain's statement that "the plan above-mentioned was well carried out," he is silent on the method used. However, when Champlain arrived back at St. Croix he mentions that their guide Secondon departed "well

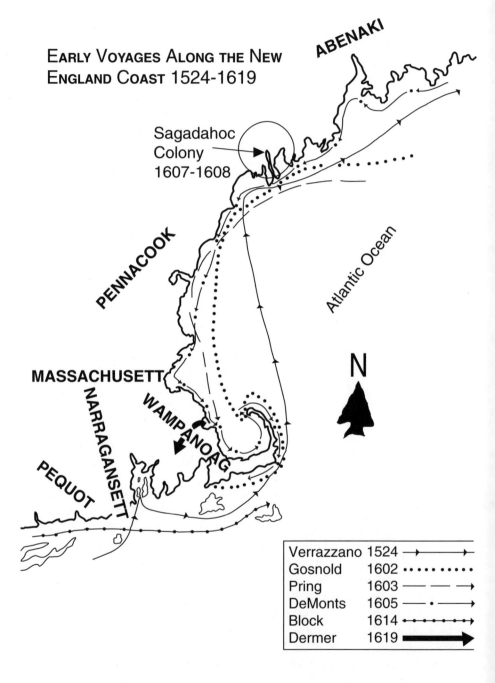

EARLY VOYAGES ALONG THE NEW
ENGLAND COAST 1524-1619

ABENAKI

Sagadahoc
Colony
1607-1608

PENNACOOK

Atlantic Ocean

MASSACHUSETT

NARRAGANSETT

WAMPANOAG

PEQUOT

N

Verrazzano	1524	——→
Gosnold	1602	••••••
Pring	1603	— — →
DeMonts	1605	—•—→
Block	1614	•–•–•–
Dermer	1619	⟶

pleased and satisfied at having made this voyage with us, and took away with him some heads of the savages that had been killed at Port Fortune [Monomoy]." Apparently the crew successfully satisfied their desire for retribution by murdering these tribesmen at Monomoy. "We withdrew," Champlain gloatingly writes, "but with the satisfaction that God had not left unpunished the misdeeds of these barbarians." Naturally, incidents of this type only served to heighten the distrust on both sides. In the published accounts of their voyages to New England, explorers such as Verrazzano, Rosier and Champlain characterized the New England Algonkians "in the rank of other salvages, who have been by travellers in most discoveries found very treacherous: never attempting mischief until . . . opportunity affordeth them certain ability to execute the same." Likewise, the Algonkians had sufficient reason to distrust the English, French and Dutch. In the decade following the second French expedition to the New England coast, the Penobscot, Massachusett, Nauset and Monomoy suffered murder, abduction and robbery at the hands of European crewmen trading along their shores. For this reason, when a Plymouth trading expedition came ashore at Monomoy some sixteen years after Champlain's visit, the native people out of fear were quite reluctant to reveal the location of their village to Governor Bradford and his men.

Poutrincourt and his crew departed Monomoy and arrived back at Port Royal in November, 1606, where he resumed his duties as Lieutenant-General of the settlement. During the spring of 1607, war broke out all along the Maine coast, from Almuchicoitt to Secondon's land on the St. John River. Several Saco warriors had murdered Panounias, a tribesman who lived in one of Secondon's villages. About the same time, a Maliseet brave named Iouaniscou ordered the execution of several captive Penobscot and Kennebec tribesmen out on Mount Desert Island, which brought the Abenaki confederation into the war. Panounias, being the first Maliseet to die in this renewed conflict, was buried with great ceremony. Champlain describes the mourning ceremony, in which Panounias' body was brought ashore in a canoe by several tribesmen (probably Passamaquoddies), whose tribe was friendly with the Abenaki, but neutral in this conflict:

> As soon as the body was brought on shore, his relatives and friends began to shout by his side, having painted their entire face with

black, which is their mode of mourning. After lamenting much, they took a quantity of tobacco and two or three [sacrificed] dogs and other things belonging to the deceased, and burned them some thousand paces from our settlement on the sea-shore. Their cries continued until they returned to their cabin. The next day they took the body of the deceased and wrapped it in a red covering, which Mabretou, chief of this place, urgently implored me to give him, since it was handsome and large. He gave it to the relatives of the deceased, who thanked me very much for it. After thus wrapping up the body, they decorated it with several kinds of 'matachiats;' that is, strings of beads and bracelets of diverse colors. They painted the face, and put on the head many feathers and other things, the finest they had. Then they placed the body on its knees between two sticks, with another under the arms to sustain it. Around the body were the mother, wife and others of the relatives and friends of the deceased, both women and girls, howling like dogs. While the women and girls were shrieking the savage named Mabretou made an address to his companions on the death of the deceased, urging all to take vengeance for the wickedness and treachery committed by the subjects of Bessabez [bashaba of the Penobscots], and to make war upon them as speedily as possible. All agreed to do so in the spring.

Towards the end of June, as Messamouet had vowed in the previous year when he was at Almuchicoitt, he assembled four hundred Mic Mac and Maliseet warriors at Port Royal to attack the Saco people. Shortly after the war party had left from Port Royal, Ralleau, secretary to Sieur DeMonts, arrived at the settlement with three other Frenchmen in a shallop from Cape Breton Island. He had orders from DeMonts that Port Royal was to be abandoned and the men were to sail for Cape Breton Island and from there be sent to France. On July 3, three shallops carrying the settlement's supplies and manned by the sailors at Port Royal, sailed the convoy up the Nova Scotia coast to Canso. Poutrincourt and eight of the crew remained at Port Royal to harvest the grain they had planted, intending to leave for Canso on August 11.

While the men harvested the grain, Mabretou arrived back at the settlement from the war with the Sacos and told the French that twenty Saco tribesmen had been killed. The Sacos and Kennebecs, while battling the Mic Mac and Maliseet, also went to war against each other. A Kennebec chief, Sasinou, killed the two most prominent Saco leaders, Onemechin and Marchin, which some of Onemechin's companions later avenged by murdering Sasinou. Abriou succeeded his father, the sachem Marchin as the head of the Saco nation, and Queconsicq succeeded his father, the sachem Onemechin. Both new sachems were seriously wounded when some of Mabretou's followers, pretending friendship, attacked them. By mid August, when the last Frenchmen left Port Royal, the three-sided war between the Saco, Mic Mac and Abenaki (Penobscot and Kennebec) was still going on. At Canso the entire French crew boarded a fishing vessel for France, the end of their three-year expedition.

Meanwhile, in England, George Waymouth's account of his voyage to the Maine coast in 1605 had prompted two interrelated groups of English merchants, from London and Plymouth, to petition the Crown for a patent to colonize the lands between 34 degrees north and 45 degrees north latitude. They were granted a patent on April 20, 1606, with the agreement that within the Virginia companies there would exist two distinct business syndicates: the London or South Virginia Company and the Plymouth or North Virginia Company. The London Company was authorized to colonize the region from 34 degrees north to 41 degrees north latitude, from Cape Fear in the the Carolinas north to Long Island, New York. The Plymouth Company was given the land between the latitudes 38 degrees north to 45 degrees north latitude, from Chesapeake Bay to the St. Croix River in the north. To avoid any disputes over territory between the latitudes 38 degrees north to 41 degrees north, neither company was permitted to colonize within a hundred miles of the other. This area was effectively a neutral zone between the colonies. The patent stipulated that each colony was to acquire all the lands fifty miles north and south of the first settlement, and a hundred miles into the interior.

In 1607, two vessels, the "Gift of God" and the "Mary and John" were dispatched to the Maine coast to establish the Sagadahoc Colony, the first English colony of Northern Virginia. Prominent in this enterprise were George Popham, Raliegh Gilbert and their Algonkian guide, Sketwarroes, who had been taken to England in 1605 by Captain Waymouth. Making landfall off the Nova Scotia coast on July 27, 1607 they sailed towards the southwest where they met Messamouet and several of his subjects. These people "used many French words," according to Captain Robert Davies, who navigated Gilbert's ship. Davies deduced that French fishermen frequented their shores. Unbeknownst to Captain Davies, the French were close by, busily preparing to abandon Port Royal.

When Captain Gilbert arrived in Muscongus Bay on the Maine coast, he took thirteen crewmen including Sketwarroes, who acted as their guide, to visit the Pemaquid captive Sketwarroes' village. The Pejepscots were suspicious when the English appeared abruptly in their village at night, and went for their bows until Sketwarroes spoke out to the sagamore Nahanda, who ordered his warriors to lay aside their weapons. Nahanda, himself a former captive from the Waymouth expedition, had been returned to Maine during Martin Pring's voyage to the region in 1606. This same sagamore now embraced Captain Gilbert, inviting his men to stay awhile as guests at Pemaquid. The English remained in the Pejepscot bark lodges for two hours before boarding their ship for the Kennebec River.

By late August, the colonists had settled on the banks of the Kennebec with the local Abenakis' approval, and were industriously erecting their fort. Captain Popham, to strengthen friendship with the natives near the settlement, made a second brief visit to the Pejepscots at Pemaquid. At the village he learned from Nahanda that Sketwarroes, who now lived at Pemaquid, had gone with his fellow tribesmen to battle the Kennebec nation. In this skirmish they killed Pememen, chief of the Kennebecs, whose father, Sasinou, was murdered earlier in the war. Apparently, the coastal Abenakis (the Casco and Pejepscot, among other tribes) had allied themselves with the Sacos.

During September, the Pejepscots returned Captain Popham's visit, paddling over to the Sagadahoc Colony to barter. The colonists had much to gain in fostering a congenial relationship with the local Abenaki tribes, because the fur trade in the region was potentially very profitable. Nevertheless, the Abenaki later told Jesuit missionaries that the English sometimes abused them, and that the Sacos were eager to destroy the Sagadahoc Colony from the beginning. The Kennebecs also exhibited an increasing hostility toward the colony, killing a colonist who went by the surname of Pateson.

By late autumn the colony contained a fort, church, storehouse and a number of houses. In the harbor the ship "Virginia" rested at anchor, the vessel a product of the colonists' labor. As winter approached, Captain Davies sailed back to England, where he was to procure supplies to be brought back to Sagadahoc in the spring. The winter was quite severe. Icy winds blew down from the north, imprisoning the "Virginia" in ice for a time. Unaccustomed to the harsh winter climate, some of the colonists perished, among them George Popham. Nevertheless, when Captain Davies arrived back at the settlement he found the colonists "in good forwardness [with] many kinds of furs obtained from the Indians by way of trade." He brought Captain Gilbert news of his father's death, and Gilbert had to leave for England in order to inherit his father's property. Disenchanted with the climate and uncertain about the Abenaki, the colonists finally decided to abandon Sagadahoc. The Abenaki, according to a letter written by George Popham, were somewhat fearful about approaching the Sagadahoc Colony, for the deity *Tanto (Kiehtan)* threatened to kill them if they went near the English. The Abenaki believed *Tanto* intended to destroy the settlement. Determined to abandon Sagadahoc, both the "Virginia" and Captain Davies' vessel were fitted out for the long voyage back to England. The Sagadahoc enterprise became the second ill-fated European attempt to establish a permanent colony in New England.

Even more than the prospect of colonizing coastal North America, European explorers hoped to discover a water passage through the continent that would lead to the Orient. The search for the supposed Northwest Passage, as this legendary waterway came to be known, brought Henry Hudson to the New England coast. He and his crew on the "Half Moon," arrived off the Nova Scotia coast in July, 1609. Sailing southwest they eventually came to the Penobscot River, where Hudson traded with the Penobscots, who, he claims could not be trusted when allowed on board the ship. In reality, these people had more to fear from Hudson than he did from them, for the crew ruthlessly rifled a Penobscot wigwam village and "drove the savages from their houses," so they could rob them of their furs. It is ironic that Hudson should refer to the Penobscots as savages in the light of his own activities. His expedition then sailed south to Cape Cod, and went on to another landfall in the latitude of Virginia, before turning north to New York Harbor. When Hudson voyaged up the river that today bears his name, he was involved in the killing of several Algonkians, and lost one of his own men during a skirmish with the Raritan tribe.

109

After Hudson returned to the Netherlands, Dutch merchants in Amsterdam realized the potential fur trade to be had along the Hudson River and acquired exclusive rights from their government to barter with the tribes living there. In 1614, the Dutch expanded their claim to south coastal New England when Captain Adrien Block sailed into Long Island Sound and the mouth of the Connecticut River, before going on to Block Island and Nantucket. The following year the Dutch built a small fort up the Hudson River. From this river the Dutch attempted to tap the fur trade among the Algonkian and Iroquoian peoples of present-day New York and New England. Early on, Dutch traders came into contact with the "Wapenocks" (Wampanoags), "Nahicans," (Niantics), "Pequatoos," (Pequots), "Morhicans," (Mohegans) and "Quiripeys" (Quinnipiacs) of south coastal New England. In his history of the New Netherland Colony, Johan De Laet describes the New England Algonkians as "a numerous people who are extremely well-looking."

While the Dutch were securing a foothold to the south, the French returned to the Bay of Fundy in the north. In 1610 Port Royal was resettled under the direction of Poutrincourt, who had obtained the abandoned colony from DeMonts as a gift. The French crown legitimized his claim to the colony on the condition that several Jesuits would be allowed to accompany the enterprise for the sole purpose of Christianizing the local Mic Mac and Maliseet tribes. Poutrincourt reluctantly conceded to this condition, and sailed to Port Royal accompanied by twenty-three Frenchmen. Landing at Port Royal in early June, they found the colony totally intact, just as they had left it in 1607. A priest named Josse Flesche baptized twenty-four of Chief Mabretou's subjects, who lived just to the south of the settlement along St. Mary's Bay. Towards late summer, Poutrincourt sent his son, Sieur de Biencourt, back to France to obtain relief for the colony which was in dire need of food supplies for the coming winter.

The following year in June, Biencourt returned to Port Royal with the Jesuit fathers Pierre Biard, Enemond Masse and another thirty-six settlers, increasing the population at the settlement to around sixty people. Though the new emigrants were welcome, they put an even greater burden on Port Royal's depleted food stores. To prevent famine during the winter, many of the colonists had to live among Chief Mabretou's people. Biencourt's arrival brought only temporary relief, because the food stores on the ship had been partially consumed during their long voyage. The Jesuit fathers also accused Biencourt of having sold some of the food stores intended for the colony, but Biencourt's name was naturally cleared through his father's authority at Port Royal. Poutrincourt, faced with starvation, had no alternative but to sail along the Maine coast where he hoped to acquire some grain from the Abenaki tribes and certain other supplies from French fishing vessels in the area. He and most of his crew left for the Maine coast, accompanied by Father Biard, who was eager to meet with the Abenaki people. They managed to procure some meager supplies from four French fishing vessels but these food stores were not enough to maintain the colony. When they arrived back at Port Royal, Poutrincourt and his entire crew resolved to return to France to buy supplies. Poutrincourt left his son in charge at the settlement, and set sail for France in July, 1611, making port there a month later.

Meanwhile, twenty-two colonists remained at Port Royal, among them the two Jesuit fathers, who spent their time learning the Mic Mac and Maliseet dialects in the hopes of starting their missionary work. Frequently, the fathers invited several of Chief Mabretou's people to their cabin to learn the language. Father Biard states:

> The task [of learning the language] was not so very wearisome as long as what was asked about could be touched or seen; a stone, a river, a house; to strike, to jump, to laugh, to sit down. But when it came to internal and spiritual acts, which cannot be demonstrated to the senses, and in regard to words which are called abstract and universal, such as, to believe, to doubt, to hope, to discourse, to apprehend, an animal, a body, a substance, a spirit, virtue, vice, sin, reason, justice, etc., - for these things they had to labor and sweat; in these were the pains of travail. They did not know by what route to reach them, although they tried more than a hundred. Meanwhile, our gentlemen Savages, to pass away the time, made abundant sport of their pupils, always telling them a lot of nonsense. And yet if you wanted to take advantage of this fun, if you had your paper and pencil ready to write, you had to set before them a full plate with a napkin underneath . . . as it was, they even became angry and went away, if we wished to detain them a little.

Toward the end of August, Chief Mabretou came from one of his villages on St. Mary's Bay to be treated for a fever. Since he was the first local chieftan to receive baptism, the two fathers naturally appreciated his influential position and were eager to help him, for Chief Mabretou was vital to the success of their missionary effort. In spite of the genuine attempt made by Herbert Louis, the apothecary at Port Royal, to cure Mabretou, the chief's health continued to fail. After suffering for five days with fever and dysentary, Chief Mabretou finally died which greatly saddened the Jesuits. Before he passed away, Mabretou vacillated on whether he should be buried with his ancestors or among the French colonists, but through Father Biard's convincing words, Mabretou decided upon the latter. "Learn our language quickly," Father Biard writes Chief Mabretou said to him, "for when you have learned it, you will teach me; and when I am taught I will become a preacher like you, and we will convert the whole country."

About this time Biencourt decided to lead an expedition to Almuchicoitt, to barter for corn. After a delay of several weeks, the group left in early October. They visited briefly French colonists living on the St. John River from whom they extracted a fifth of all their property for the privilege of settling on Poutrincourt's territory. Then Biencourt and the crew, including Father Biard, continued down the coast to the Kennebec River, where they arrived October 28, and traded with the natives, while Father Biard went over to a nearby island to celebrate Mass. Here the French heard from the Abenaki the fate of the Sagadahoc Colony. The natives told the priests the English colonists had become so unfriendly towards them that whenever they visited Sagadahoc the colonists released their dogs. On occasion they even beat some visiting Abenaki tribesmen. No longer willing to endure these English colonists, a band of Abenakis assaulted some who were out fishing on their sloops, attacking after they first pretended they wanted to trade with them. Eleven colonists were killed, and the English were so intimidated that they abandoned Sagadahoc.

Father Biard visited the Abenaki people on two separate occasions while at the Kennebec River, showing them various ceremonial objects of the Catholic faith. He taught the children how to make the sign of the cross and spoke to the village residents through an interpreter. The expedition abandoned their plan to go to Almuchicoitt, because it was now early November, and returned to Port Royal where Father Masse had been awaiting Poutrincourt's arrival from France. Long overdue, Poutrincourt's ship did not arrive at Port Royal until January, 1612. Once again the colony had narrowly escaped starvation, for the threat of famine plagued the settlement from the outset, borne of continual mismanagement by its proprietors.

Nearly six months had passed since the Jesuit fathers landed at Port Royal, and despite their continuous efforts to acquire some proficiency in the Mic Mac and Maliseet dialects, they found that an occasional visit by the natives to their cabin was an ineffective approach to learning the northen Algonkian language. Father Masse decided to live with Louis Mabretou, son of the late Chief Mabretou, hoping to gain greater exposure to the language. When Louis Mabretou next visited Port Royal, Father Masse, accompanied by a boy to assist in the Mass, departed with the chief to his village on the St. John River, where they remained for most of the summer. At one point during their stay Father Masse became extremely ill and Louis Mabretou feared he might die. Coming into Father Masse's lodge he said to him, "Listen, Father. Thou art going to die; I predict it. Write now to Biencourt and to thy brother, that thou hast died of disease, and that we did not kill thee." Father Masse misunderstood the chief's genuine fear of French reprisal if he should die among them, and he replied, "I shall take care not to do that, for possibly after I had written this letter thou wouldst kill me, and then thou wouldst take there thy innocent letter, saying thou hadst not killed me." Understanding Father Masse's reasoning the chief replied, "Well then, pray Jesus that thou mayest not die, so they will not accuse us of having killed thee." "Indeed I am doing so," assured Father Masse; "do not fear, I shall not die."

When Father Masse arrived back at Port Royal, he again found the colony in the predicament of rationing its dwindling food supplies. Rather than await starvation, the Jesuits constructed a small boat, for, as Father Biard realized, "the roads in that country [were] the rivers and the sea," and if they intended to survive they must go in search for their next meal. With this boat they journeyed along the coast and up the smaller estuaries seeking out acorns, edible roots, fish and anything else that would sustain them for another day. The Jesuits' ingenuity won them the admiration of their most persistent critics at the settlement.

In March, 1613, Captain La Saussaye along with two Jesuits, Father Quantin and Father Gilbert du Thet, and thirty other colonists, arrived from France and anchored at Port Royal. Captain La Saussaye had orders to relocate the Jesuit fathers in a more suitable place where they could undertake their mission to the native population more effectively. After considerable discussion over the most desirable site for their mission, the Jesuits finally agreed to settle on Mount Desert Island off the Maine coast. Originally when the Abenaki on Mount Desert Island heard that Father Biard preferred to settle on the Kenduskeag River, one persuasive talker tried to convince him of the islands desirability saying, "if thou wishest to stay in these regions, why dost thou not rather remain here with us, who have truly as good and beautiful a place as Kadesquit?" While he spoke the others sang praises of their island home, which they called "Penetic." Shortly afterwards, one of them cleverly called on Father Biard, pleading that he visit Asticou, their sagamore, who they claimed was extremely ill, and said they feared that if their sagamore was not baptized, he would be unable to enter heaven if his sickness proved fatal. When Father Biard reached Asticou's lodge he found the sagamore ill, but certainly not on his deathbed, for he was only suffering from a mild cold. However, the hospitality of the Penetic natives convinced Father Biard that God had ordained the island to be the site for their Catholic mission. The Jesuits appropriately called their new mission station St. Sauveur.

Probably the Jesuits would have won the affection of the Abenakis, if their work had not been suddenly interrupted by the English Captain Argall's attacks on the French settlements that same year. This captain, discovering St. Sauveur by accident, pillaged the mission, taking some of the Jesuits captive to Jamestown, Virginia, and leaving the others to find their way back to Port Royal in a shallop. When Argall returned to Virginia, the council ordered him back to the Maine coast with a larger force, where he burned the French settlements at St. Sauveur, St. Croix and Port Royal.

Though the French temporarily abandoned their settlements along the Maine coast, they immediately proceeded to rebuild Port Royal. From it, and their other settlements in Quebec, the Jesuits continued their missionary work among the Abenaki, and cast their nets even further west to include other tribal nations. In 1619, a group of Recollect fathers came again to the St. John River spreading the gospel among the Maliseet nation. This mission was abandoned after about five years, and the priests involved went to Quebec, but others belonging to this same order were back in the area of the St. John River during the 1630s. To the north, on Cape Breton Island, other missions were spreading the gospel to the Mic Mac. At the invitation of some Abenaki converts, Father Gabriel Druillettes came down from Quebec to the Kennebec River in 1646, and for eleven years he made sporadic visits to the Abenakis, gaining converts to Catholicism. When Father Druillettes departed from the Abenaki mission in 1657, these people saw few priests in their villages for the next thirty years because much of the missionary effort was being concentrated on the tribes further west. By 1689, the year when the early French and Indian Wars began in New England, the Catholic mission to the Abenaki was again underway. The "Black Robes," as the Abenaki called the Jesuit priests, won the affection of many of the Algonkian tribes in northern New England. As a result, the Abenaki became dependable allies of the French.

The English, while the French continued their exploration of the Maritimes, sent several expeditions to the New England coastline. In 1611, the Earl of Southampton and several other backers on the Isle of Wight hired Captain Edward Harlow to locate a certain island off of Cape Cod. Harlow was unable to locate this island because he "found that their plots had much abused them." Harlow attempted to seize some Algonkians, named Pechmo, Monopet and Pekenimme, who had boarded his ship to trade. In the struggle to capture them, Pechmo managed to escape by leaping overboard. Seeking revenge, he returned with several others and cut one of Harlow's landing boats from the stern, dragged the boat ashore, and filled the hull with sand, while others of the tribe stood guard in case the sailors should attempt to retrieve it. When a landing party did come ashore further down the beach, these people "sorely wounded them with arrows."

Captain Harlow accepted the loss of his boat, and sailed to Nauset where the natives again attacked the ship, and the crew staved off this assault with gunfire. In the area of Nauset, Captain Harlow managed to abduct another tribesman named Sakaweston, who ended up in England where he lived for some years. (He also spent some time as a soldier in Bohemia!). Harlow captured Coneconam, sagamore of Manamet; and Epenow, sagamore of Capawick, before he returned to England. Both these chiefs eventually ended up back in New England.

Epenow served as a guide to Sir Ferdinando Gorges and Captain Hobson when they came to New England in 1614. He led the two Englishmen to believe there was gold on Capawick in the hope they would sail to this island, where he would escape. When they arrived, Epenow's kinsmen rejoiced to discover their sagamore was alive. Epenow seized his first chance of escape in nearly three years and dove overboard swimming wildly towards some of his fellow tribesmen who had come out in canoes under the pretense of trading with the crew. Captain Hobson's men foolishly fired at Epenow which brought down a shower of arrows from the warriors in canoes. Several sailors were wounded. In the words of Sir Gorges, the successful escape of Epenow left his hope of finding gold "void and frustrated."

Captain John Smith also came to New England in 1614, charting the coastline from the Penobscot River to Cape Cod. He sailed along the shore of Massachusetts Bay before going on towards Cape Cod. Smith described Massachusetts Bay as "the paradise of all those parts," wherein were "great troupes of well proportioned people." A French vessel had been in the bay area for about six weeks prior to Smith's arrival, so the Massachuset people had few pelts to trade with the English. The English crew doubted this explanation and tried to force these tribes to trade. Tensions rose and a clash ensued in which forty warriors fought the English until they had spent all their arrows. When these warriors had retreated, Captain Smith ordered his men to seize the natives' canoes, and the Massachuset people had to pay a ransom for the canoes in the form of beaver skins. As Captain Smith's vessel sailed into another part of the bay, several warriors sought revenge by canoeing out to a group of rocks where they knew the ship must pass, and when Smith's vessel came by the Massachuset men let their arrows fly. The crew responded with gunfire killing one warrior, and wounding another in the thigh.

On this trip Captain Smith became quite familiar with the numerous tribes living in the vicinity of Massachusetts Bay. "The next I can remember by name" Smith writes, "are Mattahunts . . . then Totant [Nahant], Massachuset, Pocapawmet, Quonahassit [Cohasset], Sagoquas [Scituate], Nahapassumkeek, Topeent,

116

Seccasaw, Totheet, Nasnocomacack, Accomack [Patuxet] and the Chawmun," who lived at the bottom of Cape Cod Bay near Barnstable Harbor. Because Captain Smith understood little Algonkian he wrongly assumed the Patuxet people called their village area *Accomack*. The term is actually derived from the compound word *Sachimaccomack*, which refers to the lodging place of the Algonkian sachems and sagamores. Six years later, when the Pilgrims landed at Plymouth, Samoset told them the area was called Patuxet. During Smith's visit to this Algonkian village, his crew killed a number of Patuxets in a skirmish, but, surprisingly, the crew were at peace with these people an hour after this incident. From Patuxet, Captain Smith sailed over to Cape Cod and the Nausets, who he refers to as the people of Pawmet. Beyond Cape Cod was the island of Capawick and "those abounding Countries of Copper, Corn, People and Minerals."

Smith voyaged along the coast with two vessels and a crew of forty-five men. He used one ship, manned by eight of the crew, to map the coastline. Captain Thomas Hunt, along with the remainder of the crew, were given instructions to fish off the coast of Cape Cod and barter with the local Algonkians for furs. Once Hunt had completed this task, he was to sell his cargo in Spain. However, Hunt decided to increase his profits, and captured twenty Patuxets and seven Nauset tribesmen, whom he intended to be mercilessly sold into the bondage of the Spanish slave market. One of these captive tribesmen was Squanto, who along with some of the others was saved from this fate when certain monks in the province of Malaga in Spain purchased them. From Malaga some of the natives somehow got over to England where they proved useful to Sir Ferdinando Gorges. Captain Smith later wrote of Hunt, "this vile act kept him ever after from any more emploiment in those parts."

The abusive actions of such captains as Harlow and Hunt naturally made some of the outer Cape tribes distrust, if not despise, all Englishmen. About seven years after the tragic Hunt incident, the newly-arrived Pilgrims learned first hand of the lasting psychological anguish these abductions caused among certain Wampanoag families. The Pilgrims at Plymouth had sent an expedition out to Nauset to retrieve a child named John Billington, who had wandered from the plantation, and been found by these people. Enroute to the outer Cape, the Plymouth search party anchored overnight among the Matachees people at Cummaquid, and the Sagamore Iyanough introduced the men to an elderly tribeswoman, who, they surmised, was nearing one hundred years of age. She had asked her sagamore to meet these English visitors, for in all her years she had never met an Englishman. When they were introduced the elderly woman burst out into "great passion, weeping and crying excessively." The Pilgrims asked the reason for her sorrow, and were told the woman had lost her three sons at the hands of Captain Hunt, and now she was deprived of the comfort of her children in her old age.

Another Englishman, Captain Dermer, came to Maine in 1619 in a fishing vessel carrying Squanto, among others, intending to join up with the English Captain Rocroft at Monhegan Island. Unbeknownst to Dermer, Rocroft had been killed in Virginia. While Dermer waited for Rocroft's arrival, he decided to use a smaller boat to return Squanto to Patuxet. Dermer and Squanto landed at Patuxet where they found the village abandoned, so they travelled inland to the populous village of Nemasket. Captain Dermer met Sachem Massasoit, and redeemed a French sailor who had survived a shipwreck off Cape Cod. Dermer then left Nemasket and sailed north to Massachusetts Bay, where he rescued another French sailor who had been living with the Massachusett.

When he returned to Monhegan Island he decided to set sail for Virginia. As his ship made its way down the Maine coast the vessel broke apart during a violent storm, the crew escaped the shipwreck in a shallop and continued their voyage. Wherever the men landed they encountered Algonkian hostility, with the exception of Capawick, where when they came ashore they were warmly received by Sagamore Epenow. "I met with Epinow," Dermer states, "a Savage that lived in England, and speaks indifferent good English, who foure years since [was] carried home." Captain Dermer sailed from Capawick west, through a narrow channel, where the local tribe showered the boat with arrows. This remarkable sojourn finally ended, as Dermer moved down the coast from Long Island and arrived safely at the Jamestown settlement in Virginia.

During the 17th century, explorers, traders and colonists were agents of cultural exchange between Europe and Algonkian New England. Algonkian society was gradually transformed by the products they received from Europeans. Some of the first cultural practices to change were the indigenous peoples' use of stone tools and the art of making ceramic containers. Algonkians prized the white man's superior metal utensils, particularly such durable items as knives, hatchets and brass kettles. The Algonkians also often bartered for sheet metal, which they shaped into various implements. In some cases a native craftsman made metal arrowheads from European sheet metal by simply cutting out a square piece of brass, and folding the edges over to form a triangle. The workmanship was far inferior to the ancient Neolithic Algonkian tooling tradition of working in stone.

Ceramic skills were also greatly affected by the introduction of European utensils. When the Pilgrims first landed on the outer Cape they found several European kettles in some vacated Nauset wigwams. Apparently the tribal women prized the durability of these metal containers. In the 17th century, Algonkian clay pot designs deteriorated with the increasing use of brass kettles. Compared with the Iroquoian collared designs of the previous century pottery made by the New England Algonkians tended to be unshapely; in fact, pottery from the Historic period (1600-1726) often resembles the kettles used by the English colonists. Motifs on these inferior ceramic designs are either very simple or totally lacking.

Language also was changed by contact with the Europeans. Tribes near the St. John River occasionally spoke some French, which entered into their language from trading with French fishermen and the Port Royal colonists. John Brereton of the Gosnold expedition, and Captain Christopher Levett, who both sailed along the New England shore (the latter in 1623), remarked on the Algonkian use of some English words in their bartering with their crewmen, and even among one another. Samoset, a northern Algonkian tribesman from Monhegan Island, was quite familiar with the names of the English sea captains who visited the Maine coast from year to year, from whom he had acquired a limited English vocabulary. When the Plymouth colonists first arrived, they were so impressed with his limited English that they spent an entire afternoon asking Samoset about the land and the indigenous peoples.

Even though the Algonkian people desired European products, they were selective about what they chose to adopt. They recognized the advantage of firearms and the durability of European kettles and metal knives. Due to their constant demand for superior European swords and knife blades, the Algonkians called the English *Chauquaqock*, or "Sword-men." At the same time they tended to frown on English attire as impractical and uncomfortable, particularly the white man's coat. Because coats were a common aspect of European attire, the Algonkians also called the English *Wautacone-nuaog*, or "Coat-men." Their general rejection of the white man's clothing continued well into the period of English colonization. "English clothes are so strange unto them," Roger Williams writes, "and their bodies inured so to endure the weather. While amongst the English they keep on their apparell, but pull off all as soone as they come againe into their own Houses and Company."

Likewise, the Algonkian people rejected the more permanent English colonial housing design because it did not suit their seminomadic lifestyle. In some tribal villages certain Algonkian families tried to adopt English doorways for their wigwams, to replace their hanging mat entry ways. To do this they acquired the boards and nails from the English colonists, and a few even fastened bolts on their entrances to secure them.

As English colonization intensified the impact of Europe on the Algonkian culture, the Algonkians grew more dependent on the English economically. Attempts to Christianize the "heathen salvages" shattered tribal solidarity, as when the local sagamores had to compete with such men as the Reverend John Eliot for their peoples' allegiance. The Puritan missionary effort was intended to force English values on the Algonkians, and the acculturation reached its eventual climax in the denial of self, through the forced abandonment of their native culture.

Unfortunately for the native population, the white man brought a host of contagious diseases to New England. Most of the Europeans were sufficiently immune to these illnesses, but the native peoples had never been exposed, in their isolated state. Sometime between 1615-1618, the New England Algonkians were overwhelmed by an epidemic that wiped out perhaps half of their people. In all probability, 1617 was the peak year for mortality from this epidemic. While mapping the New England coast in 1614, Captain Smith reports seeing numerous Algonkian villages near the shore. However, when Captain Dermer visited the region five years later, he records that the coastal Algonkians had recently suffered from a deadly virus. This epidemic appears to have been a combination of several infectious diseases. "Their disease was the Plague," Captain Dermer says, "for wee might perceive the sores of some that had escaped, who described the spots of such as usually die." The elder tribal people who survived this plague told Gookin, "that the bodies all over were exceedingly yellow . . . both before they died and afterwards." The symptoms suggest an epidemic of smallpox that apparently involved jaundice.

The plague took the most lives along the coast, particularly from Maine to Massachusetts Bay, where the Massachusett nation was drastically reduced. It spread from the coast "about twenty or thirty miles up into the land." Tribes east of the Penobscot River and west of Narragansett Bay escaped this epidemic for the most part, as did the Algonkians living deep in the interior of New England. When Captain Dermer sailed from Maine to Patuxet in 1619, he observed that many of the coastal villages inhabited several years earlier were "now utterly void" of people. Among the Massachusett nation, Thomas Morton states:

> The hand of God fell heavily upon them, with such a mortal stroke, that they died on heapes, as they lay in their houses, and the living, that were able to shift for themselves would runne away and let them dy, and let there carkases ly above the ground without buriall. For in a place where many inhabited, there hath been but one left alive, to tell what became of the rest, the livinge being not able to bury the dead, they were left for Crowes and Vermin to pray upon. And the bones and skulls upon the several places of their habitations, made such a spectacle after my coming into those parts, that as I travailed in that Forest, nere the Massachusetts, it seemed to mee a new found Golgatha.

Actually, two forces caused the high death rate. One was the epidemic itself, and the other the social collapse of the village society. The plague reduced the labor force, and daily tasks went unattended. Gardens not cultivated were choked off by weeds, food supplies depleted remained unreplenished, wigwams and lodges fell into disrepair and many people, believing their gods had cursed the land, fled their villages in fear. Many villages and in some cases entire tribal populations, unprepared for winter, met their end from a combination of sickness, starvation and exposure to the elements.

By 1619, the Patuxet people had vanished. Captain John Smith gives the first and last historical reference to such peoples as the Pocapawmet, Nahapassumkeek, Topeent and Totheet, who he encountered along Massachusetts Bay in 1614. All these tribes vanished during the years of the contagion. Edward Winslow, travelling along the Winnetuxet River, a tributary of the Taunton River, noted that "thousands of men had lived there, which died in a great plague not long since," for the river banks were cleared in many places indicating that the area had been farmed intensively. When on this same journey, Winslow forded the Taunton River at present-day Raynham, he encountered two aged tribesmen who were the sole survivors of the plague in their village. Later on, when the Puritans began settling in New England, they benefited from the demise of the natives, for many of the natives' fields were ready to be farmed. The Puritans interpreted this as an act of God, who they believed had cleared the land of its "pagan natives" to make way for his people. In their minds this was the reenactment of the Old Testament story of the Israelites taking possession of Canaan through the displacement of the Canaanite people.

Algonkian casualities from foreign viruses did not end with the plague of 1617, for the native people continued to suffer from isolated outbreaks of smallpox and other viruses. In the winter of 1622-1623, the Massachusett and Nemasket experienced another "great sickness arising amongst them," followed in 1631 by a serious viral outbreak among the remnant of the Saugus tribe. Edward Johnson, the Puritan historian, relates how several English colonists attempted to assist the Saugus tribespeople during this smallpox outbreak. A "most sad spectacle" confronted them when they entered one wigwam, where they discovered an entire family that had succumbed to the virus, except an infant who lay on the ground suckling his deceased mother. In 1634, the Podunk, Tunxis, Agawam and Pocumtuck living along the Connecticut River, who had been isolated from the white man up until that time, contracted smallpox from Dutch traders coming into the Connecticut Valley. William Bradford writes:

> This spring also, those Indians that lived about their trading house there, fell sick of the small pox and died most miserably; for a sorer disease cannot befall them, they fear it more than the plague. For usually they that have this disease have them in abundance, and for

want of bedding and linen and other helps they fall into a lamentable condition as they lie on their hard mats, the pox breaking and mattering and running one into another, their skin cleaving by reason thereof to the mats they lie on. When they turn them, a whole side will flay off at once as it were, and they will be all of a gore blood, most fearful to behold. And then being very sore, what with cold and other distempers, they die like rotten sheep. The condition of this people was so lamentable and they fell down so generally of this disease as they were in the end not able to help one another, no not to make fire nor to fetch a little water to drink, nor any to bury the dead. But would strive as long as they could, and when they could procure no other means to make a fire, they would burn the wooden trays and dishes they ate their meat in, and their very bows and arrows. And some would crawl out on all fours to get a little water, and sometimes die by the way and not be able to get in again . . . . The chief sachem himself now died and almost all his friends and kindred.

That same year the Narragansetts, who were in close alliance with the Connecticut river tribes, likewise lost seven hundred of their people to smallpox.

Outbreaks of contagious viruses continued to eliminate the Algonkians well into the 18th century. In 1759, the Reverend Stephen Badger reported of the "Praying Indians" of Natick that "in the space of about three months, more than twenty of them died, all of the same disorder, which was a putrid fever; it carried them off in a few days."

The plague of 1617 altered the power balance between the seven Algonkian confederacies for some of the tribal nations went unaffected, while others, such as the Massachusett tribes, were practically obliterated. By 1620, the political jurisdiction of the Massachusett was reduced to those villages located along their bay, and west to the Nashoba and several of the Nipmuck tribes. The Pocumtuck, Nashua and Wachusett, formerly of the Massachusett confederation, sought membership among other confederations in the wake of the epidemic. Narragansett hunting parties, taking advantage of their enemy's weakened condition, began wintering in the lands of the Massachusett, taking all sorts of game. Between 1615-1625, the Mic Mac and Maliseet attacked the Massachusett nation. The Massachusett tribes that remained around the bay became so unsettled by these raids they often relocated to deceive their enemies about where they were. In a matter of three years disease reduced the Massachusett to a shadow of their former strength, as it did the Wampanoag and Pennacook nations.

The psychological impact of the contagion was so devastating to the Wampanoags that they assumed their sacrifices to the spirit Hobbamock had been rejected. They also believed this god had allowed their Narragansett enemies to escape from the plague because the Narragansetts worshipped Hobbamock with more intensity. As a result, the Wampanoag began worshipping Hobbamock as a more powerful deity than Kiehtan because they thought this latter god had not saved them from the epidemic conjured up by Hobbamock. A local Nipmuck tribe that lived near present-day Marlborough, Massachusetts, was so shaken by this plague they abandoned their wigwam village and resettled along an adjacent pond and renamed their former village ground *Whipsuppinicke*, which translates "place abandoned because of sudden death." A remnant of this tribe lived in the area of present-day Marlborough when the English began moving into the Concord and Sudbury river valleys. To the south, the Capawick people tried to appease the fury of the plague by giving away their most prized possessions. In this ceremony, as Thomas Cooper describes it,

> After the rich had thus given away all their moveable property to the poor, they looked out the handsomest and most sprightly young man in the assembly, and put him into an entire new wigwam, built of everything new for that purpose. They then formed into two files at a small distance from each other. One standing in the space at each end, put fire to the bottom of the wigwam on all parts, and fell to singing and dancing. Presently the youth would leap out of the flames, and fall down to appearance dead. Him they committed to the care of five virgins, prepared for that purpose, to restore to life again. The term required for this would be uncertain, from six to forty eight hours; during which time the dance must be kept up. When he was restored, he would tell, that he had been carried in a large thing high up in the air, where he came to a great company of white people, with whom he had interceded hard to have the distemper layed.

Before the Pilgrims arrived at Plymouth in 1620, the Algonkians of coastal New England had experienced a century of cultural exchange with the white man. Some natives had learned how to speak broken French or English from marooned European sailors, who lived among the Massachusett, Wampanoag or Nauset. A number of tribesmen had been kidnapped to England where they were tutored in English before they were returned to their homeland. Nahanda, Sketwarroes, Coneconam, Epenow and Squanto were all transported to England and returned to their tribal homelands before 1620. Three of these former Algonkian captives were influential sagamores who during tribal councils certainly told their overseas experiences to others. Their stories may be the basis for the Passamaquoddy legend titled " How Glooskap went to England and France, and was the first to make America known to Europeans."

In this legend, the Abenaki hero Glooskap crosses the ocean to England in a supernatural stone canoe. When he arrives, the citizens of London come down to the shore to see the canoe. The English want to trade Glooskap a large ship for his stone canoe, but he refuses the offer. From England he goes over to France, where the French king gives him gifts. Afterwards, Glooskap returns to the Maine coast. The legend tells how "the white men did not discover this country [America] first at all. Glooskap discovered England, and told them about it [America]. Since that time white men have come to America." And come they did, but unlike Glooskap, who returned home, the white man came to stay.

Chapter IV
"The English Are No Sachems"

When the Pilgrims anchored off of Cape Cod in November, 1620, they spent several weeks searching for a promising site for settlement. Their penetrating expeditions along the outer coast of Cape Cod Bay, and their insensitive actions alarmed the Nauset people, who observed their every move from places of concealment. When Captain Miles Standish and his men sighted occasional fleeing Nauset tribesmen they aggressively pursued them but to no avail. The Pilgrims disinterred at least two Nauset gravesites out of curiosity and stole corn from their winter storage pits. Aspinet, the Nauset sagamore, from past experience with the English and the present behavior of these newcomers, believed the Pilgrim intruders were trying to discover the Nausets' main winter village in order to do them injury. The Nausets tried to ambush Captain Standish and some of his men while they were breaking camp on a beach in present-day Eastham, Massachusetts. According to William Bradford,

> About midnight we heard a great and hideous cry; and our sentinels called Arm! Arm! So we bestirred ourselves, and shot off a couple of muskets, and the noise ceased . . . . About five o'clock in the morning we began to be stirring; and two or three, which doubted whether their pieces would go off or no, made trial of them and shot them off, but thought nothing at all . . . . Anon, all upon a sudden, we heard a great and strange cry, which we knew to be the same voices though they varied their notes. One of our company, being abroad, came running in, and cried, 'They are men! Indians! Indians!' and withal their arrows came flying amongst us . . . . The cry of our enemies was dreadful, especially when our men ran out to recover their arms. Their note was after this manner, 'Woach, woach, ha ha hach woach.' Our men were no sooner come to their arms, but the enemy was ready to assault them.

There was a lusty man, and no whit less valiant, who was thought to be their captain, stood behind a tree within half a musket shot of us, and there let his arrows fly at us. He was seen to shoot three arrows, which were all avoided . . . . He stood three shots of a musket. At length, one took, as he said, full aim at him; after which he gave an extraordinary cry, and away they went all.

The captain and his men chased the Nausets for a quarter of a mile but did not find any of them. The expedition, with no casualties from the attack, resumed the search for a settlement site until they reached Patuxet (Plymouth). The following spring, after they settled Plymouth, an area claimed by the Wampanoags, the Wampanoag sachem Massasoit visited them. Before the great sachem's journey to Plymouth, both English speaking Samoset and Squanto, had visited the newcomers. The Plymouth colonists were surprised to see Massasoit appear on the outskirts of their settlement one day in late March, 1621. He had come to establish diplomatic relations between his people and the colonists. Massasoit showed himself on a nearby hill with sixty of his warriors. The Pilgrims dispatched Edward Winslow to speak with him and present him and his brother Quadequina with gifts of knives, jewels and a copper chain. After the initial formalities, Winslow agreed to be left in the custody of Quadequina while the English held six tribesmen hostage during the sachem's visit to Plymouth. Massasoit and twenty of his men left their weapons behind and entered the town to make a mutual defense treaty with Plymouth Colony. The agreement stipulated in part that neither Massasoit nor any of his subjects should injure the colonists, and if such an incident should arise, the offender was to be immediately delivered to the Plymouth authorities. Naturally, the entire pact weighed heavily in the colonists' favor. Bradford describes Massasoit:

In his person he is a very lusty man, in his best years, an able body, grave of countenance, and spare of speech; in his attire little or nothing differing from the rest of his followers, only in a great chain of white bone beads about his neck; and at it behind his neck, hangs a little bag of tobacco which he drank [smoked], and gave us to drink. His face was painted with a sad red, like murrey, and oiled both head and face, that he looked greasily. All his followers likewise were in their faces, in part or whole, painted some black, some red, some yellow, and some white, some with crosses, and other antic works; some had skins on them, and some naked; all strong, tall men in appearance.

Massasoit probably made a peace covenant between his villages and Plymouth to protect his people against Narragansett attacks, for the Narragansetts knew the Wampanoags had lost many warriors in the recent plague.

After the treaty was concluded Massasoit and his men left, passing into the woods and promising that they would come and plant corn alongside the English in a week or so. This promise by no means cheered the Plymouth authorities, who were obviously nervous about having so many natives in the midst of their plantation. The English, ignorant of Algonkian ways, failed to realize the Wampanoags were simply being hospitable with their usage right to the planting fields around Patuxet.

After Massasoit made this first gesture of friendship, the Pilgrims thought it wise to return an official visit to Pokanoket country and see where the sachem lived and how many people were actually under his authority. Governor Bradford chose Edward Winslow and Stephen Hopkins to lead this sensitive mission, and chose Squanto to guide them there. The journey took five days. The first stop was the Wampanoag village of Nemasket where the Plymouth emissaries were treated to a meal of shad and a bread made from corn. Then Squanto guided the two men along the Taunton River which eventually brought them to Pokanoket country. When Massasoit had been sent for, Squanto suggested Winslow and Hopkins discharge their firearms when the sachem appeared. However, when one of them reached for his gun the Pokanoket women and children went into a panic from previous unpleasant experiences with the white man's deadly weapons. The village could not be calmed until the firearm was laid down and Squanto reassured the inhabitants about the Englishmen's motives.

When Massasoit arrived, Hopkins and Winslow nonetheless gave him a noisy salute by firing their muskets. The sachem welcomed them to his village and invited them into the *sachimmaacomack*, where the two emissaries gave him a red cotton coat and a chain necklace. Massasoit told them he intended to continue the peace forged at Plymouth, then donned the coat and necklace and proudly displayed himself before his people. Afterwards he spoke to the

Pokanokets at length, reminding them that he was their leader, and encouraging all the Wampanoag nation to follow him in keeping the treaty. The next day many sagamores arrived to greet the Englishmen and to express their goodwill towards the colonists. When the time came for the emissaries to go back to Plymouth, Massasoit detained Squanto and sent him among the villages to get furs for the Plymouth colonists. Another tribesman, Tokamahamon, was given the task of guiding Winslow and Hopkins safely back to their plantation.

Many sagamores agreed along with Massasoit to be allies of the English, but a minority of tribal leaders openly opposed the sachem's policy. Conbitant, the outspoken chieftan of the Pocasset, had little faith in the alliance with Plymouth. In an attempt to see how sincere the colonists were in their promise to defend Massasoit, he spread rumors that the Wampanoag sachem had been kidnapped by the Narragansetts. Conbitant also sought to injure Squanto in the hopes of cutting off communication between Plymouth and Massasoit. Captain Standish and ten armed men were quickly dispatched to Nemasket to protect Squanto for according to the Wampanoag tribesman Hobbamock, sagamore Conbitant had gone to this village with the intention of murdering Squanto. When Standish and his men suddenly entered one of the wigwams at Nemasket, he announced that they were looking for Conbitant, but the militia's intrusion caused such a panic among the women and children that some of those inside the wigwam attempted to escape out a side door. Standish assumed some of these might be implicated with Conbitant and recklessly ordered his men to fire on them, several villagers were wounded. Some of the boys in the Nemasket tribe became so frightened by the gunfire they cried out "*Neen Squaws!*," that is to say "I am a woman!" in the hopes the militia would not harm them. Others in the tribe surrounded Hobbamock, who served as the militia's guide, calling him "*towam*" or "friend."

When the militia had terrorized the Nemaskets into submission, the villagers told Captain Standish that Conbitant had been at the village earlier, but had gone back to Pocasset. Squanto, as it turned out, was unharmed at Nemasket. The next morning Captain Standish warned the Nemaskets that even though Conbitant had managed to escape, there was no safe refuge for him as long as he continued to endanger the security of Plymouth and tried to harm Massasoit. Before he returned to Plymouth with the injured tribespeople that were willing to accompany the militia, Standish also vowed that if their ally Massasoit was harmed the English would take revenge on Conbitant and his people. The sagamore of the Pocassets was intimidated by the threat and stopped challenging the Pilgrims.

In the winter of 1621-1622, a tribesman claiming to be a Narragansett messenger came to Plymouth accompanied by the Wampanoag named Tokamahamon. The messenger asked whether Squanto was presently at Plymouth, and when he was told Squanto was not at the plantation he appeared somewhat glad. The Plymouth leadership was uneasy because the messenger seemed too familiar with Squanto to be a Narragansett runner.

The Plymouth authorities temporarily detained this messenger and before his release he handed the colonists a quiver of arrows wrapped in a rattlesnake skin. Squanto, when he returned to Plymouth, identified the quiver as a war challenge from the Narragansetts. Governor Bradford deliberated at length over this apparent threat, then ordered the quiver to be stuffed with gunpowder and lead shot, and delivered to the Narragansetts by a tribal messenger. The stuffed quiver reached the Narragansett sachem Canonicus, who was so terrified he refused to even touch it. The quiver passed from Narragansett country and then from one Wampanoag village to the next until it finally ended up back at Plymouth. Even though this supposed threat from the Narragansetts proved false, the Pilgrims nonetheless took the precaution of building a stockade around Plymouth.

The next spring the Pilgrims prepared to make another trading expedition to the Massachusett nation as they had the year before, but the Wampanoag tribesman Hobbamock implored them not to go; he believed that the Massachusett people had allied with the Narragansett in a plan to murder the Englishmen when they arrived. Hobbamock, to the Pilgrims' surprise, accused the trusted Squanto of being part of the plot. The expedition leaders did not believe Hobbamock's accusations, and the expedition had started out of the harbor when they heard three discharges of ordnance from Plymouth, signals to Captain Standish to abandon the trip and return to the plantation. A Wampanoag tribesman belonging to Squanto's family had come running from the woods toward some of the Plymouth residents who happened to be outside the stockade, with his face bloody from a wound, and he shouted at the English to retreat to their fortified settlement. The Wampanoag looked nervously behind him, as if he was being pursued. He told Governor Bradford that Massasoit, Conbitant and some Narragansett warriors were gathered about fifteen miles to the west of Plymouth at Nemasket, where they were preparing to assault the colony. He claimed the sachem and his men had abused him for speaking in favor of the English but he managed to break free, and now had come to warn the colonists.

When Captain Standish, Hobbamock, and the rest of the expedition heard the account of the Wampanoag tribesman, Hobbamock immediately labeled the report as preposterous pointing out that since he was a Wampanoag pniese, Massasoit would have certainly told him of any planned assault on the English. The sachem had no reason to break off his covenant with the Pilgrims, Hobbamock said. The colonists still decided to postpone their visit to the Massachusett nation, and sent Hobbamock's wife to speak with Massasoit. When she arrived in Pokanoket country she found nothing to indicate preparation for war. She told the sachem about the alarm at Plymouth, which had falsely implicated him as a conspirator, and Massasoit became angry for the rumor had almost cost the peace agreement between Plymouth and his own people of Pokanoket.

Gradually the Pilgrims learned through the accusations made by Hobbamock, and the fact that Massasoit was unaware of what had transpired at Plymouth, that Squanto himself had started the rumor. "They begane to see that Squanto sought his owne game," Governor Bradford says, "by putting the Indeans in fear, and drawing gifts from them to enrich him selfe, making them to believe he could stur up warr against whom he would, and make peace for whom he would." Squanto even told some of his fellow tribesman that the English kept the plague at Plymouth and could release it on tribes that did not cooperate with them. Squanto schemed to ally the Wampanoag sagamores to himself and thereby unseat Massasoit from the sachemship. The Plymouth authorities, disappointed with his actions, nevertheless tempered their criticism of Squanto's double-dealing, for he was their guide and interpreter and they could not afford to do without.

132

Hoping the whole incident would be forgotten, the English re-sumed their trading expedition to Massachusetts Bay. They returned to find an infuriated Massasoit at Plymouth, who had apologized to Governor Bradford for Squanto's deceit. Squanto had dishon-ored the Wampanoag sachemship by misrepresenting his sachem. Even worse, Squanto apparently had competed with his sachem for allegiance of the Wampanoag people. The Plymouth authori-ties tried to appease the angry Massasoit in the hope of keeping Squanto from punishment by the *miawene* or tribal council. The Wampanoag sachem left, exasperated by their stalling tactics, but he sent delegations several times to demand Squanto be handed over even though Plymouth argued he was vital to the colony as an interpreter and without him their communication with the local tribes would be greatly hampered. Relations between Massasoit and the Pilgrims deteriorated giving the Wampanoag sagamores even more reason to doubt the credibility of their treaty with Plymouth. The Pilgrims, uncertain how they stood with the Wampanoags, built a fort for their own protection.

During the summer of 1622, a London merchant named Tho-mas Weston sent sixty colonists to New England. Weston's men explored Massachusetts Bay and established their settlement at present-day Weymouth, an area the Massachusett people called Wessagusset. The Pilgrims' new neighbors prospered until the first winter, when to avert starvation they began stealing corn from the Wessagusset tribe. Checkatabutt, sagamore of the Neponsets, and Obtakiest, sagamore of the Wessagussets, endured this abuse for only so long, and then conspired to get rid of these undesirable neighbors. Checkatabutt was convinced the Pilgrims would revenge any English who might be killed at Wessagusset, so he wanted to make allies of other tribes to destroy Plymouth, too. In a short time, he had persuaded the Agawams (in present-day Ipswich), Manamets, Matachees, Pawmets, Nausets, Capawicks and the vil-lage of Sokones to join in his anti-English conspiracy.

Meanwhile, the disheartening news reached Plymouth that Massasoit was near death from a prolonged illness. Edward Winslow was quickly sent to visit the sachem at Pokanoket. Hobbamock, who served as Winslow's guide and interpreter, went with him. When they arrived at Massasoit's village, the *sachimmaacomack* was so crowded they were scarcely able to enter. At the center of the throng lay the ailing sachem, who had powwows chanting over him and six tribeswomen chafing his arms and thighs to enhance circulation. Despite the sachem's weakened state, which had left him almost blind, Massasoit put out his hand to Winslow, asking him weakly, "*Keen Winsnow?*" which in Wampanoag translates "Are you Winslow?" When Winslow answered "*Ahhe,*" or "yes," Massasoit feebly uttered "*Matta neen wonckanet namen, Winsnow. ,*" or "Oh Winslow, I shall never see you again."

Winslow, after a superficial examination of Massasoit's condition, saw that the sachem's mouth was terribly furred and his tongue was swollen. Winslow rinsed out his mouth and used a knife to gently scrape his tongue free of spittle and unswallowed food. Because of his condition Massasoit had not eaten for two days, but with his throat now somewhat cleared, the sachem was able to take a small amount of nourishment made out of conserves brought from Plymouth. Within a few hours Massasoit's condition improved to the point where he began to regain his vision. After several days his overall health had so normalized that everyone in Pokanoket acknowledged that Winslow and Hobbamock had cured him. Massasoit was so impressed with his own rapid recovery that he asked of Winslow to spend one entire morning rinsing out the mouths of all the "good folk" that had taken ill in this village. "This pains I took with willingness," Winslow writes, "though it were much offensive to me, not being accustomed with such poisonous savors."

When Winslow and Hobbamock prepared to leave Pokanoket, Massasoit called Hobbamock aside and revealed that several Massachusett sagamores were conspiring to destroy the English colonists at both plantations. The sachem had been aware of this plot for some time, but he made little effort to warn the English colonists until Winslow's kindness restored his faith in Plymouth. If Winslow had failed to visit Massasoit during his illness, and the sachem had died, both English settlements would probably have come under attack.

Winslow warned Governor Bradford of the impending danger when he arrived back at Plymouth. On the Pilgrims' annual court day, which occurred shortly after Winslow's return, the Pilgrims decided that they would take the advantage and strike first. They sent Captain Standish and a company of eight men to help the colonists at Wessagusset defend their settlement. Standish devised a scheme at Wessagusset: the men invited a couple of Massachusett conspirators into the fort, under the pretense their differences could be resolved peacefully. Once these tribesmen were inside, the English murdered two warriors, Pecksuot and Wituwamat, who had actively solicited the support from neighboring tribes in their conspiracy against the English. In the end, Wituwamat's head was brought to Plymouth and displayed from the fortifications as a deterrent to other tribes. Captain Standish, after murdering the warriors, led an expedition into Massachusett country, where his men skirmished with a band of natives and then returned to Wessagusset. Back at the settlement, Weston's men prepared to abandon their colony and sail to Monhegan Island, where they could board a fishing vessel for England. Captain Standish remained at Wessagusset until Weston's men left for the Maine coast.

When the tribes allied with the Massachusett people heard the Pilgrims had killed the chief conspirators and crushed the plot, they fled into the swamps out of fear the English intended the same fate for them. Many of them died in the cold and damp from pneumonia, including Coneconam, sagamore of the Manamets; Iyanough, sagamore of the Matachees; and Aspinet, sagamore of the Nausets. These Wampanoag sagamores, all of whom were implicated in the tribal conspiracy to destroy the English at both plantations, were probably victims of the same widespread sickness that had also stricken the Massachusett and Nemaskets during the winter of 1622-1623. Evidently the Pilgrim's offensive actions at Wessaguset intimidated most of the local Algonkians into accepting Plymouth as a permanent colony, for by 1623 the Wampanoags, Nausets and several Massachusett sagamores had made peace with the English settlers.

Plymouth Colony, having survived its most difficult years, gradually expanded over the next decade to where William Bradford was able to write, "the people of the plantation begane to grow in their outward estates, by reason of the flowing of many people into the countrie, especially into Bay of Massachusetts; by which many were much enriched, and commodities grew plentiful." However, growth put pressure on the town of Plymouth, and in a short time its inhabitants were "scattered all over the bay and the towne in which they lived compactly till now was left almost desolate." When the population of Plymouth increased, the colonists began dividing the land into new townships such as Duxbury, Marshfield, Scituate, Taunton, Sandwich, Yarmouth and Barnstable. By 1633, Plymouth Colony had established trading posts at Aptucxct (present-day Bourne), and on the lower Connecticut River to purchase furs from the Algonkian tribes. Yet even though the Plymouth enterprise continued to prosper, its success was soon overshadowed by the rapid development of the Massachusetts Bay Colony.

In 1623 a group of English merchants, who were already involved with sending fishing vessels to the Massachusetts coast, decided that by establishing a colony there they could increase their profit margin. The following year they sent over thirty-two men, who started a colony on Cape Ann. This venture soon failed through unwise management of the company stocks and many of the stockholders lost their investments. A ship was sent over to Cape Ann to rescue the abandoned colonists, but a handful chose to remain in New England and moved down the coast where they built the settlement of Naumkeag, later known as Salem, Massachusetts.

A few persistent investors tried to keep the defaulting company operative, and by 1627 they were backed by several affluent London merchants. These investors financed the voyage of another twenty or more colonists who joined the others at Naumkeag. A third group of three hundred settlers, soon followed in 1629. Two hundred of these colonists joined the others already at Naumkeag, while the rest settled along Massachusetts Bay where they established Charlestown. As more English colonists arrived they founded Boston, Cambridge, Watertown, Roxbury, Dorchester, Lynn, Saugus, Medford, Woburn, and Concord.

At the same time, Sir Ferdinando Gorges and Captain John Mason, along with other investors, organized themselves into the Laconia Company. In England, the Council for New England (the successor to the former Plymouth Company) granted these two proprietors the region from the Merrimac River in the south to the Sagadahoc area in Maine, which they later divided between themselves. In 1623, two groups of colonists settled along the Piscataqua River in what is now New Hampshire. One group established themselves at the mouth of this river, naming their settlement Little Harbor which later became Portsmouth. The other group settled eight miles up river at a neck of land the local Algonkians called *Winnichahannat,* which the colonists renamed Dover.

Soon afterwards, John Wheelwright of the Massachusetts Bay Colony and several other investors purchased all the land between the Merrimac and Piscataqua rivers from the Pennacook sachem Passaconaway and his sagamores. The natives reserved for themselves the right to fish, hunt and plant within these limits. From this purchase emerged the settlement of Exeter. By 1638, English from the Bay Colony had also settled at *Winnicumit,* which they renamed Hampton, and Massachusetts settlers also established outposts north of the Piscataqua River at Kittery, York and Wells.

The Piscataqua River settlements contained only a few houses in 1631, but twenty years later there were about sixty families along the river. These towns were often havens for outspoken Massachusetts colonists, who wanted to be free from the theocratic government of the Puritans. Yet as the number of newcomers from the Bay Colony steadily increased, the Massachusetts General Court sought to advance its disputed claim over these towns to the north. Between 1641-1658, all the settlements along the Piscataqua River and Maine coast conceded authority to Massachusetts. Under this arrangement, the Bay Colony extended its jurisdiction northward to a line running from Lake Winnipesaukee in the west to Casco Bay on the Maine coast. Later on, when Robert Mason, the grandson of Captain John Mason, complained the northward extension of Massachusetts jurisdiction intruded on his inheritance, the Crown finally agreed to separate the Piscataqua settlements from the Bay Colony. This partition, in 1680, created the New Hampshire Colony, but Maine remained part of Massachusetts until the early 19th century.

Throughout the 1630s, emigration to New England increased until by 1640 the English population of the entire area was about 13,500. Immigration practically stopped after this time but within three decades the English population had increased to 51,500 through internal growth. During most of these years the Massachusetts frontier expanded outward from Boston into the interior since the rich alluvial soils attracted the Puritan settlers up the Charles and Mystic Rivers, and shortly thereafter onto the lower Merrimac, Concord and Nashua Rivers. By 1670, an irregular line of frontier towns stretched north from Marlborough to the settlements of Lancaster and Groton. Between Groton and the lower Merrimac River stood the isolated frontier community of Dunstable, not incorporated as a town until 1673. In the lower Merrimac Valley another line of frontier towns was established: Chelmsford, Billerica, Andover, Haverhill, Amesbury and Salisbury. From the mouth of the Merrimac River the frontier went north along the New Hampshire coastline, with outposts at Hampton, Exeter, Portsmouth and Dover. Beyond the Piscataqua River the frontier ended at the towns of Kittery, York, Wells and Casco. Central Massachusetts contained the isolated settlements of Quabaug (Brookfield) and Quinsigamond (Worcester), with Deerfield, Hatfield, Hadley and Springfield in the Connecticut River Valley.

In 1635, some residents of Cambridge considered moving west when they heard there was fertile land in the Connecticut Valley. The outflow of settlers from Massachusetts to this area had already begun, for that same autumn a group of families from Dorchester travelled overland and settled in what is now Windsor, Connecticut. By the following spring, a number of families from Cambridge moved to Connecticut, where they started the town of Hartford. Because their distance from Boston placed them outside the jurisdiction of Massachusetts (which some had wanted to begin with), the Connecticut settlers formed themselves into a separate colony. Lord Say and Lord Brookes, patentees of the Connecticut Valley, built a fort at the mouth of the Connecticut River, which they appropriately named Saybrook.

During this same period, Roger Williams, who had been banished from the Massachusetts Bay Colony because of his controversial interpretations of Biblical scripture, bought a tract of land from Canonicus, sachem of the Narragansetts, to found the Providence Plantation. Like the Piscataqua settlements, the Providence Plantation became a refuge from the Puritanism of the Bay Colony. In 1637, Canonicus and his nephew Miantonomo sold Aquidneck Island and other islands in Narragansett Bay to William Coddington, in exchange for ten coats and twenty hoes. According to the stipulations of this transaction, the Narragansetts then living on Aquidneck Island were given one year to vacate their homeland in the bay, so the English could begin settling there. Aquidneck Island was eventually sectioned off into the towns of Portsmouth and Newport, while the Providence Plantation encompassed the more northerly part of Narragansett country. The town of Warwick was built on an adjacent claim, and the Narragansett nation tried to keep control over the southern portion of present-day Rhode Island. In 1643, Roger Williams managed to obtain a charter from the English Crown for Providence, Newport and Portsmouth.

While the Connecticut and Rhode Island colonies were coming into their own, John Davenport left England for New England with a group of colonists and settled at Quinnipiac in present-day Connecticut. After they bought the land from the Quinnipiac tribe, they built the settlement of New Haven. Davenport, a Puritan, became the pastor at New Haven while his longtime friend, Theophilus Eaton, became governor. In 1641, the New Haveners founded Stamford, and shortly afterwards the independent towns of Guilford and Milford joined the New Haven Colony. The New Haveners reluctantly joined the Connecticut Colony in 1665.

When the English began to settle in Connecticut they encountered the Pequots, a powerful tribal nation that had recently vanquished the indigenous river peoples. The Pequots demanded tribute payments from such subjugated tribes as the Quinebaug, Podunck, Wangunk, Mohegan and Quinnipiac, and these river tribes occasionally asked both the Dutch and English to start trading posts and settlements along the lower Connecticut River, in the hope that their presence would deter Pequot expansionism. Consequently these Algonkian river tribes initially welcomed the English when they founded the towns of Hartford, Wethersfield, Windsor and Saybrook. In fact, their presence encouraged Uncas, sagamore of the Mohegans, to separate from the Pequot confederation in 1637.

Massachusetts Bay Colony insisted that the Pequots and their allies, who were opposed to English interference and domination, had murdered a number of Englishmen. In 1634, they accused the nation of killing a Virginian trader named Captain John Stone and seven of his crew, when their vessel entered the Connecticut River while enroute from Boston to Virginia. According to the Pequot account, Stone had abducted two of their fellow tribesmen, bound them hand and foot, and forced them to help pilot him up river. A small band of Pequot warriors, who saw this, trailed the vessel until Stone and his men came ashore to camp for the night. The Pequots attacked to free their kidnapped tribesmen and killed Stone and his crew. Some English, however, claimed the Pequots had boarded the captain's vessel pretending they wanted to trade, and then done away with the crew. English-Pequot relations became even further strained when it was rumored the Pequots had murdered two sailors stranded on Long Island. About this time, the tribespeople of Manisses (Block Island) were charged with killing a Bay colonist named Captain John Oldham when he went ashore there to trade with them. The Pequots tried to compensate for the death of Captain Stone by sending a gift of furs and wampum to the fort at Saybrook, but the colonial authorities of Massachusetts Bay Colony deemed the offer insufficient and demanded that the Pequots turn over the warriors implicated in Stone's death.

As tensions steadily increased, Sassacus, sachem of the Pequots, tried to persuade his adversaries, the Narragansetts, to ally with his nation. If the Narragansetts helped the English to subdue the Pequots, he argued, they would be preparing for their own eventual destruction. The Pequots, instead of openly confronting the English, planned to ambush the settlers as they worked in their fields. Sassacus had nearly convinced the Narragansetts to join him, when the Massachusetts Bay Colony sent an embassy to them, and with the assistance of Roger Williams, dissuaded them from joining the Pequots. The Pequots were aware the English were planning a military expedition against them for in a series of letters to Deputy Governor John Winthrop of Massachusetts, Roger Williams writes, "the Pequot hear of your preparations, and comfort themselves in this, that a witch amongst them will sink the pinnaces, by diving under water and making holes [in the boats], and as also that they shall [thereby] now enrich themselves with store of guns, but I hope their dreams (through the mercy of the Lord) shall vanish, and the devil and his lying sorcerers shall be confounded." Williams also relates that the Pequots and Western Niantics were resolved "to live and die together, and not yield up one."

In August, 1636, Governor Vane of the Massachusetts Bay Colony sent a troop of one hundred and twenty men under the command of Captain John Endicott to Pequot country, under orders to call this nation into account for the murder of Captain Stone. However, before the expedition sailed over to Connecticut they planned revenge on the Manisses tribal people on Block Island for the murder of Captain Oldham. On August 31st they landed and skirmished with some Manisses tribesmen who then retreated into the interior of the island. The expedition could not track down the fleeing warriors, so they burned about sixty wigwams in two villages and destroyed some of their corn. From Block Island the English crossed the sound to Connecticut. Captain Lion Gardener, commander of the fort at Saybrook, voiced his displeasure over their arrival, since, he argued, Captain Endicott's expedition would only provoke the Pequots into a war, and leave the Connecticut settlers with the consequences. When Captain Endicott met with the Pequots, they refused to hand over the tribesmen supposedly implicated in the Stone murder, and Endicott ordered his men to burn several wigwams and seize corn to punish the tribespeople for not cooperating. None of the Pequots were injured during this destruction, because prior to this incident some of the tribesmen deliberately delayed the captain at a distance, as others in the village emptied the wigwams, and then at a given signal all the Pequots had fled the area. But elsewhere Cutshamequin, a Massachusett sagamore accompanying Captain Endicott, murdered a Pequot brave. The Massachusetts militia withdrew, leaving behind several of Captain Gardener's men to confiscate the Pequot corn. As Gardener's men brought the corn to Saybrook, a band of Pequot warriors pursued them and wounded two. This was the beginning of the Pequot War, the first major conflict between the New England colonies and the Algonkian people.

Within days the Pequots went on the warpath, killing two Englishmen at Saybrook. All winter long they harassed the fort, ambushing men as they went outside. One day when Captain Gardener and ten men went a half-mile from the fort to burn a field of reeds, the captain stationed two sentinels in case the Pequots tried to ambush them. The English set the reeds afire, and four Pequot braves suddenly started up from the burning brush, along with another band of warriors at the further end of the marsh. The Pequots shot two of the Englishmen before they could escape. Gardener and the rest of his company quickly retreated towards the fort, but some sustained arrow wounds to their backs and thighs. In all, eight people were killed at Saybrook before the winter was over.

Meanwhile, the Pequots began firing on shallops on the Connecticut River between Wethersfield and Saybrook. Captain Gardener posted a warning, "that no boat or bark should pass the fort, but that they came to an anchor first, that he might see whether they were armed and manned sufficiently, and they were not to land any where after they passed the fort till they came to Wethersfield." When a shallop was ambushed up river, and one of the drowned men eventually washed ashore at Saybrook with an arrow through his head, Gardener grew even more determined to enforce his restrictions. By the spring of 1637, the Pequots had burned several warehouses on the lower Connecticut River, and they were disrupting water traffic between Saybrook and Hartford.

Having terrorized the English, the Pequots became even bolder and killed nine settlers at Wethersfied. In response, the Connecticut Colony declared war on the Pequots and raised a militia of ninety men under the command of Captain John Mason. Uncas and eighty Mohegan warriors allied with the English against the ✓ Pequots. Mason left Hartford and stopped at Saybrook where he joined his forces with Captain John Underhill's militia, sent there by the Massachusetts Bay Colony to protect the fort from the Pequots. The two captains stayed at Saybrook for five days, and planned to surprise the Pequots by marching through Narragansett country, for they believed the Pequots expected the English to attack from the west.

To carry out their plan, the English travelled east in boats to Narragansett Bay, where Miantonomo gave the expedition permission to use his lands as a staging area for the assault. It was Miantonomo who convinced the English to attack the Pequots from the east. In a letter to John Winthrop dated May, 1637, Roger Williams tells how Miantonomo held a tribal council meeting at his home in Providence. During the meeting the sachem pointed out the feasibility of using Narragansett country to stage the attack. He also revealed to Williams the location of the Pequots' three major fortified villages, and a great swamp called *Ohomowaukee* (owl's nest), which the Pequots used as a refuge for their women and children during times of war.

From Narragansett Bay Mason led his men overland to Niantic, a fortified village at the edge of Pequot country. The Eastern Niantics welcomed the expedition with reservations; they were allied with the Narragansetts, but their close relatives, the Western Niantics, were Pequot subjects. Mason feared the Eastern Niantics might warn the Pequots of their coming, so he put guards around their village, and threatened to shoot any tribesman who tried to leave. While the English were still at Niantic, Miantonomo arrived and told Mason that his own people had decided to assist the English in fighting the Pequots. The next morning the English expedition (along with five hundred Algonkian men) crossed the Pawcatuck River and made camp near the Pequot's main fort, a stockaded village on top of a hill on the west bank of the Mystic River. That night, the sentinels reported to Mason they could hear singing inside the Pequot fort as tribesmen celebrated their attack on Wethersfield.

Shortly after daybreak Captain Mason cautiously led his soldiers closer to the fort, but most of the Algonkians, excepting the Mohegans, fell behind out of fear. The soldiers made their surprise attack through the fort's two entrances and found the Pequots still asleep after a long night of celebration. Mason writes:

There being two Entrances into the Fort, intending to enter both at once . . . [a] Dog barked and an Indian crying Owanux! Owanux! which is Englishmen! Englishmen! We called up our Forces with all expedition, gave Fire upon them through the Pallizado; the Indians being in a dead indeed their last Sleep: Then we wheeling off fell upon the main Entrance . . . . Captain Mason seeing no Indians, entered a Wigwam; where he was beset with many Indians, waiting all opportunities to lay Hands on him, but could not prevail. The Captain going out of the Wigwam saw many Indians in the Lane or Street; he making towards them they fled, were pursued to the End of the Lane, where they were met by Edward Pattison, Thomas Barber, with some others; where seven of them were Slain . . . . The Captain also said, We must Burn them; and immediately stepping into a Wigwam where he had been before, brought out a Firebrand, and putting it into the Matts with which they were covered, set the Wigwams on Fire . . . and when it was thoroughly kindled, the Indians ran as Men most dreadfully Amazed. They would fly from us and run into the very Flames, where many of them perished. And when the Fort was thoroughly Fired, Command was given, that all should fall off and surround the Fort. The Fire was kindled on the North East Side to windward; which did swiftly over-run the Fort. Some of them climbing to the Top of the Pallizado; others of them running into the very Flames; many of them gathering to windward, lay pelting at us with arrows; and we repayed them with our small Shot: Others of the Stoutest issued forth, as we did guess, to the Number of Forty, who perished by the Sword.

In less than an hour about six hundred men, women and children of the powerful Pequot nation were horribly massacred, while the English sustained only two dead and twenty wounded. As the fort went up in flames, a number of grief-stricken Pequots watched from a distance, clenching their hair in their hands because of the anguish they felt for their fellow tribesmen. Mason regrouped his forces and marched along the Mystic River to Pequot Harbor where Captain Patrick and his forty men had brought the boats from Narragansett Bay. As the expedition marched down to the sea they were trailed by Pequot warriors who shot their arrows into the rear guard. The English wounded were placed on board the boats in the harbor and brought to Saybrook by Captain Underhill. The rest of the English forces marched overland through the lands of the Western Niantics, who took refuge in the swamps as the soldiers passed through their country. That evening the English arrived safely at Saybrook.

With the success of Mason's campaign, the English terrorized the Pequots even further by rewarding Algonkians for bringing in the heads of Pequot warriors. The surviving Pequots, branded as fugitives, fled west toward Munhattan. The Massachusetts and Connecticut colonies, in a joint effort, pursued these remaining Pequots as far as Quinnipiac, where they captured about two hundred old men, women and children. Some of the surviving Pequots were shipped to Bermuda and the Caribbean as slaves, while others became servants in English households. In the end, when the sachem Sassacus and some of his people made a desperate attempt to seek refuge among their Iroquoian enemies, even the sachem was executed and his head sent to Hartford by the Mohawks.

Scattered from the Mystic River to Munhattan, the Pequots were unable to find safety. Almost daily the Connecticut River tribes sent the heads of Pequot warriors to Windsor and Hartford. Their numbers greatly reduced through this crushing defeat, the Pequots finally surrendered to the English, who divided the survivors between the Narragansetts, Mohegans and Eastern Niantics. According to the terms of their submission, the Pequots could never reunite their nation, nor could they reinhabit their native land. They were forbidden to call themselves by their tribal name. Some of the remaining Pequots attempted to challenge these stipulations by resettling along the Pawcatuck River, but the English quickly dispatched an expedition to the area and plundered their village. The colonists claimed the area had become English territory by right of conquest and the country was now open to "peaceable habitation." In 1640, the Connecticut Colony examined the forests in the region intending to cut timber. Four years later, John Winthrop's son was given permission to start a settlement in Pequot country, and as English settlers moved into eastern Connecticut, the Pequots' banishment from most of their land became permanent. Remnants of the shattered Pequot confederation were settled between Niantic and New London until 1650, where they again reestablished some of their remaining people in Pequot country at a place called *Noank*, at the mouth of the Mystic River. From here, the Pequots moved to *Mashantucket* (Groton) in the early 18th century. According to the Connecticut historian John DeForest, Pequots lived at the Mashantucket reservation as late as the 1850s.

Many of the Algonkian tribes of southern New England were greatly intimidated by the sudden defeat of the Pequots. According to Edward Johnson, the swiftness of the campaign "struck a trembling terror into all the Indians round about." Several days after the battle with the Pequots at Mystic Fort, Waiandance, the Montauk sagamore on Long Island, visited Saybrook "to know if [the English] were angry with all Indians." Two Nipmuck sachems from the area of Mount Wachusett publicly reaffirmed their friendship toward the end of May, 1637. In 1642, the Bay Colony seized the Massachusett sagamore Cutshamequin, who lived in the vicinity of Braintree, acting on rumors of another possible Algonkian conspiracy. Cutshamequin was thrown into prison for a day, on suspicion that the Massachusett and Pennacook nations were plotting against the English. Forty armed men were immediately sent to Pawtucket to capture Passaconaway, but he was not at the village. Searching the wigwams they seized the sachem's son, Wannalancit, along with his wife and child. Wannalancit was brought to Boston after a near escape and later released. Masconomet, sagamore of the Agawams (Ipswich) was also accused of being implicated in the conspiracy. Even though the plot proved to be a rumor, Massachusetts Bay Colony disarmed the local sachems and sagamores of their guns for a time.

The Massachusett, Nashua, Agawam and some Nipmuck tribes submitted to the authority of the Massachusetts Bay Colony under these circumstances. They agreed to the following terms:

Wossamegon, Nashowanon, Cutshamequin, Masconomet & Squa Sachem did volentarily submit themselves to us, as appeareth by their covenant subscribed with their own hands, here following, & other articles to which they consented. Wee have & by these presents do voluntarily, & without any constraint or perswasion, but of our owne free motion, put ourselves, our subjects, lands, & estates under the government & jurisdiction of the Massachusetts, to bee governed & protected by them, according to their just lawes & orders, so farr as wee shalbee made capable of understanding them; & wee do promise for ourselves, & all our subjects, & all our posterity, to bee true & faithfull to the said government, & aiding to the maintenance thereof, to our best ability, & from time to time to give speedy notice of any conspiracy, attempt, or evill intension of any which wee shall know or hearof against the same; & wee do promise to bee willing from time to time to bee instructed in the knowledge & worship of God. In witness whereof wee have hereunto put our hands the 8th of the first month, 1643-44.

Cutshamequin

Masconomet

Nashowanon

Squa Sachem

Wossamegon

Once these tribal leaders had subjected their people to the Massachusetts colonial government, the court ordered the nomination of "such fit persons" to preach the gospel to the Algonkians, a missionary effort which was "to reduce them to civility." The Reverend John Eliot led his famous missionary drive among the New England tribes in the Massachusetts Bay Colony, where he translated the Bible into the Massachusett dialect, and brought the gospel to the Massachusett, Pennacook and Nipmuck nations. He started his missionary work in 1646 among a band of Massachusett led by Waban of *Nonantum* (Newton), who later resettled the group at Natick, Massachusetts. The Christianized "Praying Indians" were usually encouraged to separate from the rest of their tribe into new villages called "Praying Indian towns." Because of its central location to the other tribes in the Bay Colony, Eliot hoped that "Praying Indians" from Natick could eventually be sent "unto some remoter places, to teach them the fear of the Lord."

Between 1646-1674, Eliot converted about eleven hundred tribal people in fourteen different villages, from Natick in the east to the Merrimac River in the north and as far west and south as the Nashua River and northeastern Connecticut. Natick, Punkapoag, Hassanamesitt (Grafton), Okommakamesit (Marlborough), Wamesit (Lowell), Nashoba (Littleton), Magunkaquog (Ashland), Manchage (Sutton), Chabanakongkomun (Webster), Pakachoog (Worcester) and Washacum (Sterling) were the "Praying Indian" towns under the jurisdiction of the Massachusetts Bay Colony. Ironically, the land where these new Algonkian groups founded their "Praying Indian" towns was granted to them by the Massachusetts court! Eliot was convinced that despite their ancestral usage rights to tribal lands, only a legal title as defined by English law would ultimately guarantee their rights to any of their land. In a prefatory letter to the Commissioners of the United Colonies of New England, Eliot explained his rationale for having the Massachusetts court grant the "Praying Indians" their own townships. He requested that the commissioners "in all respective colonies would take care that due accomodation of lands and waters might be allowed them, whereupon townships and churches might be in after ages able to subsist; and suffer not the English to strip them of all their land, in places fit for the sustenance of the life of man."

The English tried to increase their authority over these Christianized Algonkians as early as 1647, by establishing quarterly courts in some of their villages. The court sessions handled altercations among the "Praying Indians," but their function was also to further the spread of the gospel. The colony empowered an English magistrate to oversee the governing of these "Praying Indian" towns. In 1656, Daniel Gookin was appointed to be the first superintendent of the "Praying Indian" reservations in the Massachusetts Bay Colony. He managed the affairs of the "Praying towns" with help of the "most prudent and pious Indians" who had accepted the gospel. It was Eliot's conviction that his missionary effort to the tribes would be hastened by training up "Praying Indians" to be local pastors and elders, for they would be more effective speakers of their own Algonkian dialect, than an "English young man raw in that language." The superintendent and the Massachusetts court sanctioned these Christian tribal leaders as local rulers and magistrates in the reservations.

Theoretically, the "Praying Indians" were allowed local autonomy, but the English magistrates sometimes interfered. In 1654, the Massachusetts court ordered that "whereas Showanan, sagamore of Nashaway (Washacum), is lately dead, & another is now suddenly to be chosen . . . this Court doth order, that Mr. Nowell and Mr. Eliot be sent to direct them in their choice, their eyes being upon 2 or 3 which are of the blood, one whereof is a debaust, drunken fellow, & no friend to the English; if, therefore these gentlemen may, by way of persuasion or counsell, not by compulsion, prevail with them for the choice of such a one as may be most fit, it would be a good service to the country." A "Praying Indian" named Matthew was eventually chosen as the new sagamore, but when he died he was replaced by Shoshanim (Sagamore Sam), who along with a tribesman named Monoco tried to preserve Nashua tribal customs.

It was only a matter of time before Eliot's missionary effort among the Massachusett tribes "stirred up divers other ministers and scholars, in . . . other colonies, by his words and letters to fit themselves to labour in this Indian harvest." In neighboring Plymouth Colony, Richard Bourne and John Cotton had learned some of the Wampanoag dialect, and preached the gospel from Nauset to Nemasket. By 1674 there were about six hundred and fifty converts scattered among thirty Wampanoag villages. Of these an impressive one hundred and forty-two were able to read the Wampanoag dialect, while seventy-two could both read and write the language. Only nine could read English, but many more spoke it fairly well.

Likewise, on Martha's Vineyard and Nantucket, Thomas Mayhew and his sons met with considerable success in their missionary work among the island tribes. Just prior to King Philip's War (1675-1676) there were six hundred adherents to Christianity on the two islands. The Mayhews had established nine "Praying towns." As at Plymouth Colony, many among the island "Praying Indians" could read and write Wampanoag. During the early 1670s, James Fitch, pastor of a church in Norwich, Connecticut, preached the gospel to the Mohegan tribe. About thirty Mohegan adults and their children joined together to form a "Praying town" on three hundred acres donated by Fitch and the community of Norwich. A Mohegan tribesman named Weebax was appointed as leader of these converts, despite opposition from Sachem Uncas. The tribespeople of the Narragansetts, however, resisted conversion. According to Daniel Gookin this nation was "more indisposed to embrace religion [Christianity], than any Indians in the country" because of the averseness of their sachems.

While the Puritans evangelized among the Algonkian confederacies of southern New England, the Jesuits of Quebec preached Roman Catholicism to the Abenaki in Maine. The Jesuits were fairly successful at converting this nation, for Cotton Mather mentions "that the Indians have three forts at Narridawog [Norridgewock], Narrackomogog and Amassacanty. And at each of these forts they have a chapel, and have images in them." During King William's War (1689-1697) English settlers on the frontier were often taken captive to Canada by the Abenakis, where they were usually redeemed by the French. In writing about their experiences as prisoners, several authors noted the influence of Catholicism among the Abenaki people. As a captive of the Abenaki at Pennacook (Concord, New Hampshire), Hannah Dustin observed that "in obedience to the instructions which the French had given them, the [Abenaki] would have prayers in their family no less than thrice every day; in morning, at noon, and in evening, nor would they ordinarily let their children eat or sleep, without first saying their prayers." Similarly, the Reverend John Williams of Deerfield, Massachusetts, was taken captive to Quebec where he saw two Jesuits perform Mass for a congregation of Algonkian people. On one occasion during his imprisonment, Williams tells how "my [Algonkian] master took hold of my hand to force me to cross myself, but I struggled with him, and would not suffer him to guide my hand; upon this he pulled off a crucifix from his own neck, and bade me kiss it: but I refused."

Most of the Algonkian people were extremely reluctant to accept Christianity, particularly the sachems, sagamores and powwows. The missionaries tended to draw the loyalty of their tribal subjects away, which fractured tribal unity and reduced the annual tribute payments of wampum in a nation. But tribal youth who were sometimes unable to have a leadership role under their sachem or sagamore saw Christian conversion as an alternative path to tribal leadership. They adopted the Christian faith so they could be appointed to supervisory positions over one of the "Praying towns." Sachem Uncas repeatedly complained of the Christianization of the Mohegans and tried to prevent the fracturing of his authority by publicly criticizing those who became converts. For this reason, Gookin described Uncas as "a willful man, who hath always been a opposer and underminer of praying to God." Wannalancit, sachem of the Pennacook nation, shunned the English missionaries, for he feared some of his sagamores would desert him if he converted to the Christian faith. However, in 1674 this sachem surprisingly promised to become a Christian, probably because he hoped the English would then respect Pennacook neutrality if war broke out between the local tribes and the colonists. At the same time, King Philip was rumored to be conspiring to free his people from English domination. Wannalancit told of his decision to become Christian in a speech before Eliot and others at Pawtucket:

> Sirs, you have been pleased for four years last past, in your abundant love, to apply yourselves particularly unto me and my people, to exhort, press, and persuade us to pray to God. I am very thankful to you for your pains. I must acknowledge, I have all my days, used to pass in an old canoe, and now you exhort me to change and leave my old canoe, and embark in a new canoe, to which I have hitherto been unwilling; but now I yield up myself to your advice, and enter into a new canoe, and do engage to pray to God hereafter.

Another reason the Algonkian tribes were reluctant to adopt Christianity was that when they converted they had to renounce their powwows. Without the shaman, the Algonkian believed himself to be more vulnerable to evil spirit forces. The Reverend John Eliot told the Christianized Algonkians that murder, stealing and lying were great sins, but powwowing was a worse sin, "because by them you worship the Devil instead of God." The missionaries deliberately undercut the native peoples' attachment to the powwow as a healer of ailments by encouraging the "Praying Indians" to use their own knowledge of herbal remedies without consulting the powwows. To further limit the influence of the shamans, the Massachusetts court decreed "that no Indian shall at any time powwow, or perform outward worship to their false gods, or to ye devill, in any part of our jurisdiction, whether they be such as dwell here, or shall come hither." Uncompromising Puritan missionary attitudes and intolerant colonial laws made the powwows agree with their sachems and sagamores that the Christianization of their people was unacceptable.

For the *sannup*, or common people in the tribe, the greatest hurdle to adopting the Christian faith was the Puritan insistence that the converted "Praying Indians" separate from their unconverted kinsmen and friends into exclusive "Christian Indian towns." Eliot believed the "Praying Indians" would make greater progress toward sanctification if they stopped everyday contact with their former villages. In this respect the Catholic missions among the Abenaki were better liked by the tribal leadership, for the Catholics generally made no demands to physically separate from the unconverted tribal members. In his *Indian Dialogues*, Eliot describes the Algonkian fear of social isolation from the communal family circle, which he oftentimes heard as he preached the gospel among the tribes in Massachusetts Bay Colony. In one particular dialogue a "Praying Indian" named Piumbukhuo testifies about his Christian faith to a family member called Kinsman. Kinsman hesitates to become a Christian, saying "the greatest difficulty that I yet find, is this. I am loth to divide myself from my friends and kindred. If I should change my course and not they, then I must leave and forsake their company, which I am very loth to do. I love my sachem, and all the rest of my good friends. If I should change my life and way, I greatly desire that we might agree to do it together." The sachems and sagamores occasionally attempted to subvert these separate "Praying towns" by deliberately encouraging the "Praying Indians" and unconverted tribal members to mingle, hoping to reestablish fractured kin and clan ties. Such attempts were usually found out, however, before the "Praying Indians" were reabsorbed under the authority of their former sachems and sagamores.

Why a minority of the indigenous people of New England would adopt Christianity is puzzling, considering that the Algonkians believed in allowing all people to hold their own religious convictions. Algonkian Christian conversion was the result of two factors: the psychological state of certain coastal tribes after the disastrous impact of the plague of 1617, coupled with the excessive changes in their woodland environment made by the English. The Massachusett nation was so devastated by this plague that when the Plymouth colonists made their first trading expedition to their bay they found the Massachusett in a state of disorientation. A pervasive pall of fear and vulnerability seemed to be over them, due to the sudden widespread deaths, which soon encouraged Mic Mac and Maliseet warriors from the north to make raids on them in their weakened condition. As the English rapidly assumed control of the region in the first half of the 17th century, they brought permanent changes to the landscape. They cleared land for livestock, had a more intensive form of agriculture and there was growing Algonkian dependency on the colonial economy due to the fur trade. The remaining Massachusett tribes became increasingly alienated from their precontact lifestyle. Their political and social customs disintegrated, and Eliot found ample opportunity to draw some of these people out of their bewilderment into the "Praying Indian" community, where they found what seemed to be greater structure and security.

Another factor in Algonkian conversion to Christianity was the fact that nature worship had a very accomodating world view, allowing for a wide latitude of expression and personal opinion. The Algonkian oral tradition had diverse explanations of the creation of the cosmos, the tribes' origins as a people, and totemic traditions. Wampanoag and Narragansett creation stories relate how their ancestors were first made from stones, and then later sprung from trees, while another Algonkian creation theme tells a "story of the beaver, saying that he was their Father." Tribesmen were even free to question openly the credibility of their own traditions. Roger Williams tells how an Algonkian tribesman from Connecticut, who had been exposed to certain basic Christian teachings, told the Narragansett sachem Miantonomo that souls neither went to heaven or hell, but went to the southwestern sky after death. This all Algonkians knew from the traditions of their forefathers. In response, Miantonomo said, "but how do you know yourself that your soul goes to the southwest, did you ever see a soul go thither?"

The powwows, like the sachems and sagamores, depended on their personal charisma and skill in divination, which they used for individuals or when the welfare of the entire village was threatened. However, the norm in Algonkian religion was for each tribal member to strive after a personal spiritual communion that generally did not require the tribal powwow. Where the tribal customs had been overstressed by the catastrophes of viral epidemics and extreme ecological changes, both Puritan missionaries and Jesuit teachers were able to compete with the powwows, whose credibility had diminished. Because these shamans were not part of an organized priesthood with a systematic theology, they were generally unable to formulate an effective defense against Christian missions.

In their conversion efforts, the denomination a Christian missionary belonged to made little difference. All the missionaries shared the common objective of converting the Algonkians from their nature worship to the spiritual mores of Christianity. Christian indoctrination destroyed the animistic ceremonialism practiced by these tribes, so that for the converted tribesman, the Algonkian ecosystem was denuded of its many nature spirits. The natural environment became a more exploitable realm devoid of the many animated forces that in former times a tribesman had to propitiate before he could extract anything from nature. The new mentality of the "Praying Indians" of Natick and Hassanamesitt allowed them to build meeting houses and several other stationary buildings after the English style of construction, even though the majority of the villagers continued to live in wigwams. At Natick the "Praying Indians" laid out three long streets, and bridged the Charles River. The Algonkian converts in the Christianized towns were encouraged to live in more permanent year round villages, and discouraged from following their former lifestyles as nomadic farmers. This was only partly achieved, for the "Praying Indians" continued to supplement their food supplies from time to time through gathering.

The Reverend John Eliot's effort to make the "Praying Indians" more like their English neighbors led him to insist that the Christianized Algonkians cut their hair short and wear English clothing. This was part of a greater strategy to further engage the "Praying Indians" in the colonial market economy. The English introduced the "Praying towns" of Hassanamesitt and Nashoba to animal husbandry and the cultivation of apple orchards. Residents in other towns such as Punkapoag were taught to produce cedar shingles and clapboards, which they sold in Boston. The colonists encouraged the more distant "Praying Indians" at Pawtucket and Wamesit in the Merrimac Valley to market dried fish products to the settlements in the Bay Colony. "Praying Indians" on Martha's Vineyard and Nantucket travelled up to Boston and the surrounding towns during the harvest season to find seasonal work as farm laborers among the English. Still others produced brooms and baskets, or sold cordwood in the neighboring colonial towns.

The acculturation of the "Praying Indians" was more intense than that of tribesmen who stayed with the traditional Algonkian lifestyles, but even the unconverted tribal members grew more dependent on European capitalism. The French and English colonies, early on, built trading posts to carry on the fur trade with the local tribal nations. Algonkian demand for items produced in Europe led many Algonkian tribes to excessively exploit their environment to a degree they never had before. Catholic missionary efforts toward the Mic Mac of Nova Scotia, coupled with European demand for beaver pelts, caused this northern Algonkian nation to gradually stop propitiating their nature spirits. This in turn enabled the Mic Mac to assist French fur trappers in exterminating entire beaver populations in exchange for European trade items. This radical transformation seems even more significant when one considers that most precontact northern Algonkian tribes considered the beaver to be one of their tribal totems. Likewise, the neighboring Abenaki supplied the English with thousands of fledgling ducks by slaughtering the ducklings in their breeding grounds. "One thing I cannot here omit," Samuel Penhallow says, "three days after our departure, a number of Indians went a Duck-hunting, which was a season of the year that the old ones generally shed their feathers in, and the young ones not so welled flushed as to be able to fly; they drove them like a flock of sheep before them into the creeks, where without either powder or shot they killed at one time, four thousand and six hundred; for they followed them so close, that they knocked them down with billets and paddles, and sold a great number of them to the English for a penny a dozen, which is their practice yearly, though they seldome take so great a slaughter at once."

In southern New England, the Narragansetts traded venison to the Rhode Island colonists at the price of three and a half pence a pound, a price set by the colonial authorities. According to Daniel Gookin, the Narragansetts and the neighboring "Warwick Indians" also frequently helped the Rhode Island colonists to build their stone walls, and it was also common for the Algonkians who lived near the colonies to help the English eradicate local wolf popula-

154

tions. Wolves were a constant menace to the settlers' roaming livestock. The Massachusetts and Plymouth authorities offered an incentive of several pounds of gunpowder, shot or wine for every wolf head shown to the selectman in the nearest township.

By 1670, some Algonkian tribes in the Massachusetts Bay Colony had become so involved in the colonial market economy they frequently sold pork to the English. This pork was so abundant that the English settlers began to suspect that the tribesmen were killing the colonists' free-ranging swine and reselling it to them. The Massachusetts court ordered in 1672 that all swine be given permanent marks in their ears, as proof that the swine taken by Algonkian hunters was feral.

In the space of a century and a half, the economic relationship between Algonkians and the English brought about the permanent deterioration of native culture. To a lesser degree Christian missionary efforts contributed, but unquestionably the main influences were economic, as native customs deteriorated and disappeared. This tragic acculturation had become so thorough by the 18th century that the Mohegan Christian preacher, Samson Occom reflected on his childhood as a time in his life when he was exposed to the "heathenism" of his tribal forefathers. Occom writes apologetically about the fact that his people lived in wigwams, and for the most part were still living a rather nomadic lifestyle.

In the three decades between the Pequot War and the outbreak of King Philip's War, the colonial governments increasingly intruded on the self rule of the Algonkians by trying to hold them accountable under English law. The Massachusetts court based its power to deal with the native people as subjects on several presumptions. First, the magistrates pointed out, the principal sachems and sagamores within the colony had submitted themselves to English rule in the agreement of 1643. Secondly, the colonists claimed a right to the land through the patent granted by the English Crown. Lastly, the court believed it was in the Algonkian peoples' best interests to accept their new status, "for the English were a growing and potent people." The Massachusetts magistrates established quarterly courts for their tribal subjects in places where tribes came to hear the teaching of the Bible. These court sessions were exclusively for criminal and civil cases involving Algonkians, and the sachems and sagamores were encouraged to use these courts to maintain tribal order. Usually, however, the local Algonkian leaders used the sessions to bring complaints against the English.

A frequent grievance of the native people was that the settlers' unfenced livestock trampled and grazed on their cornfields. Masconomet, sagamore of the Agawam people, brought a complaint against the inhabitants of Charlestown for allowing their swine herds to roam up into the area of Ipswich, where they ate some of the Agawam corn stores. The Massachusetts court investigated the complaint and ordered that Charlestown residents compensate Masconomet for damages. The Algonkians sometimes took matters into their own hands and shot the livestock when they found them in their cornfields. Checkatabutt, a leader of the Massachusett, paid a fine of one beaver skin for killing a pig owned by Richard Saltonstall. The court permitted John Endicott to seize property belonging to his Massachusett tribal neighbors, without evidence for a conviction, until he discovered who had shot his cow. In retaliation for killed animals the settlers occasionally burned the wigwams of area tribal families. The Massachusetts court tried to alleviate this problem by ordering that "the English keep their cattle from destroying the Indians' corne in any ground where they have right to plant, if any corne bee destroyed for want of fencing, the towne shall be liable to make satisfaction and the Indians are to be encouraged to help towards the fencing of their cornfields." To make sure the fences were effective, the Connecticut Colony appointed "fence viewers" in each of its towns where the area tribes had planting fields, and encouraged these same tribes to construct pounds to hold any stray livestock found to be damaging cornfields or underground storage pits.

Free-ranging swine herds also damaged Algonkian clamming grounds. Coastal tribes such as the Wampanoag and Narragansett ate shellfish throughout most of the year, and made a broth from clams called *nasaump*, which they used to season their bread. English swine herds would sometimes discover clam beds at low tide and devour large quantities of clams, which angered the Algonkians. However, not all swine that were killed by Algonkians were killed in retaliation. Sometimes the Algonkians shot the English settlers' swine intending to sell the pork in the colonial towns. And sometimes they butchered the animals for their fat, which they used as a skin conditioner, a more readily available substitute for the Algonkians' traditional bear grease.

156

The English plantations in Rhode Island responded to the killing of their livestock by trying to make the Narragansett people answerable to English law. A statute enacted in 1659 gave Rhode Island magistrates the power to imprison any tribesman found to have willfully damaged or stolen English livestock. If the accused was unable to make restitution, then the court had the authority to "condemn such offender or offenders to be sold as a slave to any forraigne country of English subjects." Similarly, the Connecticut Colony announced that neighboring sachems and sagamores would be held responsible if any of their tribal subjects damaged English property "either by spoiling or killing of cattle or swine either with trappes, dogges or arrowes." Connecticut colonial law demanded that tribal leaders pay a double fine if it was discovered that the damage was deliberate.

The Algonkian nations soon realized that their former willingness to have the English settle in their midst was unwise, for the English almost always took away their usage rights to tribal land which the English colonists now considered their private property and under colonial jurisdiction. When the Algonkians lost their usage rights they also lost access to resources they needed and their customary seasonal life cycles. Formerly, Aquidneck and adjacent islands in Narragansett Bay once belonged to the Wampanoag and Narragansett nations, but the English established the settlements of Portsmouth and Newport, which gradually began to restict Wampanoag and Narragansett usage rights to the islands. In 1644, for example, Massasoit was granted a temporary invitation to come ashore on Aquidneck Island with ten men to hunt for five days. He was given permission to kill ten deer provided he and his men presented their kills to colonial authorities at Portsmouth before leaving from the island. The Narragansetts were still using the trees on this island after 1638 to get bark shingles for their wigwams, although by this time Aquidneck Island was supposed to have been vacated for English occupation. The Rhode Island settlements "ordered that no Indian shall fall or peel any trees upon the Islands, and that if any be found so doing . . . it shall be lawful for all that so find them, to bring cause to be brought the Parties so offending before the magistrates, who shall order and punish them according to the Law." Even the annual Algonkian practice of setting the woodland undergrowth on fire was now restricted. The Narragansetts, under the jurisdiction of the Rhode Island settlements, were prohibited from starting any fires that could not be put out on their immediate departure. Connecticut Colony held the sagamore of the Tunxis people liable for fire damage to some English properties because of a fire started by a tribesman named Mesupeno. The court judged that the Tunxis sagamore "pay unto the General Court . . . yearly, for the term of seven years, the full sum of eighty fathom of wampum, well strung and merchantable, the first payment to be made in October next ensuing, at the Session of the Gen: Court, and so to be paid yearly at the Sessions in October, until the term be expired (that is to say) seven payments."

The Algonkians, besides being fined by the colonial courts, also suffered various corporal punishments for crimes such as sabbath breaking, drunkeness, trespassing, stealing, verbal threats, and murder, particularly when these violations occurred in areas under English colonial jurisdiction. Plymouth court records during the 1650s and 1660s increasingly reveal the tragic erosion of Wampanoag tribal autonomy and the intrusive expansion of colonial authority over the Algonkian people. A Wampanoag tribesman named John was committed to prison for allegedly stealing a gun and an axe from a Taunton resident named William Harvey. The Englishman never appeared in Plymouth court to testify against John, who was released from prison after having "undergone much hardship." Even though his guilt had never been proven, he was nevertheless ordered to report to William Harvey to compensate him for the so-called stolen items either through work or payment. In another case, Plymouth magistrates found a Nantucket tribesman named Tetannett guilty of "pilfering and stealing sundry thinges" from John Mayo of Eastham. Tetannett was sentenced to be publicly whipped, and ordered to return to the island. A few years after this incident, the Plymouth court found nine Wampanoag men guilty of illegally going aboard the boat of one Simon Stevens as he was sailing along Cape Cod. Three of the tribesmen were sentenced "to be whipt att the post att Plymouth, which accordingly was performed," because they had stolen a cask of liquor from the vessel. The other six were accused of being accomplices to the crime, and were ordered to pay a fine of ten pounds in either Indian corn, pork or feathers to the colony.

In certain cases Algonkian men and women were punished for statements and actions that the English thought threatened their personal security. The Massachusetts court ordered the whipping of two tribeswomen "for their insolent carriage, and abusing [of] Mrs. Weld." In another court case that involved the Plymouth Colony, a tribesman named Repent was similarly whipped after he was found guilty of threatening to shoot the governor of the colony. On another occasion, five Wampanoag men entered the house of Robert Shelley of Barnstable on a late winter evening and so frightened his family by their sudden intrusion that the court sentenced these five to be placed in the stocks on the sabbath. They were also required to serve the Shelley family for the equivalent of five shillings worth of work. Algonkian people accused of breaking English law were not even allowed the clemency sometimes granted by their sachems. In 1658, Plymouth authorities learned that several Massachusett tribesmen had been murdered. According to the governor of the Bay Colony, a suspected accessory to these murders was then living under the protection of Sachem Massasoit. Disregarding the sachem's pardon for the man, the Plymouth court ordered:

> Forasmuch as we have been informed, both by letters from the Governor of the Massachusetts and otherwise, that a certain Indian called Pohkenonpamitt, who is suspected to have been accessory to the murder of some Indians belonging to them, has been ordered and is sheltered and protected by Ossamequin [Massasoit's other name] and his son, that he cannot be brought forth to a legal trial. This court has ordered, that the chief marshall go to Rehoboth, and take with him Lieutenant Peter Hunt, Mr. John Browne, and John Allin, and in their defect or absence such as shall desire, and go to Ossamequin and his son, and from the governor and court advise him to deliver the said Indian suspected unto him, that so he may come to a legal trial, also assuring them that if he be not guilty he shall have no wrong, but in case they shall refuse to deliver him, the marshall shall then use his best care and prudence himself to apprehend him and censure him and take care that either by the constable of Rehoboth or some other he be conveyed to the Massachusetts, where the charges shall be repayed them.

When Algonkian tribesmen living within the jurisdiction of the New England colonies committed a felony such as murder, they were seldom, if ever, returned to the tribal council of their nation, even if the incident involved the death of another tribesman. Instead, the accused was required to appear before an English colonial court, where the suspect was sometimes judged by a mixed jury of English colonists and Algonkian men. In Rhode Island, an imprisoned Narragansett man named Iankesick went on trial for the murder of another by the name of Ossawan. Before the trial, the magistrates voted that the verdict would be decided by a jury consisting of six Englishmen and six Narragansetts. Likewise, in the tense months just prior to King Philip's War, Plymouth Colony arrested several Wampanoag men suspected in the death of a "Christian Indian" named John Sassamon. The tribesmen were found guilty by a jury of both Plymouth colonists and "Praying Indians." An Algonkian tribesman found guilty of premeditated murder faced hanging on the colonial gallows or death before a firing squad.

Murders among native people were often due to feuds between Algonkian tribal groups, or incursive strikes by Mohawk raiding parties. In 1669, the Connecticut Colony responded to intertribal feuding by decreeing that "whereas it is to manifest to this Court that the natives about notwithstanding all counsel and advice to the contrary given them by the authority here, have and still do proceed to commit murder and kill one another within the English plantations and upon English land . . . this court doth order that for the future whatever Indian or Indians shall willfully and violently fall upon any Indian or Indians within this colony . . . and murder him, he shall be put to death." Apparently the Puritan motive for heightening the penalty for murder between tribal members was partly a theological concern. The Connecticut magistrates believed that they were responsible before God to "take off the guilt of blood" from their lands, so they would not incur divine judgement. Because Old Testament law demanded death for premeditated murder, the Connecticut magistrates believed themselves to be morally just in executing anyone found guilty of this crime.

The English colonial authorities were also concerned to control intertribal warfare between the various Algonkian tribal confederacies, particularly when these conflicts involved one of their tribal allies. The colonists were blatantly partial to their Mohegan allies whenever the tribe became involved in a dispute with the Narragansetts. After the defeat of the Pequots in 1637, the Mohegans, ⌐

under Sachem Uncas, assumed they had legitimate usage rights to certain lands in eastern Connecticut; their Narragansett enemies, under Sachem Miantonomo, strove to counter Mohegan access to these areas. Even though both sachems agreed to appeal to the English at Hartford and Boston concerning these difficulties, it did not prevent the two nations from attacking one another. As early as 1638, a Mohegan force attacked the Wunnashowatuckoogs, a Nipmuck tribe allied with the Narragansetts. Intermittent hostilities continued on both sides until 1642, when both the Connecticut and Massachusetts Bay colonies intervened. Sachem Miantonomo was summoned to Boston, where he gave satisfactory answers to their inquiries, leaving the Massachusetts authorities to believe some of the accusations leveled against Miantonomo were false. But the next year Sachem Uncas complained about Narragansett belligerency to the Commissioners of the United Colonies, a New England colonial confederation established in 1643 for the purpose of presenting a united English front against potential Algonkian hostilities. The Mohegan sachem accused Miantonomo of being behind a series of plots to have him assassinated, which was not difficult for the United Commissioners to believe, since the Narragansett sachem was also reported to have solicited south coastal tribes along Long Island Sound to assist him in making war against both the English and Dutch. The constant feuding between these two sachems finally broke out into a more serious conflict, when warriors under the Narragansetts' ally Sagamore Sequasson of Connecticut, shot an arrow at Uncas as he was travelling downriver on the Connecticut. The Mohegans retaliated by attacking Sequasson's village, where they killed some tribal defenders and burned a number of wigwams. Miantonomo gathered about a thousand of his finest warriors for a retaliatory strike, and set out for *Mohegoneak* in the autumn of 1643, determined to punish Uncas with a humiliating defeat. As the Narragansetts approached the Thames River in eastern Connecticut, they were seen by a Mohegan scout, who quickly warned Uncas. Rather than wait for his adversary, Uncas mustered about four hundred braves and met the Narragansetts in battle. Using both firearms and arrows, the Mohegans forced the Narragansetts to retreat. Because Sachem Miantonomo was wearing a coat of mail, his retreat was greatly encumbered, and he was captured and turned over to Uncas.

Miantonomo did not remain in the custody of the Mohegans, but as Uncas' prisoner, he was delivered to the English at Hartford, and the colonial authorities had the responsibility of sentencing him. Naturally, the magistrates of the United Colonies favored their Mohegan allies, so when they convened at Boston they decided there would never be peace between the two Algonkian nations as long as the Narragansett sachem lived. Also, Miantonomo's attempt to raise an Algonkian alliance against the New England colonies worried the commissioners. Therefore, they allowed Uncas' brother to execute Miantonomo outside the jurisdiction of the English colonies by striking him in the head with a tomahawk. The Narragansett people were enraged by this unwarranted act, and they would have staged a renewed offensive against the Mohegans, but the United Colonies could raise a force against them, so for the time being the Narragansetts maintained the peace. Nevertheless, they did not forget the humiliating death that the English magistrates had allowed Miantonomo to suffer.

The Narragansetts and Eastern Niantic nations, now having even more reason to wreak vengeance on their Mohegan adversaries, joined forces against Uncas in 1644. When word reached the English that Sachem Uncas had again suffered casualities, and that his people could not leave their fortified areas safely, the United Colonies decided to counter Narragansett hostilities. The English sent forty soldiers from Boston to Mohegoneak, where they were to be joined with companies from Hartford and New Haven to protect Uncas in his fort from his enemies. Before the English could dispatch an even larger military force to invade Narragansett country, the principal Narragansett chieftans Pessacus, Mexano and Witawash, accompanied by others, came to Boston to reaffirm their friendship with the English. After some discussion the English magistrates decided the Narragansett leaders and their Eastern Niantic allies, who were under the leadership of Sagamore Ninigret, ought to pay a yearly tribute in wampum to defray the cost of colonial preparations for the potential conflict. In August, 1645, both sides agreed to a treaty containing twelve stipulations, the principal six being:

1. [The Narragansett and Niantic] should pay or cause to be paid at Boston to the Massachuset Commissioners the full sum of 2000 fathom of good white wampum, or a third part of black

wampumpeag, in four payments; namely, 500 fathom within 20 days, 500 fathom within 4 months, 500 fathom at or before next planting time, and 500 fathom within 2 years next after the date of these presents, which 2000 fathom the Commissioners accept for satisfaction of former charges expended.

2. Whereas there are sundry differences and grievances betwixt Narragansett and Niantic Indians, and Uncas and his men, (which in his absence cannot now be determined) it is hereby agreed that Narragansett and Niantic sagamores either come themselves or send their deputies to the next meeting of the Commissioners for the Colonies, either at New Haven in September 1646 or sooner . . . promising to give a full hearing to both parties [Narragansett and Mohegan] with equal justice, without any partial respects according to their allegations and proofs.

3. The said Narragansett and Niantic sagamores and deputies do hereby promise and covenant to keep and maintain a firm and perpetual peace, both with all the English United Colonies . . . and with Uncas the Mohegan sachem and his men; with Ousamequin [Massasoit], Pomham [Shawomet sagamore], Socanoket [Pawtuxet sagamore], Cutshamakin [Massachusett sagamore], Shoanan [Nashua sagamore] Passaconaway [Pennacook sachem], and all other Indian sagamores and their companies who are in friendship with or subject to any of the English.

4. The said Narragansett and Niantic sagamores and deputy do hereby promise and covenant that within fourteen days they will bring and deliver to the Massachusetts Commissioners on the behalf of the colonies four of their children; viz, Pessacus his eldest son, the son [of] Tassaquanawit, brother to Pessacus, Awashawe his son and Ewanghos' son a Niantic, to be kept as hostages and pledges by the English, till both the forementioned 2000 fathom of wampum be paid at the times appointed, and the differences betwixt themselves and Uncas be heard and ordered; and till these articles be underwritten at Boston by Janemo and Wipetock.

5. The Commissioners for the United Colonies do hereby promise and agree that at the charge of the United Colonies the four Indians now left as pledges shall be provided for and that the four chil-

dren to be brought and delivered as hostages shall be kept and maintained at the same charge. That they will require Uncas and his men, with all other Indian sagamores before named, to forbear all acts of hostility against the Narragansetts and Niantic Indians for the future.

6. Lastly they promise that if any Pequot or other be found and discovered amongst them who hath in time of peace murdered any of the English, he or they shall be delivered to just punishment.

Despite these treaty stipulations, Sachem Uncas continued to complain to the English about Narragansett hostilities as late as 1649. In fact, the Mohegans told the commissioners the Narragansetts had even gone as far as to ask the Pocumtuck and Mohawk tribes to help them in their protracted feud with Uncas. New troubles arose in 1653 when the Eastern Niantic sagamore Ninigret, who was a confederate of the Narragansetts, became involved in a conflict with a tribe on Long Island. When this struggle erupted anew the next year, the United Colonies again prepared to go to war against the Narragansett and Niantic, for the Long Island tribe was on friendly terms with the English. When Ninigret refused to appear at Hartford in September, 1654, concerning the complaints that had been brought against him, the United Colonies voted to send a joint expedition to Niantic. By October, militias from Massachusetts, Connecticut and New Haven converged on the Eastern Niantics, where the intimidated Ninigret agreed that the Pequots living under his sagamoreship would be organized into separate tribal communities. These new Pequot villages had their own tribal leaders, answerable to the Commissioners of the United Colonies of New England. The colonies requested the villages be formed to impair the Eastern Niantic ability to wage war on their Long Island enemies. Ninigret claimed this conflict was in self defense because the Long Island tribe had attacked them out on Block Island.

Soon afterwards, Sequasson complained to the court magistrates at Hartford about the sagamore of the Podunk tribe. According to Sequasson, the Podunks were harboring a tribesman named Weaseapano who had killed a sagamore, and then fled to the protection of the Podunk sagamore Tantonimo. Now, both Sequasson and his newly-found ally, Uncas, requested that six to ten of

Weaseapano's friends be put to death in retaliation for the murder. Tantonimo pleaded that this request was unjust, pointing out that the murdered sagamore had been behind the killing of Weaseapano's uncle. The Connecticut court, hoping to resolve the dispute, summoned the three chieftans to appear before the magistrates at Hartford.

The Podunks said they were willing to give wampum as satisfaction for the murder, but Sequasson and Uncas said the offer was unacceptable. The Hartford magistrates wearied, with the verbal accusations of both sides, pressured the Podunk sagamore to release Weaseapano to them, and he appeared to agree. However, during the court proceedings Tantonimo slipped out with his men and went back to their fort at Podunk. The English magistrates sent a message to the Podunks to hand over the accused, and appointed a committee of four deputies to negotiate with both sides. Sequasson and Uncas eventually agreed to accept Weaseapano alone as full satisfaction, but the Podunks now claimed they did not dare to apprehend him because he had the support of so many friends at the fort. The Connecticut magistrates, unwilling to get involved any further, decided to leave the Algonkians to themselves, and the governor, in a lengthy speech, said he hoped they would exchange wampum as compensation, and preserve the peace. If they could not do this, he added, any warfare was to be carried out away from Hartford to the west of the Connecticut River.

In 1657, the Narragansett leadership asked the Massachusetts court to allow them to enter the intertribal war between the Podunk and Mohegan. The Podunk had enlisted the aid of their fellow member tribes in the Pocumtuck confederation, who in turn called on the Narragansett and Mohawks. The Pocumtuck had already successfully assisted their Podunk allies in a substantial victory over Sachem Uncas in which they had "kild so many of his men"; consequently, the Massachusetts magistrates refused to allow the Narragansett to join their allies—this time out of fear the growing alliance would overwhelm their Mohegan allies. When the authorities of the Bay Colony denied the Narragansett request they again showed partiality towards the Mohegans, reminding the Narragansett sachem and sagamores that they had made a covenant with the English not to war against any Algonkian nation allied with the United Colonies. The Massachusetts magistrates informed the Narragansetts:

We take notice, that you are mindful of the covenant made with the commissioners, at Boston, in the year 1645, which is 12 years ago, not to war with any Indians that are in friendship with the English, without the consent of the commissioners, and therefore like well their coming now for advice in so great a case, . . . but do require you, according to your covenant, and as you desire the continuance of our friendship, to forbear any hostile attempt against Uncas, or any other Indians in friendship with us, till you have liberty from the commissioners of the colonies [United Colonies] so to do, to whose next meeting we further refer you for final resolution in all cases of differences, and him or any others.

Again and again the United Colonies of New England under-mined Algonkian self-determination in tribal warfare by intruding on the sovereignty of the sachemdoms. When the Wabaquasset Nipmucks willfully witheld their annual tribute payment to the Narragansetts in 1667, the Narragansetts sent about a hundred and twenty warriors to the Nipmuck village of Quatisicke, where they held the native inhabitants in suspense for a day. These warriors exacted the customary wigwam mats, firearms, shot, deer pelts, wampum, kettles, trays and stores of dried berries. After they left, the Nipmucks protested to the Massachusetts court. The court magistrates summoned representatives from both nations to ap-pear at the next court session, because the incident had occurred in the jurisdiction of the Bay Colony, and the raid was viewed as an incursion against "friendly Indians" allied with the colony. The English considered this another intolerable Narragansett violation of the covenant of 1645.

The Massachusetts court appointed a committee of eight En-glishmen, to hear the complaints on both sides. At the court ses-sion, in the spring of 1668, the Wabaquasset Nipmucks testified they had never paid tribute to the Narragansetts, and that they were a sovereign people who had always chosen their sachems through a twelve-member council. They encouraged the commit-tee to consult such neighboring Algonkian leaders as King Philip, sachem of the Wampanoag nation, who they said would confirm the truth of their statements. However, when the Wabaquasset Nipmucks then agreed at this hearing to "submit to the gospel of the Lord Jesus Christ, and for the future to live under the govern-ment and protection of the Massachusetts, unto to whom they yielded up themselves and people," the court decided to grant them subject status within the Bay Colony. This ploy by the Nipmucks prejudiced the court against the Narragansetts even more, and the magistrates reneged on their former willingness to have these Nipmucks pay the Narragansetts annual tribute in an amount set by the court, providing if the Narragansetts could prove previous Wabaquasset involvement in their confederation.

Even though later Narragansett testimony proved to the court "that the Nipmuck Indians, especially those at Quatisicke, were subject to them," the colonial magistrates now informed the Narragansetts that the Wabaquasset Nipmucks were to be subjects of the English. The Narragansetts were not willing to challenge the combined force of the United Colonies of New England over the loss of the annual tribute from Quatisicke. They bowed to the decision by returning the tribute they had taken from the Nipmucks the previous year.

Similarly, the Pennacook tribal nation's autonomy was tragically reduced by the power of the Boston magistrates. In May, 1662, the Pennacook sachem Passaconaway petitioned for a land grant from the Bay Colony. In the petition, this formerly influential sachem was reduced to begging the court to grant the Pennacook people a tract of ground along the Merrimac River, an area that was originally Pennacook land! The Massachusetts Bay Colony responded to this request by granting the Pennacook sachem a portion of land one-and-a-half miles wide on both sides of this river and running about three miles long, comprising the area of present-day Manchester, New Hampshire. The Pennacooks were also given part of their former ancestral planting grounds near the confluence of the Souhegan and Merrimac rivers, since, in the words of the court, "there is very little good land in that which is now laid out unto them."

In a little less than a century of interaction with the English and French, the Algonkian nations in New England had seen their culture deteriorate beyond repair. When they traded for European goods they were opened to forces that in the end undermined their way of life, as they gradually assumed aspects of European culture, and grew to depend on it economically. From the beginning, some Algonkians were impressed with European material culture, or intimidated by their military advantage, but there were also others who viewed the European intrusion on their people with contempt. The Narragansett chieftans declared that Sagamore Waiandance of Long Island "must give no more wampum to the English, for they are no Sachems, nor none of their children shall be in their place if they die; they have no tribute given them; there is but one king in England, who is over them all, and if you would send him 100,000 fathom of wampum, he would not give you a knife for it, nor thank you." These same chieftans also complained that the English had taken their tribal land and "with axes felled the trees; their cows and horses eat the grass, and their hogs spoil our clam banks." They feared that the English hunting practices would eventually reduce the Algonkian tribes to starvation.

By the mid-17 century some sachems and sagamores felt the white man's influence on Algonkian tribal society had become intolerable. They knew their diminished authority was on the verge of being eclipsed by the English magistrates in Boston, Hartford and Plymouth. Increasingly, the New England colonies' so-called "Indian subjects" grew suspicious about their tenuous future alongside the English. The Mohawk War of the 1660s did much to justify their suspicions.

Chapter V
"As High As The Sun Is Above The Earth"

The Mohawk War (1664-1671) began with a dispute between the Dutch settlers and the Esopus tribe, who lived along the Hudson River in New York. In 1659, a group of local settlers murdered an Esopus tribesman. His people, justly incensed against the Dutch for this unwarranted assault, retaliated by killing a number of settlers and burning some Dutch houses, barns and harvest stores. During the following spring the two sides reached a peace agreement with the help of the Mohawks and Mahicans, who encouraged the Esopus tribe to lay down their arms. However, within three years the tribe again attacked the Dutch for encroaching on their lands, and after a year of renewed hostilities, the Dutch invited the Esopus people to meet with them at Fort Amsterdam, where a treaty was signed in May, 1664.

Meanwhile, the Mohawks were fighting a war with the Sokoki nation of Vermont. Some Algonkian tribes in northern New England had even been aided against the Mohawks by the French, who came down from Quebec in 1663 to attack a Mohawk fort. The Pocumtuck nation on the Connecticut River became concerned war might spread into their valley, and when the Mohawks raided the neighboring Sokoki village of Squawkheag (Northfield), the Pocumtuck made peace overtures to the Mohawks. The New Netherland Colony also urged the Mohawks to avoid conflict with the Pocumtucks that would affect the Dutch beaver trade. In the spring of 1664, the Mohawk sachem, Saheda, led an embassy east to Pocumtuck to reaffirm the peace. The New Netherland Colony sent two Dutchmen to accompany him to repay the Mohawks for their mediation in the Esopus dispute. Unfortunately, this peace embassy was somehow murdered while in Pocumtuck country.

The Mohawks immediately accused the Abenaki, Pennacook, Sokoki and Pocumtuck nations of conspiring in this treacherous act, but they held off from widening the war on the Pocumtuck tribe until the next spring. The delay was to their advantage, for in the interim the English seized New Amsterdam from the Dutch and in a treaty with the Mohawks they promised "not to assist the three nations of the Ondiakes (Abenakis), Pennacooks and Pocumtucks." The treaty also stipulated that if the Mohawks were defeated by these three Algonkian nations, they would receive accomodation from the English. By accepting the terms of this treaty, the English authorities in New York openly encouraged the Mohawks to make war on the Algonkian tribes in New England.

The Mohawks went to war against nearly all the New England tribes, with the probable exception of the Narragansett people, who paid tribute to them from time to time. In the first year of warfare, Mohawk raiding parties made excursions deep into Algonkian territory. Cambridge residents became alarmed in 1665, when the town constable apprehended five Mohawk warriors on the outskirts of the town, who were planning to ambush area Algonkian tribesmen. Each of these warriors had a gun, pistol and hatchet, and a long knife which they wore fastened around their necks. They were temporarily imprisoned at Cambridge and later removed to Boston, where they were questioned by the court.

Their imprisonment created a stir among the neighboring Algonkian tribes, who according to Gookin, "flocked into Boston, in great numbers, not only to see those Maquas [Mohawks]," but also to earnestly plead with the English to have these enemy warriors executed. The English magistrates directed the imprisoned warriors to tell their sachem that the Mohawks were to cease their attacks on the "Praying Indians" within a forty-mile radius of Boston. The Mohawks were told these Christianized tribesmen could be distinguished from the other Algonkians because they wore English clothing and cut their hair short.

Naturally, the Algonkian people who lived under the supposed protection of the Massachusetts government were offended by the release of the Mohawks. According to Daniel Gookin, when some of the local Algonkian tribesmen tried to convince the English to put the warriors to death, they told them, "these Maquas are unto us, as wolves are to your sheep. They secretly seize upon us and our children, wherever they meet us, and destroy us. Now if we had taken five wolves alive, and should let them go again, and not destroy them, you Englishmen would be greatly offended with us for such an act, and surely, said they, the lives of men are of more worth than beasts." Despite the English attempt to pacify their tribal subjects over the release of the Mohawk captives, the local Algonkians remained deeply dissatisfied with this decision.

The Mohawks ignored the directive relayed to their sachem by the English magistrates in Boston, and their raiding parties continued to attack the New England tribes. War parties repeatedly terrorized the Pennacooks, murdering a group of Nameskeag and Wamesit people on the north side of the Merrimac River near Pawtucket. Two more tribespeople were killed during a surprise attack on Wamesit, and the Nashuas and Quabaugs lost a considerable number from Mohawk raids, as did the Massachusett and Pocumtuck. In fact, the Mohawks destroyed the tribal fort at Pocumtuck in 1666. Even the distant Abenaki suffered casualities during this war. However, the Algonkians also did considerable damage to the Mohawks in their retaliatory strikes. Ten years after this conflict a Mohawk chieftan recalled, "We have had a long time of warr with them nations in former yeares, and at that time have received many damages, with a great losse of our Indians."

Throughout the Mohawk War the United Colonies of New England maintained a neutral stance, claiming it was wrong for the English to side with the local Algonkians against the Mohawks, when the English could not tell who were the aggressors. They also pointed out that the Mohawks had not disturbed the English settlements, and so to declare war on them would be imprudent. But the French in northern New England supported their Abenaki and Sokoki allies, supplying them with guns and ammunition. The French even battled with the Mohawks. The difference between the French and English attitudes toward the Algonkian struggle during the Mohawk War did not go unnoticed by the New England tribes.

At times Mohawk attacks became so relentless they caused a general panic among the native people in New England. Whenever the Algonkians spotted a Mohawk war party in their lands, they gathered into their forts, where they sometimes remained for weeks, and some Algonkian people became afraid to venture onto their planting fields, fishing weirs and hunting grounds. The Nashobas, a small tribe under continual Mohawk attack, eventually deserted their village temporarily, and moved closer to the safety of the English settlements. Some of the native people in the Massachusetts Bay Colony became so unsettled and impoverished from this conflict they hired themselves out as field workers to the English settlers, in order to get food and clothing for themselves.

In 1669, the Abenaki, Pennacook and Sokoki sachems convinced some of the Algonkian tribes in southern New England to join with them in a final attempt to strike back. The Massachusett and Nipmuck nations mustered about seven hundred warriors between them, and marched toward Mohawk territory under the leadership of Sachem Josiah Checkatabutt. Their march to the nearest Mohawk fort of Caughnawaga was slowed by their almost daily need to hunt, fish and gather roots in order to stockpile the provisions they needed for a successful seige against the stockade. Checkatabutt's forces at times stayed for several days at Algonkian villages along the way, both to boast of their valour and to recruit more volunteers. The warriors arrived at the easternmost Mohawk fort after a two-hundred mile trek, and found their enemies somewhat unprepared for a long seige seeing how some of the Mohawks were abroad at the time. Checkatabutt and his warriors surrounded the fort for several weeks; the Mohawks sent out one party of warriors that was driven back. Eventually sickness broke out in the Massachusett camp, and with provisions nearly gone, the expedition turned for home. On their way back a Mohawk force circled out ahead of them, ambushed the Algonkians at a pass flanked on both sides by swampland, and although Checkatabutt's men fought valiantly, in their vulnerable condition the sachem and some fifty of his best men were lost. According to Reverend Eliot, a number of prominent Algonkian sachems and sagamores fell in this "imprudent expedition." This was the last campaign the Massachusett nation led against the Mohawks. Two years later the English arranged a peace between the Mohawks and the Algonkian tribes of southern New England, but this treaty proved to be short-lived.

It is no coincidence the Wampanoags entered into a war against the English shortly after the first peace between the Mohawks and the Algonkian tribes in southern New England. The Mohawk War was one significant factor in the timing of King Philip's War, a brief, but intense conflict between the United Colonies of New England and the Wampanoags. When Massasoit's eldest son Wamsutta assumed the Wampanoag sachemship in 1661, subsequent to the outbreak of the Mohawk War, and again after this conflict ended in 1671, their was a flurry of rumors concerning a potential Wampanoag uprising against Plymouth. Yet, during the years of intertribal warfare with the Mohawks, the rumors of a Wampanoag uprising against the English ceased. Algonkian preoccupation with the Mohawk War may have temporarily dissuaded the Wampanoags and their allies from opposing Plymouth.

Before the outbreak of the Mohawk War, Wamsutta, along with his younger brother Metacom, demonstrated their goodwill and desire to continue the forty-year alliance with Plymouth Colony by asking the court to grant them English names. Wamsutta was named Alexander and his brother was given the name of Philip. In spite of the gesture, some Plymouth authorities remained suspicious of the new Wampanoag leader because Alexander was "estranging land, and not selling it to our [Plymouth] collonie." This fueled the rumors that the Wampanoags were conspiring with the Narragansetts to attack the English. Alexander was ordered to appear before the Plymouth authorities, and when he failed to show, Plymouth sent Major Josiah Winslow with ten armed men to bring the sachem in. The English found Alexander and his chief men in one of the Wampanoag hunting houses at Munponset, present-day Halifax, Massachusetts. At first Alexander refused to cooperate, but after receiving counsel from one of his men, the sachem agreed to accompany Winslow as far as Duxbury to meet with a few of the Plymouth magistrates. After this meeting Alexander and some of his people agreed to remain at Winslow's residence in Marshfield, where they awaited the Plymouth governor's arrival from Eastham. However, before Governor Prence (Prince) arrived, Alexander took ill and was forced to leave with his men. Shortly thereafter Alexander died at Pokanoket. As was customary, his brother Philip became the new Wampanoag sachem. One of his first acts was to reaffirm the treaty with Plymouth Colony; then, to demonstrate his goodwill and sincerity, King Philip asked the Reverend John Eliot to send him some books, so he could learn to read English.

No sooner had a treaty been effected between the New England Algonkians and the Mohawks in 1671, then the Wampanoags were again accused by Plymouth of plotting to destroy the English. How much of this was simply English suspicion of the native people as opposed to a genuine threat of hostilities is uncertain, but continual rumors of a Wampanoag uprising increased tension between the two sides. In April, 1671, King Philip was summoned to Taunton, where the English demanded the Wampanoags renew their peace covenant with Plymouth and surrender their guns. The condescending manner of the Plymouth authorities toward King Philip in the Taunton Treaty, dated April 12, 1671, is worth noting:

> Whereas my father, my brother, and myself, have formerly submitted ourselves and our people unto the king's majesty of England, and to this Colony of New Plymouth, by solemn covenant under our hand, but I have of late, through my indiscretion, and the naughtiness of my heart, violated and broken this my covenant with my friends, by taking up arms with evil intent against them, and that groundlessly; I being now deeply sensible of my unfaithfulness and folly, do desire at this time solemnly to renew my covenant with my ancient friends, and my father's friends above mentioned, and do desire that this may testify to the world against me, if ever I shall again fail in my faithfulness toward them, (whom I have now and at all times found kind to me,) or any other of the English colonies; and as a real pledge of my true intentions, for the future to be faithful and friendly, I do freely engage to resign up to the government of New Plymouth all my English arms to be kept by them for their security, so long as they shall see reason. For the true performance of the promises, I have hereunto set my hand, together with the rest of my council.

The sachem and some of his men made a token gesture by handing over their firearms, but the majority of the Wampanoag warriors refused to cooperate. They often obtained guns from unscrupulous traders, even though the New England colonies had passed laws to control the sale of firearms to the area tribes. Many Algonkian tribesmen were adept marksmen, and a few were skilled gunsmiths who had served apprenticeships under English gunmakers. With firearms they were better able to defend themselves and hunt for game, and when Plymouth Colony demanded the Wampanoags voluntarily surrender their guns, the warriors were understandably uncooperative.

Unable to agree about disarming, both Plymouth and King Philip appealed to the Commissioners of the United Colonies at Boston. The Wampanoag sachem made his appeal in person, and the Com-

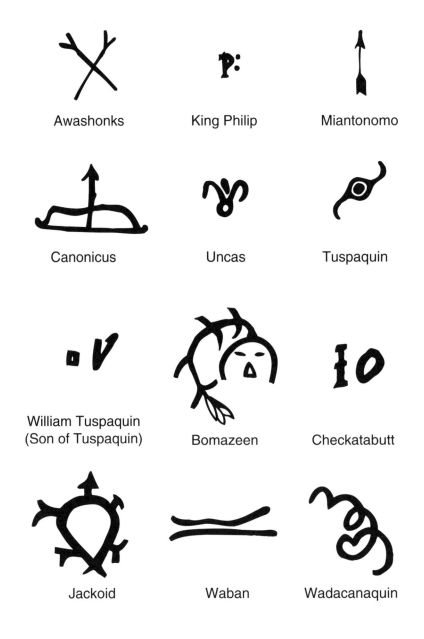

Awashonks   King Philip   Miantonomo

Canonicus   Uncas   Tuspaquin

William Tuspaquin
(Son of Tuspaquin)   Bomazeen   Checkatabutt

Jackoid   Waban   Wadacanaquin

ALGONKIAN SIGNATURES

missioners agreed to act as arbiters in this dispute. That September they met with both sides at Plymouth. At the hearing the arbiters found Philip was avoiding the English request that the Wampanoags surrender their firearms. He was also reprimanded for disregarding a summons to appear before the Plymouth magistrates. In the end King Philip signed a new treaty drawn up by Plymouth in which he agreed to pay the colony a fine of one hundred pounds "in such things as [he] had." To curtail the Wampanoags from selling land to Rhode Island colony, the Plymouth magistrates ordered King Philip to submit all future land transactions to them for approval. That same year nearly all the tribes on Cape Cod signed "fidelitie" agreements with Plymouth Colony promising to reveal any "plott or designe contrived against the English . . . by any other Indians."

During the winter of 1674-1675, a Christianized tribesman named John Sassamon died under suspicious circumstances. Plymouth Colony suspected agents of King Philip. According to Cotton Mather, Sassamon was the son of "Praying Indians," but he had temporarily fallen away from the faith, and reverted to his former ways. He became secretary to King Philip, and he learned of the sachem's secret plans to destroy the English. Abandoning his post, Sassamon went to the governor of Plymouth Colony with his information and shortly thereafter his body was found in a frozen pond near Nemasket. Though his murderers had attempted to make his death appear to be an accidental drowning, several bruises on his head suggested foul play. Besides this, a local Algonkian named Patuckson claimed he had actually seen Tobias, a counsellor to King Philip, and several other tribesmen kill John Sassamon. Plymouth officials, acting on his testimony, ordered Tobias and later his son Wampapaquan, along with another man named Mattashunannamo to be arrested. After trial by a jury made up of both "Praying Indians" and Englishmen, the three tribesmen were convicted and sentenced by the Plymouth Court to be executed. Tobias and Mattashunannamo were hung on the 18th of June, 1675, while Wampapaquan was shot before a firing squad several weeks later. About this same time Peter Nunnuit, husband of Squa-Sachem Weetamoo of the Pocassets, told Captain Church that "there would certainly be war, for Philip had held a dance of several weeks continuance, and had entertained the young men from all parts of the country." He also added King Philip feared that he, too, would be summoned by the Plymouth Court as a suspect in John Sassamon's murder.

The Plymouth authorities did not want to back King Philip into a corner, so they ignored the possibility of his involvement in John Sassamon's death. Nevertheless, King Philip expressed his displeasure over the court proceedings by permitting his braves to bear firearms as they wandered in the vicinity of Swansea. Responding to this threat, Plymouth Colony ordered a militia watch in all the towns adjacent to King Philip's lands. As the atmosphere grew even more intense, King Philip directed the women and children in his village to take refuge among the Narragansetts. Meanwhile, "many strange Indians" from several places flocked into Sowams and Kikemuit to assist the Wampanoag sachem.

The Plymouth Council wrote a letter to King Philip, in a final attempt to resolve their differences peaceably. They advised him to dismiss the "strange Indians," and restrain his own warriors from alarming the settlers at Swansea. The Plymouth Colony also assured the sachem in their letter that the English had no intention of harming him or his people, for Philip had told Squa-Sachem Awashonks of Sakonnet that "the Umpame [Plymouth] men were gathering a great army to invade [his] country." King Philip sent no response to Plymouth by the 17th of June, the day before the outbreak of the looting of some English properties, and Plymouth now accused him of being "very high and not persuadable to peace."

In fact, King Philip's attempt to unite his people against the English invasion they expected met resistance. Many members of his tribal nation did not support him, nor did most of the neighboring Algonkian nations who were rumored to be in agreement. In the spring of 1675, Squa-Sachem Awashonks of the Sakonnet tribe entertained six emissaries from King Philip, who tried to draw her people into the conspiracy against Plymouth Colony. When Awashonks hesitated to join them because she found the motives questionable, Philip's threat to her was that he would dispatch his men to do some damage to several English houses and kill a few head of cattle in Sakonnet country. This, he believed, would provoke the colonists into action against the Sakonnets, who they would assume the culprits in this vandalism. While the six emissaries from King Philip were still at her village, Awashonks invited Captain

Church of the Plymouth militia to meet with her. Church tried to convince the squa-sachem that "it might be most adviseable for her to send to the Governor of Plymouth, and shelter herself and people under his protection." When the war broke out it was partly King Philip's attempt at intimidation that created the ill-feeling between the Sakonnets and Plymouth, and even then, by the spring of 1676, the majority of Sakonnets were again won over to Plymouth as "Indian allies", and sent to fight against King Philip.

A week before hostilities began, Rhode Island sent several magistrates to King Philip in the hope of avoiding war. The colonists suggested to Philip that a group of impartial arbiters might resolve the differences between the Wampanoags and Plymouth Colony. King Philip, after listening to the magistrates, thanked them for their sincerity and voiced his displeasure over deciding any issue through warfare. He also expressed his resentment over the Christianization of his people, and he demanded the Wampanoags be treated as equals by the English in the colonial courts. He may have been referring to the three tribesmen who had been arrested for the murder of Sassamon, two of whom had already been executed. Also, King Philip said, his people were discouraged by the loss of their lands, the settlers' unfenced livestock, and the sale of alchohol to the Wampanoags. He also insisted that his brother Alexander had been poisoned by the English. Despite all these points of contention, the magistrates left the session somewhat encouraged by the sachem's presence. Philip was unwilling to discuss any of these issues with the colonial governors, whom he considered to be mere subjects of the English king. On an earlier occasion he had demanded an audience with the Crown.

When the two Rhode Island magistrates arrived home, they received a letter from the Plymouth governor, Josiah Winslow, which said that the Plymouth militia had set up headquarters ten miles from King Philip's village. Plymouth intended to subjugate the Wampanoags through force. Now King Philip's fear of an English invasion of Pokanoket was about to be realized. Several days earlier, in the Swansea area, some unrestrained Wampanoag warriors had pillaged a few abandoned houses. An old man and a boy returning to their home to secure their property, surprised several warriors ransacking one of the houses. The youth fired on them and killed one of the warriors. On June 25, the Wampanoags retaliated by killing nine colonials at Swansea. With these opening salvoes King Philip's War began.

During the first weeks of the war, King Philip's forces made frequent hit-and-run attacks on the peripheral residents of Plymouth Colony. To the English colonials, guerrilla style warfare was a profoundly new method of fighting, unlike European military tactics. These warriors "possessed themselves of every rock, stump, tree or fence that was in sight firing upon them" according to Captain Church. Only by imitating these Algonkian tactics could the colonial militias hope to gain the advantage in battle. Trying to prevent hit-and-run warfare on other colonial settlements, the English sent a joint military expedition of soldiers from both Plymouth and Massachusetts to the Pokanoket village of Kikemuit. They hoped to trap King Philip and his forces on Mount Hope Peninsula, but the Wampanoags had retreated into the swamps around Pocasset, where they now collaborated with Pocasset Squa-Sachem Weetamoo. Earlier, before any hostilities began, Weetamoo had realized war was imminent, and asked permission from the Rhode Island Colony to move her people across the bay for safety. After the colony denied her request, Weetamoo supported her former brother-in-law's campaign against the English.

The Plymouth militia wanted to march toward Pocasset while the Massachusetts forces entered Narragansett country, intending to make "peace with a sword in their hands," if the Narragansetts joined King Philip's cause. After the English met with some of the older Narragansett tribesmen, they spent four days negotiating a treaty. The Narragansetts assured the English they would not join with the Wampanoags, but were further forced to agree to several stipulations that placed them in opposition to King Philip. The Narragansetts were ordered to "use all acts of hostility against the said Philip and his subjects, entering his lands or any other lands of the English, to kill and destroy the said enemy." To make sure the Narragansetts honored the treaty, the English took four of their braves hostage.

Meanwhile, Church and the Plymouth militia arrived in the lands of the Pocassets, where King Philip's forces had already burned some houses in Middleboro and Dartmouth. The English searched out the Wampanoags in their planting fields, and charged on a few at work in their bean gardens, only to fall into an ambush. Immediately gaining an advantage, the warriors drove the Plymouth militia towards the seashore. All that afternoon Church encouraged his men to hold their ground until a sloop rescued them from the beach and carried them to Rhode Island. After he strengthened his forces with some soldiers from Massachusetts, Church returned to Pocasset, where he temporarily trapped King Philip's forces in a swamp. Church's men were soon assisted by other Massachusetts troops, who lost about ten men from enemy gunfire.

Wampanoag forces withdrew into the furthest recesses of the swamp, but King Philip knew this place could give refuge only temporarily. Waiting until nightfall, the sachem and about a hundred and fifty of his best warriors ferried themselves across the Taunton River on crudely constructed rafts. To speed their flight, the Pocassets left about a hundred of their women and children behind. After submitting themselves to "the mercy of the English," these women and their youngsters were grouped together with another eighty captives who had surrendered a month earlier. Most of these women and children were shipped to the Spanish slave markets. As for King Philip and his warriors, they were pursued by Captain Henchmen and sixty-eight soldiers from a garrison at Pocasset. The warriors escaped to the northwest into Nipmuck country. A combined party of Rehoboth residents and Mohegan mercenaries under the command of Lieutenants Thomas and Brown, overtook King Philip's rear guard and killed twenty-three of his men as they fled through the area, but the majority of the Pokanoket and Pocasset warriors escaped to the wilderness of interior Massachusetts.

King Philip's flight into Nipmuck country was a major setback for the English colonists, for now their foes were in a position to incite the Nipmuck and Pocumtuck nations to join their ranks. Interior New England was also a better place for the tribesmen to continue their war effort. It gave them a wider area to operate from, compared to the restricted range of the Wampanoags' homeland, which was hemmed in by English settlements. Even more important, the warriors were now able to receive guns and ammunition more easily from the French and their Abenaki allies. There was even an outside chance, which later proved to be a reality, that King Philip would seek aid from his old adversaries, the Mohawks.

Before the Wampanoag warriors moved into interior Massachusetts, the Nipmucks under the leadership of Matoonas had already assaulted the town of Mendon on July 14th, killing five or six residents. The Massachusetts government, doubting the sincerity of Nipmuck friendship, especially with King Philip now roaming in their midst, sent Captains Wheeler and Hutchinson to make a peace treaty with them. The Nipmucks had promised to sign a covenant with the English on August 2. As the two captains and a party of Brookfield residents approached Miminimisset, the tribal seat of the Nipmuck nation, they were ambushed by two hundred warriors. Sixteen men were killed, including Captain Hutchinson, and many others were wounded. The English forces fell back towards Brookfield, and reached the settlement just before the Nipmucks attacked it. Brookfield residents, having heard the distant echoes of gunfire, had already gathered into one of their garrison houses, where the soldiers and residents withstood a two-day seige. Major Willard arrived with forty-eight men, forcing the Nipmucks to retreat. The greatest fear of the English was now confirmed: King Philip's War was spreading.

By mid August, Philip and his forces had moved into the upper Connecticut Valley, where they convinced the local river tribes of the Pocumtuck confederation to go on the warpath. The residents of Hatfield and Hadley demanded the Norwottucks hand over their guns as a precautionary measure, but the tribe abandoned their fort that very night to join forces with King Philip. English soldiers under the command of Captains Lathrop and Beers pursued the Norwottucks to a hill about ten miles north of Hatfield. There a battle ensued in which twenty-six tribesmen and ten Englishmen were killed. Up river, King Philip's forces quickly retaliated by murdering ten residents at Northfield, and then they burned much of Deerfield to the ground. On August 26th, Captain Beers and thirty-six men set out from Hadley to bring supplies to a garrison house in Northfield. While enroute they were ambushed by several hundred warriors, who killed over half the company on the spot. The survivors made a disorderly retreat to Hadley, and the next day a one-hundred-man expedition set out to help evacuate the Northfield garrison.

Major John Pynchon, the Commander-in-Chief of the English forces in the Connecticut Valley, called his captains to a meeting, where they decided that soldiers would be restationed among the towns of Northampton, Hatfield, Deerfield and Hadley. In mid-September, Captain Lathrop and eighty men, sent to guard a shipment of corn going from Deerfield to Hadley, were ambushed by about six hundred of King Philip's warriors as the convoy made its way along a narrow trail. The Battle of Bloody Brook, as this confrontation later came to be known, cost the lives of seventy-two Englishmen and ninety-six Algonkians. Hubbard described this disaster as the "most fatal day that ever befell New England."

The Agawam tribe, from near Springfield, was encouraged by the success of their Wampanoag, Nipmuck and Pocumtuck compatriots in the upper Connecticut Valley, and plotted to destroy the English. Under cover of darkness, the Agawam received some three hundred warriors into their fort about a mile outside of Springfield. The English townsfolk had considerable confidence in the sincerity of the Agawam friendship with them even after a tribesman named Toto warned of the impending danger. On the morning the attack was supposed to come, Lieutenant Cooper rode out to the Agawam fort, but as he approached the stockade he was fired upon. He rushed back to town and warned the residents, who would have certainly suffered casualities had not Major Treat, a Connecticut officer in the valley, already been informed of the plot the night before. Treat marched from Westfield with his forces to the banks of the Connecticut River, while Pynchon came down from Hadley. Before the Agawam tribe retreated into the woods, they managed to burn thirty-two houses in Springfield.

On October 9th, seven hundred warriors made a daring assault on Hatfield, where a considerable number of English soldiers were stationed. Tribesmen killed nine Englishmen and burned several barns before they were driven off. After this raid attacks by King Philip's allies began to subside because the tribal forces broke up and retired to several different winter quarters. While King Philip and some of his warriors wintered in the vicinity of Albany, others of his men wintered with the Nipmucks who had settled down between Mount Wachusett and Lake Winnekeag in present-day Ashburnham, Massachusetts. Still others of Philip's men had also found winter refuge among the Narragansetts. In a little more than three months of fighting, the warriors of King Philip and his allies had created a path of death and destruction from Plymouth Colony to the frontier towns in the Connecticut Valley.

182

Meanwhile, the member tribes of the Pennacook nation under Sachem Wannalancit felt the strain of hostilities to the south and west. To avoid being drawn into King Philip's War, Wannalancit moved north to the tribal seat of Pennacook, near present-day Concord, New Hampshire. The Nashua and Wachusett sagamores of the Pennacook confederation, however, sided with the Wampanoag and Nipmuck nations, while some of the Wamesit people at their village on the south side of the Merrimac River attempted to maintain a precarious neutrality.

The Massachusetts Governor and Council dispatched "Indian runners" to Wannalancit, with a message asking him to come to Chelmsford from Pennacook with a few of his men. At Chelmsford, the message went, the Reverend John Eliot and Daniel Gookin would await the sachem's arrival, and would reaffirm the friend- ship between the late Passaconaway and the English. Wannalancit refused to come and the Massachusetts authorities consequently believed the Pennacooks might be conspiring with King Philip. Captain Mosely was dispatched to Pennacook with a one-hundred- man militia, and just before his arrival at Pennacook, Wannalancit and his people withdrew into the nearby woods, apparently fore- warned of the militia's march up the Merrimac River Valley. Some of the tribesmen watched from concealment as Mosely and his men arrived, found the Pennacook fort empty of inhabitants and, on Mosely's orders, torched the wigwams and their winter storehouses of dried fish. According to Daniel Gookin, the Pennacooks could have ambushed the soldiers at any time, but Wannalancit restrained his men who were enraged by the militia's unwarranted razing of their village. In the end, Mosely's destruction of Pennacook con- vinced Wannalancit to withdraw even further into northern New England to avoid being entangled in King Philip's War.

Shortly after the burning of the Pennacook village, the English increasingly harassed the Wamesits. This tribe was falsely accused of burning a haystack belonging to a Chelmsford resident named James Richardson. Lieutenant Richardson apprehended most of the Wamesit men and then forced them to march to Boston to answer charges. As the Wamesit men passed through Woburn, a militia exercising their arms on the village green fired on the tribes- men, killing one of them. The English colonist who fired the fatal shot, surnamed Knight, was arrested and tried. In the end the jury acquitted him, as he testified to the court that his gun went off by accident. The jury was sent out a second time to rethink their decision, but they refused to alter the verdict. In Boston, some of the remaining Wamesit were released after giving an account of themselves concerning Mr. Richardson's haystack, but three tribesmen still under suspicion were detained.

On November 15, 1675, a barn belonging to the same James Richardson was burned and again the Wamesit were accused of committing arson. A group of local residents took up arms and went to Wamesit, where they ordered the people to come out from their wigwams. When some of them came out of their homes, two of the English colonials, named Lorgin and Robins, opened fire with buckshot killing one Wamesit boy and wounding five others. The murderers were put on trial, but these, too, were found innocent, to the disappointment of Daniel Gookin and others.

The Wamesits now realized their lives were in continual jeopardy, so they went in search of Wannalancit in his northern retreat. But they were unable to find him and returned to their village on the lower Merrimac River. They now petitioned the Massachusetts Governor and Council to remove them from the area because they did not want to be further blamed for the mischief done by "other Indians," but the request was neglected. The Wamesits left six elderly persons behind, and made a second trip to find their sachem. The remaining villagers who had been left behind in one wigwam, suffered a torturous death when some Chelmsford residents set their dwelling on fire. The wearied Wamesit travellers, after risking starvation and exposure to the cold, managed to find Wannalancit. They joined with fellow tribesmen from Pennacook, Nameskeag, Naticook and Pawtucket.

During the first months of King Philip's War, the Narragansetts deliberately avoided assisting the English against the Wampanoags, even though they had promised in their treaty to assist them. Their failure to keep their promises was understandable, since the English intimidated this nation into signing a peace covenant in the first place. The English soon came to suspect the Narragansetts of planning to join King Philip in the spring and the English magistrates, to justify an immediate campaign against them, used several arguments. First of all, they claimed the Narragansett nation had deliberately ignored the articles of peace. Secondly, settlers around

Rhode Island reported bands of Narragansett warriors had assisted King Philip in ravaging the Connecticut River Valley settlements and, in fact, had seen some of their wounded returning home. Lastly, the English were certain Weetamoo had gone for refuge to the Narragansetts after she fled into Nipmuck country with King Philip.

If this was insufficient evidence, there was always the controversial incident at Wabaquasset to fall back on: some time in August, 1675, the Wabaquassets, who lived just north of the Narragansetts, seized over a hundred Wampanoag warriors. When the English learned of this, they sent Lieutenant Mason to secure the prisoners. However, before he arrived, a force of Narragansett warriors swept down on Wabaquasset and forced the tribespeople to release their captives. Though the Narragansetts delivered seven heads to the English, which they claimed were Wampanoag warriors, some of the colonial settlers of Rhode Island believed this to be a cover up, for they claimed to recognize one of the tribesmen who was beheaded. This incident alone was enough to convince the English the Narragansetts were secretly supporting King Philip.

Consequently, when the Commissioners of the United Colonies met at Boston, they decided to raise an army to attack the Narragansetts at their winter quarters. Seven hundred colonial soldiers came from the Massachusetts and Plymouth colonies to join three hundred sent by Connecticut. Three hundred and fifty Mohegan braves and a number of "Praying Indians" also joined the expedition. Under the Plymouth governor, Josiah Winslow, who acted as Commander-in-Chief, were Major Appleton, who lead the Massachusetts forces, Major Bradford who commanded the Plymouth soldiers and Major Treat who conducted those from Connecticut. Captains Mosely, Johnson, Mason and Gorman were the more noteable captains in this expedition.

On December 9, the Massachusetts troops started out from Dedham and three days later they crossed the Blackstone and Pawtuxet rivers to Wickford, Rhode Island. Here they joined forces with Mosely, who, in passing through Narragansett country, captured some tribesmen by surprise. One of these captives betrayed his own people by offering to guide the English to the main fort of the Narragansett nation. Meanwhile, Appleton and Mosely remained at Wickford until they heard the Connecticut troops had arrived at Pettaquamscott. The soldiers had hoped to receive shelter in a garrison house at Pettaquamscott, but the occupants had been murdered and the place had been razed. That night, consequently, most of the men bivouaced in a snow-covered field. On the following morning the entire army marched over to the Narragansett fort, which was located on an island in a large swamp. Had it not been their fortune to discover a four-foot gap at one of the corners in this stockade, it is probable the English would have never gained such quick entry into the fort. The first soldiers who forced themselves through this opening were quickly cut down by the Narragansetts but, others pushed their way into the stockade, where a pitched battle ensued. William Harris later writes:

> They ran up to the very muzzles of the Indians' guns, up to their portholes, and fired at them. They leaped over the Indians' breastworks, and ran into their fort, driving them out and slaying many of them (although how many is not known for certain), but only with the loss of many a brave, valiant man. The most tragic ordeal for the poor wounded men was the extremity of cold which killed many of them, it being then very cold. That night the troops marched to their quarters, having much difficulty with the wounded men for lack of sufficient accomodations and because of the bitter cold weather. But if they had pursued the enemy the next day, they were told, the Indians, thinking that the English after some time would pursue them, marched out a good distance and then came around not far from the place where they had been before. But no pursuit was made because of cold, floods, wounded men, and lack of convenient supplies, until about spring.

The Great Swamp Fight, as this battle later came to be known, gave the English their first substantial victory in King Philip's War. However, the English sustained numerous casualities: six captains and eighty soldiers died, and another one hundred and fifty were wounded. The Narragansetts lost an estimated six hundred men, besides women and children who were casualities. With their fort now taken, some of the Narragansetts sought refuge among the Nipmucks. Toward the end of December, 1675, Captain Prentice returned to Narragansett country and burned nearly a hundred abandoned wigwams. As the Narragansett on their exodus north passed by Warwick they confiscated two hundred sheep, fifty head of cattle, and fifteen horses from the town. Just before they entered Nipmuck territory, a pursuing company of soldiers overtook their rear guard, and killed or captured about seventy Narragansetts. The main body managed to escape into the woods between Brookfield and Marlborough.

With the added strength of these Narragansett warriors, King Philip and his allies concentrated on destroying the frontier towns surrounding Boston. In February they attacked Lancaster and Medfield with such fury that both these towns were abandoned. About forty residents were killed and some twenty women and children were taken captive from the two settlements. Two weeks later King Philip's forces attacked the more easterly parts of the Bay Colony again, burning a few houses and barns at Weymouth. On March 13, 1676, the Nipmucks burned most of Groton to the ground, which forced the townsfolk to seek refuge in neighboring Chelmsford and Billerica. Soon afterwards the warriors attacked Marlborough, Rehoboth and Providence. A month later Sudbury was attacked. This new wave of attacks prompted Plymouth Colony to dispatch Captain Pierce with fifty English soldiers and twenty "Praying Indians" from Cape Cod to the area about the Blackstone and Pawtuxet rivers, where he sighted a large force of warriors who had made the earlier raids in Massachusetts. As Pierce led his forces down one side of the river, some of these warriors circled from behind to enclose the company in a ring of gunfire. Pierce and his men, greatly outnumbered, all perished.

Suddenly the flagging English morale was raised when a company of Connecticut soldiers under the command of Captain Denison killed over seventy warriors and captured Canonchet, sachem of the Narragansetts. "It was sufficient matter of rejoicing to all the colonies of the English," writes William Hubbard, "that the Ring-leader of almost all this mischief . . . died himself by that sword of war which he had drawn against others." Shortly afterwards Denison made another successful expedition against the Narragansetts, where the English killed a number of warriors, and — of greater military significance — seized one hundred and sixty bushels of Indian corn.

King Philip and his allies continued to attack the frontier towns, but the prolonged war effort was steadily depleting their food reserves. In wartime they feared to remain in any one place, for the English forces would easily discover them. Unable to plant and cultivate their cornfields, Philip's men reverted entirely to a hunting and gathering existence. Due to their increasingly desperate situation, Mary Rowlandson notes "the chief and commonest food was ground-nuts. They eat also nuts and acorns, artichokes, lily-roots, . . . and several other weeds and roots that I know not. They would pick up old bones and cut them to pieces at the joints, and if they were full of worms and maggots they would scald them over the fire to make the vermine come out, and then boil them and drink up the liquor, and then beat the great ends of them in a morter, and so eat them. They would eat horses' guts and ears and all sorts of wild birds which they would catch: also bear, venison, beaver, tortoise, frogs, squirrels, dogs, skunks, rattlesnakes, yea, the very bark of trees."

To ensure their day to day survival and remain undetected by the English militias, Philip's men often divided into smaller groups. Some of King Philip's forces remained near Plymouth Colony and in Nipmuck country, while others of his allies moved west of the Connecticut Valley and north of the abandoned settlement of Deerfield (Pocumtuck) in the area of present-day Turners Falls. At the latter place, which the Pocumtucks called *Peskeompscut,* the warriors had camped near a waterfall to take advantage of the annual salmon run. The English soon discovered their wigwams and raised an army of a hundred and fifty men to attack. On May 18, 1676, Captain Holyoke led his soldiers upriver to the falls and in the early morning hours they took the encampment by surprise. William Hubbard says:

> When they came near the Indians' rendezvouze, they allighted off their horses, and tied them to some young trees at a quarter of a miles distance, so marching up, they fired amain into their very wigwams, killing many upon the place, and frighting others with the sudden alarm of their guns, and made them run into the river, where the swiftness of the stream carrying them down a steep fall, they perished in the water, some getting into canoes, which proved to them a Charons boat, being sunk, or overset, by the shooting of our men, delivered them into the like danger of the waters, giving them thereby a passport into the other world: others of them creeping for shelter under the banks of the great river, were espied by our men and killed by their swords; Capt. Holyoke killing five, young and old, with his own hands from under a bank. When the Indians were first awakened with the thunder of their guns, they cried

'Mohawks, Mohawks,' as if their own native enemies had been upon them; but the dawning of the light, soon notified their error, though it could not prevent the danger.

The scattered survivors regrouped their forces, and charged the English, forcing them to make a disorderly retreat. Gaining the advantage, the warriors attacked the company's rear guard repeatedly. About thirty-eight soldiers died, and tribal casualities were much higher. A week later the same warriors retaliated by burning houses and barns in Hatfield.

The impact of the Mohawks in King Philip's War has generally been overlooked by most New England historians, although recent research by historians such as Richard Melvoin in *New England Outpost*, points to the Mohawks as a significant factor in the eventual defeat of King Philip and his tribal allies. Just as the Pequot sachem Sassacus had done forty years earlier, King Philip sought out negotiations with the Mohawk leadership in the winter of 1675-1676, to ask for their assistance in defeating the English. The Wampanoag sachem apparently had difficulties in convincing the Mohawks to go on the warpath against the English, so he tried to win them over through a treacherous scheme. According to a suspect account written by Cotton Mather, King Philip's men murdered a party of Mohawks, whose corpses were then left in the woods. When these bodies were discovered by some of their fellow tribesmen, King Philip attempted to convince them the English were responsible. He might have succeeded in this hoax had not one of the Mohawks, who Philip's men left for dead, been only wounded. This Mohawk warrior made his way home, where he told his countrymen the truth.

The English were concerned King Philip might convince the Mohawks to join him. The Connecticut Governor and Council suggested to Governor Andros of New York that he encourage the Mohawks to attack King Philip's warriors, which he did. The Mohawks, wanting revenge for their murdered tribesmen, with the English behind their efforts, ambushed King Philip's forces near Albany in early May and Philip's forces fled. The Mohawks pursued them across the Hoosic River Valley and killed about fifty of King Philip's men. The Mohawks then began an all-out campaign against the New England Algonkians. Their raiding parties made no distinction between King Philip's forces and those Algonkian tribes which were neutral in this war. Many of King Philip's warriors, recalling the havoc their Iroquoian enemies had inflicted on them during the Mohawk War, fled eastward before this renewed Mohawk onslaught only to be attacked by various militias of the United Colonies of New England. At the same time, some of Philip's warriors gave up their plan to get powder from the French, as reported by Mary Rowlandson's son Joseph, because some of their scouts were killed by a party of Mohawk warriors. Rowlandson writes, they "were going to the French for powder, but by the way the Mohawks met with them and killed four of their company which made the rest turn back."

Fearing possible Mohawk attacks, King Philip and his allies did not use western New England as a base of operation to receive supplies from the French. By late June, many of the Wampanoag, Narragansett and Nipmuck forces had gone back to their tribal lands to escape Mohawk hostilities. Also, dissension between Philip and some of his tribal confederates, along with the outbreak of "fevers and fluxes" among them, led some warriors to abandon the Wampanoag campaign against the English. King Philip and his captains slipped back into Plymouth Colony, along with their remaining warriors. There, in their old territories, they continued the war against the English. The Massachusetts government, seeing an opportunity to further weaken King Philip's forces, offered the "hope of mercy" to all those who surrendered within a two-week period. Of course, "hope and mercy" included the possibilities of either slavery or execution.

During the last weeks of the war, a company of Connecticut soldiers under the command of Major Talcott began an extermination campaign against the remaining warriors. Hardened by the atrocities of war, the major and his men ignored many of their pleas for mercy, and he ordered his soldiers to execute all those who were taken prisoner. The news of this campaign so frightened the remainder of King Philip's forces that many turned themselves over to the officials of Rhode Island, Plymouth and Massachusetts Bay colonies. William Harris describes the sudden collapse of the Algonkian war effort:

> Since that time many Indians have been captured, others slain, and others have come in and surrendered, more than two hundred of them. Commonly now they come in and to the English, and imme-

diately go out with the English to fight against the Indians who so recently were their friends. Thus the Indians are now a great terror to each other, and are afraid of the sight of each other, seeing how their former friends have suddenly become their deadly enemies and by all craftiness they can manage, betray them into the hands of the English.

In July, King Philip and some of his warriors were sighted in the area of Taunton but the arrival of Captain Church and his militia scattered the Wampanoags across the Taunton River into the woods near Pocasset. Weetamoo's naked body was later found on the bank of the Taunton River, which led the English to believe she had drowned while attempting to flee across the river. Her head was cut off and set on a pole in Taunton. During a series of skirmishes around Pocasset and Pokanoket most of King Philip's men were either killed or taken captive; among them, his chief captains Akkompoin, Tyasks and Quinnapin. In one of the skirmishes Church's forces overtook Philip's wife and son, who were later sold into slavery. By mid August, the Wampanoag sachem and a few of his men were hiding in a swamp near Pokanoket. With the help of an Algonkian warrior named Alderman, who knew Philip's whereabouts, Church and Captain Sanford of Rhode Island surrounded the swamp. As King Philip tried to escape he was shot twice by Alderman. Church ordered the sachem's corpse to be drawn and quartered, and the soldiers triumphantly brought his head to Plymouth, where it was displayed on a gibbet for the next twenty years!

Annawon, who had served on the Wampanoag tribal council to sachems Massasoit, Alexander and Philip, escaped from this swamp only to be apprehended by Church in late August. On the night of his surrender this great Wampanoag pniese handed over to the Plymouth captain a pack containing Philip's personal possessions saying, "Great Captain, you have killed Philip, and conquered his country; for I believe that I and my company are the last that war against the English, so suppose the war is ended by your means; and therefore these things belong unto you." The pack contained three beautifully designed black and white wampum belts, one of which reached to Church's ankles when placed on his shoulders. All the belts were edged with hair that had been dyed red. According to Annawon, this dyed hair was acquired from the Mohawks. The old warrior also handed Captain Church a red cloth blanket,

191

which may have been the remnants of the red coat that Edward Winslow had given Massasoit some fifty-five years earlier. Two days later, the Captain sent Annawon and his small band of warriors to Plymouth, where the Wampanoag pniese was later executed along with Tuspaquin, the sagamore of Nemasket.

The war that was to liberate some of the Algonkian tribes from the English came to a tragic end. While some of King Philip's scattered forces sought amnesty, others distrusted this English gesture and fled. Some of the dispersed Wampanoags resettled at Skatecook, among the Mahicans. Others of the Pocumtuck and Nipmuck sought refuge among the Algonkian tribes of northern New England, as did some of the Narragansetts, who were later adopted into the Abenaki nation. About four hundred tribal people, including a considerable number of Nashuas, went to live among the Cocheco tribe along the Piscataqua River in New Hampshire. Because the Nashuas had joined in King Philip's War against the United Colonies of New England, they were apprehended by Captain Hathorne in September, 1676. Those who were subjects of the neutral Pennacook sachem Wannalancit were released; the remaining two hundred were brought down to Boston. Sagamore Sam, tribal leader of the Nashuas, and about seven of his chief counsellors were hung there, and the rest of the tribal people were sold into the foreign slave market. Over two thousand English colonists died in the war; some fifty colonial settlements had been attacked, and twelve totally destroyed. Thousands of Algonkian people had died or been enslaved and the remaining tribal confederacies in southern New England were shattered. There were truly no immediate victors in this conflict.

Even though King Philip's War ended in 1676, the possibility of raids by fugitive Algonkian warriors who had retreated northward kept the frontier towns on alert. In September, 1677, a mixed band of warriors, including some of the dispersed Norwottuck tribe, returned to the Connecticut Valley to seek revenge on the English for the war. The warriors were supported by French authorities in Canada, who offered the tribesmen payment for any captives taken. The group attacked both Deerfield and Hatfield, killing thirteen residents and capturing twenty-one others. At first the English thought the Mohawks were the culprits, until one of the captives from Deerfield, Benoni Stebbins, escaped from his captors and identified them as river tribesmen who had fled the valley after King Philip's War.

The Mohawks were suspected of these raids because they continued to attack the Algonkian tribes in New England after King Philip's defeat. Both English colonials and the neighboring "Praying Indians" saw their skulking war parties. In fact, according to Edward Rawson who served as secretary of the Massachusetts General Court, four Mohawk warriors "lodged in Hatfield and were kindly [treated] the night before" the attack on this town in 1677. The English encouraged these Mohawk assaults on the New England Algonkians, but the Massachusetts colonial government had intended the Abenaki, Saco and Sokoki tribes to be the sole victims of these raids. These tribes had gone on the warpath against the English colonists along the Eastern frontier of Maine and New Hampshire in September, 1675. These hostilities were simultaneous but separate from King Philip's War, and continued after the defeat of the Wampanoag sachem.

The war between the colonials and the Abenaki and Saco was caused largely by English mistreatment of the Saco nation. Along the Saco River lived Squando, sachem of the Saco people. One day Squando's wife was passing downriver in a canoe with her youngster, when several sailors, who had heard that Algonkian children could swim at an early age, purposely capsized the boat. The child was swept headlong into the river current, and the mother immediately dove underwater to retrieve her child, but the youngster died soon afterwards. Squando blamed these uncaring English seamen for his child's death, and the Saco swiftly attacked. On September 12, 1675, the family of Thomas Wakely was massacred on the Presumpscott River. Six days later, Captain Bonithon's house at Saco was set to the torch but his family managed to escape across the Saco River to the garrison house of Major Philips.

At the Philips garrison the Philips and Bonithan families withstood a seige as the Saco burned a house, sawmill and grist mill nearby. The Saco warriors used a strategy to drive the English from the Philips garrison: during the night the din of axes and other tools came from the sawmill. The next morning, the warriors came toward the garrison house pushing a four-wheeled cart they had built, with a shield along the front to protect them. The cart was stuffed with birch, straw and gunpowder. The garrison defenders held their fire until the cart and warriors came within pistol shot. One of its wheels became stuck in a rut, when the warriors tried to force it forward, they carelessly exposed themselves to gunfire from the right flank of the garrison. Six of the Saco tribesmen were killed and another fifteen wounded. Then the warriors abandoned their engine of war and called off the seige of the Philips garrison.

From Saco, the war spread down the coast to the Piscataqua settlements. Warriors attacked Oyster River (now Durham), where they burned houses, killed two residents, and took another two captive, although these later escaped. They attacked Hampton and Exeter as well as Newichewannock, where they killed some fifteen people. The initial response of the English to these raids was defensive, but early on about twenty men, mainly from Dover, asked Major Waldron, commander of the militia, to be allowed to fight the Saco on their own terms. Here, as elsewhere during the two wars with the Algonkian nations, the English gradually realized that, like their "Indian enemies," they would need to ambush their opponents using smaller parties of men if they ever hoped to defeat them. The Dover men scattered in the woods, where a small party discovered five warriors in a field near an abandoned house. The unsuspecting tribesmen were gathering corn to roast in a fire. The Englishmen crept near the house, rushed on the warriors, and subdued two tribesmen as the others escaped.

In mid October, the Saco attacked the settlement of Salmon Falls (Berwick). This was followed by renewed alarms when skulking warriors were seen near Dover and Exeter. By the end of November, about fifty colonists had been captured or killed along the Eastern frontier. The Massachusetts government could not provide enough supplies to defend the Eastern frontier, since they were trying to defend the frontier communities exposed to the attacks of King Philip. Major General Denison, commander of the Bay Colony militia, ordered the majors who oversaw the regiments in the Piscataqua area to send an expedition to the headwaters of the Saco River to attack the Saco and their allies. The tribes had settled for the winter at a fort in Pequaket country, roughly between Lake Ossipee and Little Ossipee Pond. This fort had been built several years earlier by English carpenters the Saco had hired to construct a strong fort to protect their people from Mohawk attacks. But the

English expedition did not set out, because of the harsh winter of 1675-1676. By mid-December the woods lay under a four-foot blanket of snow, and the men had no snowshoes to trek into the hilly interior.

The winter season also depleted the Saco nation's dwindling food stores. The tribe was nearly reduced to starvation, and after losing about ninety warriors in the war, they sued the English for peace. Major Waldron mediated the peace negotiations, but after a treaty was signed the Eastern frontier settlements had only a brief respite, for by August, 1676, hostilities broke out anew between the English and the neighboring Kennebec and Arosaguntacook tribes. In September, an expedition of two companies under the command of Captains Joseph Syll and William Hathorne was sent to relieve the outposts beyond Piscataqua. The companies found "the eastern settlements were all either destroyed or deserted, and no enemy was to been seen," and so they returned to Piscataqua. They marched up into Pequaket country in November, hoping to find tribesmen near the fort, but they came across no warriors during their nine-day expedition into the interior.

These two military companies had marched into Pequaket country mostly because of a Penobscot tribesman named Mogg, who had come to Piscataqua with a peace proposal. Mogg claimed a hundred tribesmen were gathered near Ossipee, and that he had been sent by the Penobscot sachem Madokawando, who wanted to make a peace treaty with the English. Mogg was taken to Boston where a treaty was drawn up and ratified by Sachem Madokawando on November 6. It stipulated that any tribes on the Eastern frontier who renounced this treaty and chose to continue hostilities against the English would be considered enemies by all parties who had entered into the terms of the peace. As a show of good faith Madokawando helped bring about the return of two English captives.

Mogg had guaranteed the treaty with his life, so the English sent him to neighboring Abenaki tribes to negotiate for the release of other captives. When he failed to return within three days, the English suspected foul play, but an English captive who escaped from the Abenaki the following January claimed Mogg was alive and well, and that he derided the Massachusetts governor's kind entertainment of him at Boston. Since Mogg was surety for the treaty, his behavior suggested the recent truce would be short-lived, and so a two-hundred-man militia, including sixty Natick "Praying Indians," sailed from Boston under the command of Major Waldron in February, 1677. The expedition skirmished with various Abenaki tribes at Casco, Pemaquid and Arrowsic Island. Thirteen tribesmen died in these encounters, although Waldron's forces returned to Boston in March not having lost a single man.

The prospects for peace now seemed dim. The Massachusetts government decided to use the Mohawks to reduce the Abenaki tribes. Major John Pynchon of Springfield and Major Richards of Hartford travelled to Mohawk country, where the tribe assured them they would begin hostilities against the Algonkians. A problem with the English strategy soon emerged, however, for Mohawk raiding parties made little distinction in their attacks between friendly tribes such as the Pennacook, Natick and Sakonnet (which the English called *Netops* from an Algonkian word meaning "friend,") and the adversary tribes belonging to the Abenaki nation. The Pennacook nation was first alerted to this fact in mid March, 1677, when Wannalancit's son caught sight of an unfamiliar war party while he was hunting at Amoskeag (Nameskeag) on the Merrimac River. The warriors called out to him from the opposite bank in a language that he could not understand. When he ran into the woods they fired their guns at him, and shortly afterwards warriors appeared in the woods near Dover. Waldron sent out eight of his "Indian allies" to discover who the war party might be. The warriors, who were Mohawks, attacked the party killing five as the others escaped. Two of those who fled reported to the English that "the Mohawks threatened destruction to all Indians in these parts without distinction." And so it proved true, for between 1677-1678 the Mohawks attacked the Natick "Praying Indians" in the Bay Colony, killing three and carrying twenty-four off into captivity. It was later discovered some of these Natick captives had been adopted by Mohawk families.

During the spring of 1677 the Abenaki again attacked along the entire Eastern frontier from the Kennebec to the Piscataqua settlements of Wells, Kittery and Portsmouth. Fifty English soldiers and ten Natick "Praying Indians," commanded by Captain Swaine, marched to Piscataqua to protect the towns. Soon afterwards the Penobscot warrior Mogg was killed during an attack at Black Point. The attacking war party fled in canoes, some eastward and others south towards Kittery, where they slaughtered some sheep. As these warriors turned north towards Wells they released their captives, fearing their prisoners would encumber their escape from a Mohawk war party they suspected was in the area.

The Massachusetts colonial government expected further attacks on the Eastern frontier and authorized Captain Benjamin Swett and Lieutenant Richardson, to lead an expedition of forty Englishmen and one hundred Natick "Praying Indians." They marched upriver to attack the Kennebec tribe at their fort at *Taconock*. When they arrived in the Kennebec Valley, the regiment pursued the warriors toward their fort, but at a predetermined point, the Kennebec tribesmen unexpectedly turned back to attack their pursuers. In the battle Swett was killed and about sixty of his men were either killed or wounded.

In August, Major Andros, who was then governor of New York, sent soldiers by sloop to take possession of frontier land in Maine that had been granted to the Duke of York. The soldiers built a fort at Pemaquid to defend the area from French encroachment. The presence of the English soldiers disposed the Abenaki nation toward peace. They restored fifteen captives and some fishing vessels to the English. All during that autumn and winter, the new garrison at Pemaquid was not attacked. In the spring of 1678, Major Shapleigh of Kittery and two other colonists from Portsmouth were appointed as commissioners by the Massachusetts government to formulate a treaty with Sachem Squando and his allied chieftans. The treaty was completed at Casco and area tribes brought in the remainder of the English captives in their possession. One stipulation of the treaty was that the former English inhabitants could return to their abandoned settlements on the condition that each family paid the Abenaki one peck of corn annually. Major Pendleton, who owned a neck of land at the mouth of the Saco River, had to pay one bushel annually to the appropriate tribal sagamores. By agreeing to pay, the English had for the time being conceded their continued use of these lands depended on Abenaki consent.

As the decade drew to a close, the French and their Abenaki allies arranged a peace with the Mohawks. The Massachusetts colonial government, to protect the "Praying Indians" of southern New England from any further Mohawk assaults, sent Major Pynchon to

Albany, where he negotiated a treaty between the Mohawks and the "Praying Indians." The Mohawks handed a wampum belt to Pynchon as a symbolic gesture of their longtime friendship with the English colonists. More significantly, however, the treaty marked the end of nearly four years of hostilities between the Mohawks and their Algonkian adversaries, during which the English colonies exploited long-standing intertribal animosities to advance their own cause.

Throughout these wars the "Praying Indians" were persecuted and deprived of rights and property by the English. Popular colonial sentiment turned against the "Praying Indians" because of Algonkian atrocities on English settlers during King Philip's War and the struggle along the Eastern frontier. The Natick Indians and others showed their loyalty through military service to the United Colonies of New England, but even so prejudice remained. In fact, their military service to the English in these wars was often derided. "The Indians called Christians feigning loyalty," writes William Harris of Rhode Island, "sometimes obtained gunpowder and gave or sold it to the enemy Indians, or threw it under trees for the enemy to take. When they go out with the English against the enemy Indians, some of them shoot up into the trees, as other Indians have revealed." Such stories increased the rumors of "Praying Indian" complicity with the enemy.

Early on in King Philip's War, the Massachusetts Court began to yield to the English colonists demands that "Praying Indians" be restricted in their mobility. By late August, 1675, the Massachusetts Bay Colony had dismissed the "Christian Indian" militia companies from military service. "Praying Indians" within the colony were forced to relocate to one of the five designated Praying Indian towns of Natick, Punkapoag, Nashoba, Wamesit and Hassanamesit. A "Praying Indian" could not travel more than one mile from any of these five villages unless accompanied by an Englishman, and any "Praying Indian" found outside the one-mile radius could be shot as an "enemy Indian." These restrictions were a hardship for the "Praying Indians" who gathered native foodstuffs and materials as a large part of their livelihood.

That autumn, suspicious fires were set at Chelmsford which were later attributed in part to a hostile tribesman named Nathaniel. Also, an empty building in Dedham was burned. Many of the English living near the "Praying Indian" towns became convinced the "Praying Indians" should be relocated to one place. The Massachusetts magistrates were eventually swayed by their petitions, and the Natick Indians were the first to be removed under this insensitive measure. They were given one hour's notice to gather their possessions and move to Deer Island in Boston Harbor. On their arrival in the harbor some of the Natick tribespeople wept because they feared the English planned to ship them out of the colony. The Massachusetts Court "ordered that none of the said Indians shall presume to go off the said islands voluntarily, upon pain of death; and it shall be lawful for the English to destroy those that they find straggling off from the said places of their confinement, unless taken off by order from authority, and under an English guard."

After the natives' forced departure from Natick, some of the surrounding English residents plundered the vacated wigwams, taking guns, ammunition, and other property, most of which was never returned to its owners after King Philip's War was over. During the winter of 1675-1676, the "Praying Indians" at Punkapoag, Nashoba and Okkommakamesit were also interned at Deer Island, bringing the number of "Christian Indians" there to over five hundred. Despite the order of the Court "that the country treasurer take care for ye provision of those Indians that are sent down to Deer Island, so as to prevent their perishing," these people suffered inexcusable hardship due to the lack of adequate clothing, food and shelter. Their dietary mainstay was shellfish during much of their winter confinement on this wind-swept prison, and malnutrition and exposure took a toll. During the following year after these "Praying Indians" had been moved to adjacent Long Island in Boston Harbor, they were now brought up to Cambridge by the Massachusetts Court. Most of them were women, old men, and children, because the younger "Praying Indian" men had recently volunteered for military service on the Eastern frontier under Captain Hunting. With King Philip's War over in southern New England, the remaining "Christian Indians" were relocated to the estate of Thomas Oliver near the Charles River, where they remained through the summer. In the autumn, most of them returned to their former living places at Nonantum, Natick, Punkapoag and Nashoba. At this time, Daniel Gookin estimated, they numbered about six hundred, of whom a little over a hundred were men.

The Natick Indians were the largest group of "Praying Indians" that remained in the Bay Colony after King Philip's War. They were divided into four groupings: about twenty-five lived at Medfield; another fifty resided near the garrison house at Natick; a third group of about sixty lived near Cowate (Charles River Fall); and nearby, a fourth group of about seventy-five were settled at Nonantum (Newton). In all, the Natick "Praying Indians" numbered about two hundred. Some were former residents of Hassanamesit, Magunkaquog, Okkommakamesit and Wamesit. As the declining "Praying Indian" populations increasingly converged near Natick, other "Praying Indian" towns came to an end. By 1700, the town of Marlborough had assumed control of the lands formerly belonging to the "Praying Indian" village of Okkommakamesit. Fifteen years later, the "Praying Indian" village of Nashoba was incorporated into the town of Littleton. Five hundred acres was reserved to the descendants of the Nashobas, who lived out their remaining years along the shores of Nagog Pond.

After 1676, the New England frontier towns and the Algonkian nations remained at peace for a little more than a decade. During this brief respite, the English repopulated the settlements that had been deserted. The frontier in this period extended from western Connecticut to coastal Maine, and the long line of isolated settlements consisted of three sections: the Connecticut Valley frontier, the Massachusetts Bay frontier, and the Eastern, or Maine frontier. The Connecticut Valley frontier began at Simsbury and Hartford, Connecticut. Crossing into Massachusetts, it included the settlements of Springfield, Westfield, Northampton, Hadley, Hatfield, Deerfield and Northfield. Between the Connecticut Valley and eastern Massachusetts stood several isolated towns such as Brookfield, Rutland and Worcester. The Massachusetts Bay frontier began at Marlborough, and stretched north towards the Merrimac River, where it took in the outposts of Lancaster, Groton and Dunstable. The Merrimac Valley contained the frontier settlements of Chelmsford, Billerica, Andover, Haverhill, Amesbury and Salisbury. At the mouth of the Merrimac River the Eastern frontier began, which included the New Hampshire towns of Hampton, Kingston, Exeter, Portsmouth, Dover and Oyster River (Durham). Across the Piscataqua River in Maine, the frontier ended with the outposts of Kittery, York, Berwick, Wells, Cape Neddick, Scarborough (Black

Point), Falmouth (Casco) and Yarmouth. Nearly all these towns suffered considerable hardships from Abenaki and Maliseet raids between 1689-1726, particularly the Massachusetts Bay and Eastern frontiers.

As the shock of King Philip's War passed, the English immediately tried to resettle abandoned frontier towns such as Groton and Dunstable, which were both reclaimed between 1678-1682. When the first families returned to Groton in 1678 from neighboring communities, they found sixty-six homes burned, and only six still standing intact. The former residents, in their petition to resettle the area, informed the Massachusetts Court of the poverty and housing shortage at Groton. By 1680, some forty families had returned, as compared to the sixty families who lived in Groton before the war. Dunstable, though abandoned during the conflict because of its isolated position, remained intact. The reconstruction so necessary at Groton was not needed at Dunstable, where the people simply resumed laboring to reclaim their neglected fields. Most of Dunstable's former residents returned before 1682 to the town; where about thirty families resettled. Lancaster weathered a destructive raid in King Philip's War, but recovered within the next decade. Chelmsford, like the other frontier towns in the Merrimac Valley, suffered slight damage in the conflict. Among the coastal New Hampshire towns, Algonkian warriors had attacked Oyster River, Berwick, Dover and Exeter. At the isolated outposts in southern Maine, although they were ravaged by raids, were almost all reestablished by the time of King William's War (1689-1697).

The reasons for King William's War remain unclear. Cotton Mather suggests that the controversy over boundary lines between the French and English in Maine caused renewed hostilities. A Frenchman, surnamed Baron de St. Castine, had lived among the native people for years, carrying on a lucrative fur trade with the Abenaki tribes from the Penobscot to the St. Croix rivers. One of his wives was the daughter of Madokawando, the sachem of the Penobscot nation, who controlled the same lands that had been granted to the Duke of York (later to become King James II). The heir to the English throne had built a fort at Pemaquid in 1677 to prevent the French from intruding on his grant. Later a new line of division was drawn up to the disadvantage of Baron de St. Castine,

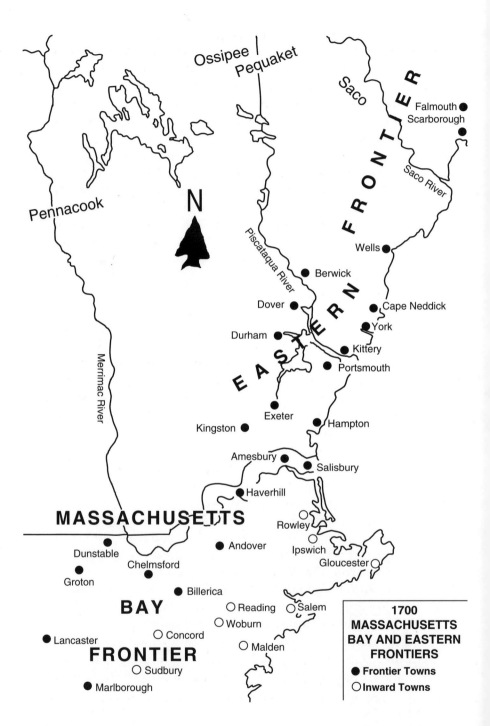

Ossipee | Pequaket

Saco

Falmouth ●
Scarborough ●

Saco River

F R O N T I E R

Pennacook

N

Piscataqua River

Wells ●

● Berwick

Dover ● ● Cape Neddick

Durham ● ● York

E A S T E R N

● Kittery

● Portsmouth

Merrimac River

● Exeter

Kingston ● ● Hampton

Amesbury ●

● Salisbury

● Haverhill

MASSACHUSETTS

Rowley ○

Dunstable ● ● Andover

Ipswich ○

Chelmsford ● Gloucester ○

● Groton

● Billerica

BAY ○ Reading ○ Salem

○ Woburn

● Lancaster ○ Concord

FRONTIER ○ Malden

○ Sudbury

● Marlborough

1700 MASSACHUSETTS BAY AND EASTERN FRONTIERS
● Frontier Towns
○ Inward Towns

for part of his claim came under English control, and the English now considered him an intruder on the domain of King James II. Consequently, in the spring of 1688, Governor Andros, who headed the newly created Dominion of New England, took forceful action to dislodge St. Castine from the area, and plundered his fort and house. In retaliation, St. Castine incited the Abenaki tribes to attack the English.

Another reason hostilities resumed may have been the English failure to pay the Abenaki tribes their yearly tribute of corn. The English also used seines on the Saco River, which reduced the Abenakis' annual catch of salmon and other fish. Internationally, the power struggle between England and France intensified toward the end of the 17th century as England's new ruler, William of Orange (King William III), and the French king, Louis XIV, became colonial rivals in North America and trade rivals in India. There was also religious friction between Anglican England and Catholic France, and both empires wanted to expand their sphere of influence over the Netherlands. For these reasons, England and France engaged in a series of wars from 1689 to 1763. Each war the two empires fought in Europe, with the exception of Lovewell's War which was exclusively a colonial conflict, had its counterpart in their North American colonies. The English colonists gave the colonial wars names that were different from the European titles for them. The wars are:

In Europe:
1689-1697 War of the League of Augsburg
1702-1713 War of the Spanish Succession
1740-1748 War of the Austrian Succession
1756-1763 Seven Years' War

In North America:
1689-1697 King William's War
1703-1713 Queen Anne's War
1722-1726 Lovewell's War (Dummer's War)
1744-1748 King George's War
1754-1763 French and Indian War

During these wars French authorities in Quebec often retaliated by using their tribal allies as pawns against the New England colonists. The northern Algonkian tribes played a significant part in

King William's War and Queen Anne's War. Though friction between the French and English colonists occurred, only rarely did the two sides engage in open conflict. Instead, Mic Mac, Maliseet and Abenaki war parties threatened the English frontier settlements. What motivated these tribes to do the bidding of the French? Such prominent seventeenth-century New Englanders as Cotton Mather and the Reverend John Williams accused the Jesuits of inculcating hatred of Protestants in their Algonkian converts. But it is debatable how much the native people understood of Christian theology. At best the converts, who were always a minority among Native Americans, knew how to make the sign of the cross and were familiar with a few other aspects of Roman Catholicism. The idea that "Romanized Indians" knew enough about theological differences to be prejudiced by Jesuits against the English colonists in New England is a Puritan concoction.

Even the claim that the Algonkian nations were trying to retake lands they had lost in King Philip's War is doubtful. Some of the displaced tribesmen from southern New England had joined with the Saco, Pennacook and Abenaki nations, and they probably told the northern sachems and sagamores to fear further English encroachment from the south. But Abenaki attacks along the Eastern frontier were generally defensive in nature, and aimed primarily at preserving Abenaki territorial integrity rather than retaking lost Algonkian hunting and planting grounds in southern New England.

However, English encroachment on Abenaki tribal lands may have contributed to the outbreak of King William's War and Queen Anne's War, for the outward expansion of the New England frontier had virtually ended after 1665, except for the Eastern frontier in Maine. Frontier expansion stopped partly because of the devastation of King Philip's War. But in the late 17th and early 18th centuries Massachusetts Bay residents were still relocating to the Maine coast in search of fishing and the wealth of timber as well as freedom from the religious strictures of the Bay Colony. Some were willing to settle along the Maine coast "partly from the fertility of the soil," as Samuel Penhallow a New Hampshire colonial official points out, "the plenty of timber, the advantage of fishery, and several other inducements." Penhallow admits some of these new arrivals on the Eastern frontier were "chiefly culpable in causing the first breach between them and us [Abenaki and English]; by invading their properties and defrauding them in their dealings." The French colonial authorities seized the chance to unite with local Abenakis, who feared further English encroachment. The Abenaki were a ready force to unleash on the English with minimal loss to the French.

To the English colonials the Abenaki raids on their towns sometimes seemed to be impulsive but the Abenaki strategy was apparently to ruin the encroaching English outposts by surprise attacks. If raiding parties came across a mill during their attacks they usually burned it; they knew the loss of a mill, along with the slaughtering of livestock, could gravely cripple a frontier settlement. Nothing was more frightening to a frontier resident than to wake in the early morning hours to the sound of gunshots. A letter from Richard Waldron dated June 28, 1689, gives a vivid description of the Dover attack, the first major Abenaki assault of King William's War.

About eight o'clock in the morning, a few hours after the assault, came ashore here [Portsmouth, New Hampshire] from Dover John Ham and his wife, who went hence last night homeward with Mrs. Heard (they living within a mile of Major Waldron) and about break of day going up the river in a canoe, they heard guns fired but notwithstanding proceeded to land at Major Waldron's landing place, by which time it begun to be light, and they saw about twenty Indians near Mr. Coffin's garrison, shouting and shooting, as many more about Richard Otis's and Thomas Pain's, but saw their way to Major Waldron's, where they intended immediately to secure themselves; but coming to the gate and calling and knocking received no answer, yet saw a light in one of the chambers and one of them say (looking through a crack of the gate) that he saw sundry Indians within the garrison which supposed had murthered Major Waldron and his family, an thereupon they betook themselves to make an escape . . . . Quickly after they [Indians] set sundry houses on fire. This is all the account we have at present, which being given in a surprise, may admit of some alterations; but doubtless the most of those at or about Cocheca [Dover] are destroyed.

In the Dover attack the Abenaki and their allies killed twenty-three and took twenty-nine captives. Five or six houses, along with the mills, were burned. This was the first major Algonkian assault since the attack on Deerfield in 1677, and frontier residents from Connecticut to the Maine coast viewed it with apprehension. The governor and council at Boston, when they received news of the attack, warned the outlying towns, "that so they might provide for their security and defence." Events soon proved the tragedy at Dover was the beginning of what would become an accepted way of life on the New England frontier. Except for outlying towns such as Chelmsford, which was used as a staging area for the deployment of colonial forces, most of the Massachusetts Bay and Eastern frontier communities lost numerous lives and property from tribal assaults in this period. Nevertheless, during three decades of intermittent frontier warfare (1689-1726), only a few of these "candlesticks" in the wilderness were actually extinguished.

Although many of the northern Algonkian tribes attacked the English settlements, the Mohegan, Mahican (Skatecook), Natick, Sakonnet and some of the Pennacook were allies of the English. A minority of soldiers that defended the towns on the Eastern frontier were recruited from the Pequot-Mohegan tribe. At Berwick, ninety-five Pequot-Mohegan men were posted for defense. Sometimes the Pennacook served as scouts, and reported the movement of the Abenaki tribes to Captain Thomas Henchman at Chelmsford, who in turn informed the governor and council at Boston. Captain Henchman wrote to the council on June 22, 1689, that two Pennacook messengers, Job Maramasquand and Peter Muckamug, told him of the war parties' plan to attack both Dover and Dunstable. The Pennacook messengers told Henchman they acted as spies so that "if damage be done, the blame shall not be on them [Pennacook], having given a faithful account of what they hear." Apparently the tribe was helping the English not so much out of friendship, but to preserve themselves by remaining neutral. Usually the information given by the Pennacook was reliable, as was this warning of Job Maramasquand and Peter Muckamug. Six days later came the attack on Dover. Ironically the council had sent a messenger to alert Dover of its impending doom, but he was delayed at the ferry landing in Newbury, Massachusetts, and the unsuspecting town was ravaged before the warning arrived.

After the massacre at Dover, which is considered the beginning of King William's War (1689-1697) warfare along the frontier rapidly increased. Sporadic raids left only a few residents dead in each settlement. But Groton, Billerica and Haverhill suffered devastating attacks in King William's War. At Groton, twenty-two people were killed in 1694, and about ten at Billerica a year later. In 1697, northern Algonkian assaults at Lancaster and Haverhill cost the lives of sixty-one settlers. On the Eastern frontier, when the fort and settlement at Falmouth (Casco) were destroyed, many English left the eastern settlements. Most retreated to the fort at Wells. In January, 1692, an Abenaki war party bypassed Wells to attack York, where forty-eight English settlers were killed. Later that same year a raid on Sandy Beach (Rye) cost the lives of another twenty-one English villagers. The attacks on the Piscataqua settlement of Oyster River in 1694 and Sagamore's Creek (Portsmouth) in 1696, resulted in the deaths of one hundred and eighteen English colonials. In many of these raids garrison houses and barns were plundered and burned, and valuable grist mills and livestock destroyed.

The New England colonies responded to these northern Algonkian attacks by taking the war into tribal domains. In 1689, Captain Noyes marched to Pennacook, found the place temporarily vacated, and ordered the corn destroyed. Captain Wincol went to Winnipesaukee where it was believed the tribes had retreated, but when Wincol found most of the warriors gone he ordered their corn plantings to be cut down. By the end of August, seven or eight companies under Major Swaine from the Massachusetts Bay Colony were deployed eastward, soon followed by Captain Church from Plymouth Colony, with a force of both Englishmen and Sakonnet tribesmen. Church's forces skirmished briefly with some warriors in the vicintiy of Falmouth (Casco). After ranging the adjacent areas, where he visited the garrison houses at Black Point (Scarborough), Blue Point (Scarborough) and Spurwink (Cape Elizabeth), Church led his men north to the Kennebec Valley, but could not find the Kennebec tribal nation. Before the onset of winter he received orders from the Massachusetts government to secure the garrisons with suitable officers and return home. In all, Church made four expeditions during King William's War.

In 1690, having attained the rank of major, he overran an Arosaguntacook fort along the Androscoggin River. Most of the Arosaguntacooks were alerted to the arrival of colonial forces under Church and Captain Pike by a tribesman nicknamed "Young Doney," who had seen the English coming. The Arosaguntacooks fled out the north entrance of their stockade as the English forces came in on the south side. The Arosaguntacooks fled so hurriedly they left behind several English captives from earlier raids. Once in the fort the English captured one Arosaguntacook tribesman and some women and children. Church consented to their "being knocked in the head for an example, ordering them all to be buried," excepting two elderly tribal women, and several younger women and their children who were the families of the Arosaguntacook and Pennacook chieftans. All the victims of this merciless and brutal action were women and children. Before Church left the fort he ordered their corn stores be destroyed. On a third expedition, in 1692, Major Church went east with his forces to the Kennebec Valley, where he attacked the tribe's fort at *Taconock*. The Kennebec burned their fort before they retreated into the woods, to prevent the English from plundering their goods. Church, once inside the stockade, razed the remaining wigwams and ordered the corn stores ruined. Four years later, Church attacked even further east, along the Bay of Fundy.

The New Hampshire settlements were temporarily separated from Massachusetts after King James II fled the English throne, and Bostonians unseated the king's hated viceroy, Governor Edmund Andros. Andros' removal led to the demise of the Dominion of New England, an unpopular union of the New England colonies with New York and New Jersey. The New Hampshire colony, faced with the pressure of King William's War and the difficulties of creating a working government, asked Massachusetts to again come under their jurisdiction in 1690. The reunion lasted two years, during which time Massachusetts asked the New Hampshire towns to choose two residents from each to meet with the Justices of the Peace of the province. They were to charge the inhabitants for the cost of the "Indian war."

Meanwhile, the Massachusetts government tried to meet the threat of Mic Mac, Maliseet and Abenaki raids by quartering soldiers on the frontier. Towns not designated as "out towns" were obligated to contribute men for frontier duty. These soldiers protected townspeople as they worked in their fields, and scouted the woods near each settlement to prevent surprise attack. While the soldiers' presence was a comfort to the frontier residents, it could also be a burden, to judge by a petition from the inhabitants of

Dunstable. On July 23, 1689, the residents petitioned they were much "obliged to your honors for your last supply of men, notwithstanding finding ourselves still weak and unable both to keep our garrisons, and to send men out to get hay for our cattle . . . therefore we humbly intreat your honors to send and supply us with twenty footmen for the space of a month to scout about the towne while we get our hay; and the towne being very bare of provisions by reason of billeting soldiers all the last winter, we doe intreat your Honors to send a supply of meat. Without this help we cannot subsist."

If some of the frontier communities felt burdened by the soldiers' presence, others disliked just as much the labor and cost of refurbishing the garrison houses for defense. Almost every frontier town sent petitions to the governor and council concerning the expense of defense. A petition from Groton in 1694 complains of their "constant (in these later times) standing upon our guard, and considerable charge of building and repairing forts, for our owne and the countryes safety and securing their majestyes subjects, both here and in the inmost places."

These petitions indicate that northern Algonkian attacks made life on the "outward borders" difficult. The Massachusetts government, concerned "out town" residents would abandon their settlements, passed the Act of 1694, a court order which stipulated that frontier residents were prohibited from abandoning their communities, except when they could present legitimate reasons. All offenders were to be punished by the forfeiture of their abandoned property. This act was reissued several times, but it was never successfully implemented. The law was nearly impossible to enforce over such a broad area, and in fact frontier residents still deserted their lands whenever they felt compelled to leave. At Dunstable nearly two-thirds of the inhabitants had left by 1696. In fact, so many townspeople had abandoned the community the Massachusetts Court granted Dunstable a tax abatement of fifty pounds. Even the more secure settlement of Chelmsford sent a petition that the war had driven "away no less than ten families not only out of the Town, but most of them out of the province (many more being upon the wing)." Why did these residents leave the frontier? The increased taxes, defense costs and the Act of 1694 pressured some to move back into the "inward towns," but the almost weekly news of northern Algonkian attacks, and the deaths or capture of frontier residents was a more pressing concern.

The Abenaki and their tribal allies took captives partly because prisoners could be ransomed by French officials in Canada. Hostage-taking was not a new practice to the Algonkian people of New England, for in their raids on each other they often abducted tribeswomen and children to replenish their villages. Before attacking a frontier town a war party often sent out spies to determine to take the community by surprise. If the pattern of settlement in an "out town" was widespread, then the Abenaki, Maliseet or Mic Mac (Cape Sable) warriors would divide themselves into several parties. In this way they could make simultaneous attacks in different parts of the town and throw the colonial defenders into momentary disorder. Once the attack was over, captives were generally taken to a predetermined location away from the settlement, where they sometimes met other prisoners from nearby "out towns" that had been attacked that same day. Prisoners who were seriously wounded or too weak to make the northward trek to Canada were usually done away with by a swift blow to the head. The surviving captives were then divided into several parties, which made it difficult for the colonial militias to pursue them.

Some English captives enroute to Canada observed how their northern Algonkian captors put marks on trees showing how many English captives they had, and how many townspeople they had killed on each raid. Jeremy Belknap in his *History of New Hampshire* writes that as late as the mid-18th century a few of these carved war tallies were still visible on very old trees around Lake Winnipesaukee.

> I have heard of two specimens of an Indian Gazette, found in New Hampshire. One was a pine tree, on the shores of Winipiseogee river, on which was depicted a canoe, with two men in it. This is supposed to have been a mark of direction to those who might come after. The other was a tree in Moultonborough, standing by a carrying place, between two ponds. On this tree was carved the history of one of their expeditions. The number killed and prisoners, was represented by so many human figures; the former were marked with the stroke of a knife, across their throats, and even the distinction between the males and females was preserved.

Captured English colonists were usually forced to serve the warrior who had first claimed them. Algonkian captors kept a close watch on prisoners forced march into North country, because they might escape as long as the war party was still near English settlements. Male captives were sometimes pinioned to the ground during overnight encampments until the group got far enough away from the "out towns." When the warrior troop neared their destination captives were less restricted. Quintin Stockwell and other captives taken from Deerfield in 1677 spent their first nights among their captors "staked down, and spread out on [our] backs; and so [we] lay all night, yea, so we lay many nights." Once Stockwell and his fellow captives were about thirty miles north of Squawkheag (Northfield), their captors considered them beyond the reach of the English, and allowed the prisoners to gather firewood. Likewise, when the young John Gyles of Fort Charles (Pemaquid) in Maine was taken captive in 1689, he was marched off with his arms bound, but when he arrived in the St. John River Valley his captor had him serve as porter during inland winter treks in search of moose. In fact during his first year of captivity Gyles helped his Maliseet captors fish for salmon at their weirs, cultivate corn, and gather edible roots from the woods.

These hostages were sometimes psychologically and physically abused by their captors, even though there might be those in the tribe who sympathized with their condition. On several occasions Quintin Stockwell was threatened with torture and execution. One day he fell behind his captors due to his frostbitten feet, and when night fell he crawled under a tree, separated from the group. Before long one of the tribesman came searching for him, and when he saw Stockwell's condition he wrapped his coat around him, and had him pulled to the next camp in a toboggan. Of course, Stockwell's ransom price in Quebec may have had something to do with the warrior saving his life. The captive John Gyles was the unfortunate victim of physical abuse during his first months among the Maliseets. "A captive among the Indians," he writes, "is exposed to all manner of abuses, unless their master, or some of their master's relations, lay down a ransom; such as a bag of corn, a blanket, or the like, which redeems them from their cruelty for that dance."

"That dance" or the "ring dance" Gyles refers to was a practice among tribes who had lost members in battle with English militia-

men. Captives were placed in the center of a ring of dancing tribesmen, repeatedly taken out and roughed up by the dancers, and
thrown back into the center of the ring, again and again until they
were overwhelmed by exhaustion. Sometimes this abuse resulted
in their death. During the dance the tribespeople taunted their
captives with threats, Gyles says, chanting, "Shall we, who have lost
relations by the English, suffer an English voice to be heard among
us?" At other times they would order their prisoners to get up and
"sing and dance Indian." Gyles mentions he was scarcely able to
walk for several days after one of the dances. Nevertheless, though
some tribal villagers were entertained by the dances, others felt
compassion for the captives. Gyles tells how the younger tribal men
once came looking for him, to stand him with another captive at
the center of one of their dance rings. But his would-be persecu-
tors never found him, for John's "Indian master" tipped him off in
advance and showed him where to hide in a swamp until the young
warriors had gone.

The adolescent John Gyles lived as a captive among the Maliseets
of the St. John River area for six years before he was ransomed by a
Catholic priest named Father Simon. During his captivity Gyles
learned the northern Algonkian dialects, and when he returned
to Boston in 1698, the Massachusetts Governor and Council used
him as an interpreter four times between 1698 and 1726. A minority of young English captives became acculturated and never returned to English society. Silas and Timothy Rice of Westborough,
Massachusetts were taken captive in 1704, adopted into Iroquoian
society, and given the new names of Tookanowras and
Oughtsorongaughton. Oughtsorongaughton returned to
Westborough in 1740, thirty-six years after being taken from what
was then part of Marlborough, and visited his relations. He remem-
bered his capture clearly. Later in his life Oughtsorongaughton
became a chieftan in the Iroquois nation. He is one of fourteen
signatories who ratified the Treaty of Fort Stanwix in 1768, the treaty
which established new boundaries between the Six Nations of the
Iroquois and the English colonies.

Colonial captives of the Algonkians in both King Philip's War
and the early French and Indian Wars (King William's War, Queen
Anne's War and Lovewell's War) wrote narratives about their experiences. Some wanted to leave personal memoirs for their children,

212

and others, such as Mary Rowlandson and John Gyles, wrote as public testimony of their miraculous preservation through the sovereignty of God, to testify to "God's goodness" and "the infinite merits of Jesus Christ." These narratives contain some valuable observations on Algonkian tribal customs.

Gyles, who was an unadopted tribal servant in the Maliseet hunting and gathering society, records the northern Algonkian ceremony of calling for volunteers to attack the New England frontier towns. According to Gyles, the leader of an expedition held a feast of dog flesh, which they believed made them courageous, before he called for volunteers. During a certain part of the meal, he held up the decapitated dog's head with its bared teeth, and sang a war chant. The song often named the English frontier towns the leader planned to attack. When he finished singing, he pointed the dog's threatening snout at the tribesman who was invited to join him as his second in command. If the warrior accepted, he would take the dog's head in his hands and sing. To decline the invitation, a tribesman simply turned the snout of bared teeth towards another in the circle. The dog's head passed from one person to another, until the chief man had enlisted enough warriors for a strike.

When King William's War ended in 1697 the raids stopped along the frontier, but according to Samuel Penhallow, four years later the Abenaki again threatened the English. Governor Dudley of Massachusetts and other colonial officials, trying to avoid war, met with the Abenaki at Falmouth, Maine in June, 1703. Sachems from the Penobscot, Norridgewock, Pennacook and Pequaket assured the governor through their tribal orator Simmo, "that as high as the sun was above the earth, so far distant should their designs be of making the least breach between each other." Before the meeting ended the tribal leaders presented Dudley with a belt of wampum, and invited him to the two stone pillars called the "Two Brothers," which had been erected during an earlier treaty. As an affirmation of peace all those present that day placed a stone near the pillars.

But no sooner had the treaty been confirmed, when fighting flared up along the entire frontier, this time under the name of Queen Anne's War. Along the Massachusetts Bay frontier attacks were less severe, even though the war lasted two years longer than the previous conflict of King William's War. Nearly every "out town" suffered from renewed attacks. In 1704, an attack on Lancaster was foiled by the quick arrival of the militia. Colonists were waylaid at Marlborough, Groton and Dunstable. An attack on the Harnden family in Reading, Massachusetts momentarily brought the atmosphere of frontier warfare back into the hub of the Bay Colony. Four townspeople were killed in this raid, and the war party carried off several children, but the youngsters were recovered by a pursuing party of local residents. Warriors also attacked Amesbury and Kingston, New Hampshire, killing some livestock. Five English were also killed at Exeter, and Dover was attacked several times.

Across the Piscataqua River in Maine, all the frontier communities suffered bitterly. The town of Wells, which had stood its ground in the previous war, now lost thirty-nine people in a surprise attack. Five settlers were ambushed at Berwick, and nineteen died in neighboring Scarborough. Early in the war, warriors attacked York, shot several residents and took several captives. Kittery came under attack, and even the fort at Saco felt the northern Algonkian fury, where eleven men were killed and twenty-four taken captive. According to Penhallow, by 1705 French authorities had one hundred and seventeen captives, while their tribal allies were estimated to have another seventy.

One of the more devastating raids during Queen Anne's War occurred in 1704 on the Connecticut Valley frontier at Deerfield, Massachusetts. Forty-nine English townspeople were massacred and over one hundred were taken captive to Canada. The Deerfield attack was followed several months later by a raid on Northampton, where nineteen died and three were taken captive to Canada. In 1711, another band of warriors bypassed Northampton for Simsbury and Waterbury, Connecticut, where four settlers died. Because the northwestern settlements of Connecticut were more exposed to attack the colony deployed militias in the woods between the Housatonic River and Hartford. To further secure these towns the Connecticut General Court later passed an "Act for Better Securing our Frontiers Against the Skulking Indians." The act forbade all Connecticut tribesmen to hunt or travel "in the wilderness or woods, east of Ousatunnuck (Housatonic) River, westward of Connecticut River, southward of the Colony and Province of Massachusetts, northward of the road that goes thro' the towns of Farmington, Waterbury, New Milford, Danbury and Ridgefield, till further order; and that . . . whatever Indian be found within those limits without leave or order of the Governour and Council . . . will be reputed an enemy."

The outlying towns of Massachusetts continued to petition the governor and council with their familiar requests. A petition from Groton in 1704 concludes the residents were living like soldiers, and unless they received more assistance from the Massachusetts government, it would be impossible for them to maintain the town.

When the Peace of Utrecht brought a cessation to the conflict between England and France in 1713, the hostilities between their colonies in North America ended. On July 13, 1713, delegates from the Kennebec, Arosaguntacook, Norridgewock, Pennacook, Pequaket, Saco, Penobscot and Maliseet nations met with the English at Portsmouth, New Hampshire and signed a peace treaty. Under the terms of the agreement, the tribes were forbidden to come near any of the English settlements south of the Saco River. The sachems were also required to confess they had broken the treaty with the English that they signed in the presence of Governor Dudley in 1703.

The English, encouraged by the peace, resettled along the lower Kennebec Valley at Topsham, Augusta and Georgetown. However, the Abenaki tribesmen became enraged by settlers along the Eastern frontier who encroached northward. The Abenaki killed several herds of cattle. In August, 1717, the English and Abenaki tribes reaffirmed the treaty of 1713, but their agreement was short-lived, for by the summer of 1721 the Abenaki were threatening to destroy the English if they remained in the Kennebec Valley. When the settlers ignored the ultimatum, the Abenaki again attacked the New England frontier. The Massachusetts and New Hampshire colonies in response declared war on the Abenaki tribes in 1722. Commonly called Lovewell's War (1722-1726), to commemorate the bounty hunter Captain John Lovewell of Dunstable, this completely American conflict between the northern Algonkians and the New England colonists is also known as Dummer's War, because most of the war occurred during the Massachusetts governorship of William Dummer.

The Abenaki and their allies immediately attacked the towns on the Eastern frontier again, with deaths at Yarmouth, Scarborough and Berwick. Along the Massachusetts Bay frontier, warriors raided the western section of Amesbury, and killed two people at Dunstable. During the winter soldiers in the "out towns" were provided with snowshoes at the expense of the Massachusetts government. Tribal attacks, though less frequent in the winter, were still a possibility, and snowshoe companies were already organized in many frontier settlements. In Chelmsford, Captain Robert Richardson commanded a snowshoe company of thirty-nine men, who often scouted the woods along the lower Merrimac River in search of the "Indian enemy." In 1726, after fighting for about four years, the Abenaki tribes wearied of the renewed conflict, and made peace with the English at Falmouth, Maine. During the negotiations the Abenaki explained they had renewed the war because the English continued to encroach on their land, and were also responsible for the fatal beating of two Abenaki tribesmen. While the English denied the charge of encroachment, they did acknowledge that some of their people had murdered the two tribesmen.

These agonizing years of sporadic warfare caused the deaths of many frontier residents, but the effect on the Abenaki and Maliseet nations was even more disastrous. The English militias repeatedly made campaigns into the White Mountains and interior Maine to drive the northern Algonkian tribes from their strongholds. In Queen Anne's War, the colonials made several expeditions in the area of the Saco River. Colonel March led a company of soldiers on a campaign against the Pequaket people in 1704, where six tribesmen were killed, and others taken prisoner. Three years later, Colonel Hilton, along with two hundred and twenty soldiers, descended on some Algonkian encampments at Scarborough, killing over twenty warriors. Another colonial militia moved up the Saco River in 1711 and killed five tribesmen. Towards the close of Queen Anne's War (1703-1713), Colonel Walton and a company of soldiers ranged the area between Ossipee and Lake Winnipesaukee, but found only deserted wigwams, for these Algonkian groups had joined with stronger tribes in Maine.

The English also fought campaigns against the tribes in the Kennebec and Penobscot valleys. Captain Church commanded an expedition of five hundred and fifty men, fourteen transports and thirty-six whaleboats. Descending on Penobscot in 1704, the English and their "Praying Indian" allies killed and captured a large number of Frenchmen and Abenaki tribespeople, before they sailed east and burned most of the French coastal settlements between Passamaquoddy and the Minas Basin in the Bay of Fundy. In 1724, Captain Harmon and two hundred soldiers surprised the inhabitants of Norridgewock. The English forces massacred twenty-six Abenaki villagers and Father Ralle, who had established a Catholic mission among the Norridgewock people. The English then burned all the wigwams. After this massacre, most of the Norridgewocks fled to Quebec, where they resettled among the St. Francis Indians. At this time, the Norridgewock tribe numbered around one hundred and fifty people, of whom only twenty-nine were warriors. Colonial militias and scouting parties in quest of scalps attacked even such seemingly inaccessible tribes as the Coos (Cohas) and Pemigewasset. Six residents from Northampton, Massachusetts travelled up the Connecticut River to a fort at *Cowassuck* belonging to the Coos tribe, where they murdered seven tribesmen, six of whom they scalped. A fifty-man expedition to the upper Merrimac River in 1712 killed eight tribesmen and took a considerable amount of plunder. In 1720, Captain Baker led a scouting party of thirty-four men on a campaign against the Pemigewassets. Leaving Northampton, they went up the Connecticut River Valley and crossed over to the Baker River. They came upon a group of tribesmen whom they fired on, killing Waternummus, sachem of the Pemigewassets. With their leader dead, the remaining tribesmen tried to flee toward the river, but they were slaughtered by a pursuing party of Baker's men. Before leaving, Baker ordered his men to confiscate the tribespeoples' beaver skins and burn their wigwam.

Scalping was practiced by both sides in the frontier wars. By the time of Queen Anne's War, the French and their "Indian allies," along with the English, were scalping, often for bounty. Massachusetts and New Hampshire offered bounties for northern Algonkian scalps, which encouraged frontier militias to pursue the "Indian enemy" far into the North country. When Queen Anne's War began in 1703, New Hampshire paid upwards of forty pounds for every scalp. Three years later this amount was raised another ten pounds to volunteers acting independently from the colonial militias. The practice of offering bounties for scalps put an additional drain on the over burdened colonial treasuries. "The charge of the war was by this time so great," writes Samuel Penhallow, "that every

Indian we had killed or taken, cost the country at least a thousand pounds." However, colonial governments continued to offer bounties because they were an effective method of defeating the Abenaki and their tribal allies. By 1724, Connecticut offered fifty pounds for every scalp taken in defense of its northwestern towns, while New Hampshire paid up to one hundred pounds a scalp, to further encourage volunteers to defeat the tribes on the Eastern frontier.

One of the most persistent bounty hunters in the Bay Colony was Captain John Lovewell of Dunstable. Between 1724 and 1725 he led four campaigns into Pequaket country. On his fourth expedition he and forty-four men marched to Ossipee and built a small fort for their defense. The captain left eight men as guards while the rest scouted the forests forty miles northeast of Ossipee, near present-day Lovewell Pond. The men were ambushed near the pond by a Pequaket hunting party, who battled them for ten hours and then withdrew, having killed the Captain and most of his company. Even though the Pequakets were victorious that day, repeated expeditions by bounty hunters eventually forced the tribe to seek refuge in Canada. In less than two years the English had killed over thirty-five Pequaket warriors, including Paugus, sagamore of the Pequaket people.

By the summer of 1725, northern Algonkian raids along the frontier decreased, and colonial militias ranging northern New England found many abandoned wigwam villages. About the same time, Saquarexis and Nebine, two Abenaki men in the custody of the English, were released on parole, on the condition that they had liberty to visit their people. When they returned to the English they told them that "the Indians were generally disposed to a peace, for that the losses they met with, and the daily terror they were under, made their lives miserable." The English, following up on this report, sent Saquarexis and Nebine a second time to their tribes, who told them that the Abenaki wanted a peace with the English. New Hampshire chose Colonel Walton and Massachusetts selected Colonel Stoddard and Mr. Wainwright to act as commissioners. They were sent to St. George, Maine, to hear what the tribal leaders had to offer. The two sides worked out the preliminaries to an end of the hostilities, with the Penobscot nation as the guarantor for the other tribes, to see that their warriors would not molest anymore of the English "out towns."

After this initial conference, the colonial commissioners decided the remaining provisions of the treaty should be worked out at Boston. Two tribal leaders, Ahanquid and Sauguaaram, accompanied the English commissioners to Boston. Once the treaty provisions were established the two Abenaki representatives were returned to the Maine coast in an English vessel, and they promised that within forty days other tribal embassies would come in to work out a final decision on all issues. Nearly eighty days passed while the English waited for the others to come in from their seasonal encampments. In the meantime a band of warriors attacked Dover, killed three people and took one captive. They made other attacks at North Yarmouth and Damaris Cove. While some of the English were convinced the Abenaki were using the treaty process to buy themselves time to execute a worse design on the New England frontier towns, others conjectured that warriors from Canada were responsible for the recent attacks. Finally, in November, 1725, the other chieftans fulfilled the Penobscot promise by coming in to confirm the peace. This treaty placed the blame for the war on the Abenaki, even though their tribal leaders had pointed out that encroachment on their lands, and the murder of their fellow tribesmen led them to retaliate against the English. The treaty also stipulated that all captives on both sides were to be exchanged without price. And, in a final stipulation, the Penobscot nation agreed to take up arms with the English against any tribe that continued to jeopardize the security of the frontier towns. The final ratification ceremonies for this peace were scheduled for Falmouth in May, 1726. During the following year, disagreement over the ratification site delayed the ceremony until August, when the Penobscot sachem Wenemovet and some of his principal men signed the treaty on behalf of the Norridgewock, Wawenock, Arosaguntacook and the St. Francis Indians in Canada.

It is difficult to know how many casualities the Abenaki, Maliseet and Cape Sable Mic Mac tribes had during these years of fighting. According to Penhallow, an accurate estimate was impossible because the Algonkians customarily carried off their dead before retreating. Nonetheless, Penhallow says that one-third of the Abenaki population had died by 1726. Also, the tribal solidarity of such groups as the Norridgewock and Pequaket had been shattered. Warriors had fallen during the years of the early French and Indian Wars; others had succumbed to contagious viruses spread into their river valleys through the French and English. Captain Church mentions an outbreak of smallpox in Boston, while he was preparing for a second expedition against the Abenaki in 1690. Some of his men contracted smallpox as they returned from the Maine coast to Piscataqua later that same year. Two years later, a more serious smallpox epidemic "remarkable for great mortality" among the English, swept through the Piscataqua towns of Portsmouth and Greenland, New Hampshire.

Trade and military expeditions in North country soon carried outbreaks to the Abenaki and Maliseet peoples. About the same time the smallpox epidemic ravaged coastal New Hampshire, John Gyles, who was then in his fourth year of captivity along the St. John River, saw the immense devastation of these viral outbreaks among the northern Algonkian tribes. He writes:

> In the latter part of summer, or the beginning of autumn, the Indians were frequently frightened by the appearance of strange Indians, passing up and down this river in canoes, and about that time the next year died more than one hundred persons, old and young; all, or most of those who saw those strange Indians. The priest said it was a sort of plague. A person seeming in perfect health would bleed at the mouth and nose, turn blue in spots, and die in two or three hours. It was very tedious to me to remove from place to place this cold season. The Indians applied red ochre to my sores, (which had been occasioned by the affray before mentioned,) which by God's blessing cured me. This sickness being at the worse as winter came on, the Indians all scattered; and the blow was so great to them, that they did not settle or plant at their village while I was on the river, [St. John] and I know not whether they have to this day.

In 1726, Samuel Penhallow describes the twenty-three years of frontier warfare as "the sound of the trumpet, and the alarm of war" which had "prevented the growth of our eastern settlements." Now that northern Algonkian opposition had been shattered, the New England frontier began to expand again. As early as 1721, a section in northeastern Dunstable became Londonderry, New Hampshire; then in 1732, another section in the southwestern part consolidated into the community of Townsend, Massachusetts. In 1726, a group of Essex County residents gathered at Haverhill, where they drew up a petition asking the Massachusetts court for permission to settle in the Pennacook region of New Hampshire, an area that was claimed by both the Bay Colony and New Hampshire due to a boundary dispute. Three years later settlers from Massachusetts began to move into the upper Merrimac Valley. Massachusetts erected Fort Dummer in present-day Brattleboro, Vermont to protect its western settlements in the Connecticut Valley. Fort Dummer is generally accepted as the first permanent English settlement in Vermont. The fort encouraged colonial proprietors and their families to found the outposts of Paquoiag (Athol, Massachusetts) and Upper Ashuelot (Keene, New Hampshire) between 1732-1737. In the ensuing decades, settlers moved into present-day southeastern Vermont, where they founded the new frontier towns of Brattleboro, Dummerston, Halifax, Marlboro, Newfane, Putney, Rockingham, Townshend, Westminster and Wilmington. The frontier, slowed for sixty years, was again moving north and west into the interior.

The new towns being built in northern and interior New England replaced the earlier frontier communities as "out towns." When hostilities with the northern Algonkians broke out again in King George's War (1744-1748) and the French and Indian War (1754-1763), the new outposts faced the same threat of dangerous isolation and attack from the north. New Hampshire towns such as Keene, Walpole, Winchester and Hinsdale were raided by warriors out of Canada, and frontier residents were again killed or taken captive. Occasionally these war parties still slipped into the Bay Colony. The family of John Fitch was taken captive in 1746 from their garrison in that part of Lunenburg that became the town of Ashby, Massachusetts in 1767. About eighty warriors attacked their garrison house, killing two soldiers and taking the family of seven captive. English residents from the neighboring communities of Lunenburg, Groton and Lancaster quickly organized a pursuit party in response to the alarm of musket fire, and the sight of smoke from the burning garrison. They followed the tracks of the war party a short distance until they came across a piece of paper tied to a tree limb. It was a message from John Fitch, advising his Lunenburg neighbors not to pursue them, for his captors promised the Fitch family their lives would be spared if the rescuers gave up. The English stopped their pursuit, and the Fitch family survived the trek to Canada. After the war the Fitch family returned to the area, except for Mrs. Fitch, who enroute home died from the exhaustive ordeal.

One of the last campaigns the English carried out against the northern Algonkians was directed at the St. Francis Indians of Quebec. This Algonkian group had absorbed many displaced tribal people from northern New England during the French and Indian Wars. The English saw the St. Francis tribe as the source of continued Algonkian raids on the new "out towns." In September, 1759 Major Robert Rogers and about two hundred rangers were sent out from Crown Point, New York to reduce this tribe that lived on the St. Francis River. They arrived in the area after a twenty-one day march, and while the tribe was asleep the soldiers massacred thirty tribespeople in their wigwams and then burned the village. Major Roger's rangers rescued five English captives from the village, and lost eight men during the battle. Warriors from St. Francis pursued Roger's forces as they retreated toward Lake Memphremagog. Most of the scattered rangers would have perished in the wilderness, had supplies not been shipped up the Connecticut River from Fort Number Four at Charlestown, New Hampshire.

One of the last raids on the northern New England frontier towns by tribesmen out of Canada came during the American Revolutionary War (1775-1783). By this time the British controlled all of Canada, having defeated the French in 1763. To discourage the former Thirteen Colonies from succeeding in their revolt against the British Empire, tribes allied with the English Crown were used to ravage the American frontier towns. On October 16, 1780, three hundred Iroquoian warriors led by a British lieutenant named Richard Horton, attacked the American inhabitants of Royalton and Randolph, Vermont. Residents in the two towns suffered at least nine dead and twenty-six taken captive. The attackers burned twenty-one houses, sixteen barns, and slaughtered over 150 head of livestock. Colonel John House of Hanover, New Hampshire led an undisciplined American militia in pursuit of the warriors, but other than a brief skirmish with the warriors' rear guard, the British led force escaped to Canada. All the captives obtained their release within a year, excepting Adan Durkee, who died in a camp at Montreal.

The Abenaki, the last of the former seven Algonkian confederacies in New England, had been greatly weakened by being drawn into the protracted power struggle between the French and English. Between 1700-1710, the Abenaki tribes of the Penobscot and Passamaquoddy numbered about one hundred and fifty men, while other tribes "westward of Penobscot" had about three hundred warriors. Sixty years later the Penobscot tribe contained about one hundred men. In southern New England isolated tribes of the former Pequot, Narragansett, Wampanoag and Massachusett confederacies remained scattered from Cape Cod to Connecticut.

On Cape Cod, the Mashpee repeatedly registered complaints their property rights were being violated by their English neighbors, but they got little sympathy from Plymouth Colony in the years right after King Philip's War. In fact, the Plymouth Court passed a law in 1682 to further restrict the Mashpees seasonal movements. The remaining tribespeople in Plymouth Colony needed to have travel permits from their English overseers in order to move from one place to another. If a tribesman was found out of bounds he was either to be fined five shillings or publicly whipped. Between 1767 and 1802, the Mashpee numbered between two hundred and ninety and three hundred and eighty. Well into the 18th century many Mashpee people continued to live in traditional wigwams made from sedge.

Other tribal groups were situated in south coastal New England at Charlestown, Rhode Island, Montauk, Long Island, and in the Connecticut communities of Stonington, Groton, Lyme, Farmington, and New London. The combined Algonkian population of Connecticut and Rhode Island in 1774 was two thousand eight hundred and forty-five. Some of these tribespeople had intermarried with African American freemen, because the social isolation of both Native American and African American people from white society tended to bring the two groups together. According to a census taken in 1754, there were almost three thousand African American slaves in Massachusetts. Actually, the number of African Americans living in Massachusetts in 1754 was higher, for freemen were not counted in this particular census.

Between 1714 and 1715, the Mohegan people living in the township of New London, and the neighboring Niantics, lodged a complaint with the Connecticut government that the English encroached on their planting fields. The Mohegans complained that two Englishmen, Joseph Woolcot and Henry Hall, forcibly "set up a frame of an house within the lands of the Mohegan country . . . and they kept watch and ward with arms by the said house, and threatened the death of any that should oppose them." The Connecticut government, after hearing the report, granted a writ to the sheriff to arrest Woolcot and Hall. Soon afterwards, two Niantic men, Mazeen and Ombehunt, informed the Connecticut authorities that some Englishmen had deliberately intoxicated people from their village, in order to defraud them of three hundred acres of planting grounds which the English wanted to enclose as pasture for livestock. The Connecticut magistrates appointed overseers from Groton and New London to recover the fields, and to "take care that the whole three hundred acres aforesaid be kept in the best manner for the use of the said Indians in planting."

At the Quinnipiac reservation in New Haven, which formerly had been about twelve hundred acres supporting 200 tribespeople, the population continually dispersed to neighboring Connecticut towns. By the end of the 18th century most of the Quinnipiacs had left the reservation, and in 1773 Samuel Adam, a Quinnipiac who lived at Farmington, sold the last of the Quinnipiac planting fields. While some of the remaining tribes in south coastal New England dispersed to neighboring towns like the Quinnipiacs, others joined an Algonkian exodus to the Oneida nation in New York, lead by the famous Mohegan pastor, Samson Occom.

Chapter VI
"The Mohegan Lands Should Forever Belong To The Mohegan Indians"

During the 1730s and 1740s a religious revival called the Great Awakening swept across New England. To the Algonkian people in south coastal New England it seemed at first nothing more than "a strange concern among the white people." However, as time went on, local church pastors became inspired by the dynamic Congregational minister, Jonathan Edwards, and the Calvinist Methodist evangelist, the Reverend George Whitefield. There was a movement to revive Christian missions to the scattered tribes in southern New England. By the summer of 1739, several pastors in Connecticut were preaching the message of Christian salvation to the Pequot-Mohegans in the towns of Stonington, Groton and the tribal village of Mohegan.

A sixteen-year-old Mohegan youth named Samson Occom, influenced by the the Reverend James Davenport at Mohegan, decided to accept the Christian faith. Despite his lack of formal education, young Samson learned to read and write with the help of several English neighbors. It's not surprising that Samson's intense desire to read the Bible soon gained the attention of the Reverend Eleazar Wheelock, pastor of the Second Congregational Church in Lebanon, Connecticut. Samson's mother, Sarah Occom, sometimes attended Wheelock's church. In 1743, Wheelock invited Samson to come and live with his family at Lebanon. For the next four years Wheelock tutored Samson in reading, writing and theology, and afterwards he continued his studies under the guidance of Reverend Benjamin Pomeroy of Hebron, Connecticut. The latter part of his education was brief, however, due to a medical problem that periodically impaired Samson Occom's eyesight. His eye condition prevented him from pursuing a more intensive study of theology at Yale.

225

When he was about twenty-five years old he expressed a deep desire to become a Christian missionary among the Mohegan and neighboring Montauk and Shinecook tribes. He served as a schoolmaster and preacher at Montauk from 1749-1760. The village of Montauk, located on the outer end of Long Island, then had a tribal population of about one hundred and sixty. Here, in 1751, Occom married Mary Fowler, a Montauk tribeswomen, by whom he had ten children. As his missionary work at this village gradually became widely known, a group of pastors from Connecticut and Long Island arranged for Occom to become a beneficiary of the Society in Scotland for Propagating Christian Knowledge.

The organization provided Occom with only 180 pounds in support during his twelve years at Montauk, which in his diary he attributes to English discrimination against Native Americans. "Now you see what difference they made between me and other missionaries," Occom writes, "they gave me 180 pounds for twelve years service, which they gave for one year's service in another mission." However, lack of financial support did not diminish his desire to continue as a missionary at Montauk. By the first winter, about thirty Montauk children attended his school, where he taught them to read and write English.

Besides working as a schoolmaster, Occom led religious services four times a week: once at mid-week and three times each Sunday. At the services he expounded on the scriptures in the Mohegan language, and led the Montauk congregation in singing Christian hymns in Mohegan, some of which he had written. While he lived in the Montauk village Occom led a seminomadic life, moving his wigwam with the tribe to the planting grounds in spring, and to the more thickly wooded areas in winter. Even though the Montauk and Shinecook tribes attempted to pay Occom for his services as village schoolmaster, he still had to supplement his income by cultivating a garden, raising pigs, woodworking and using his skills as a bookbinder.

Occom is the first Native American known to have written for publication. His familiarity with the Montauk tribe led him to write "An Account of the Montauk Indians on Long Island," which was published posthumously in 1809. He also penned "Ten Indian Remedies from Manuscript Notes on Herbs and Roots," and composed such Christian hymns as "Now the Shades of Night are Gone" and

"Waked By the Gospel's Powerful Sound." His most widely read work is "A Sermon Preached at the Execution of Moses Paul" (1772). Paul was a Native American who while drunk murdered a white person in Bethany, Connecticut. He was tried and hung in New Haven, and Occom's sermon was delivered to the congregation and condemned man, as was customary. Occom impressed a distinctly personal stamp on the sermon for it is directed at three audiences: one message to the condemned man, another more placatory message to the whites, and still a third message to the Native Americans in the congregation. In the sermon he emphasizes the rational and spiritual equality of "Negroes, Indians, English, or of what nation soever." Apparently Occom knew himself to be a more effective preacher than most of his English contemporaries. In the preface to his published version of the sermon, Occom writes, "the sermons that are delivered every sabbath in general, are in a very high and lofty stile so that common people understand little of them. But I think they can't help understanding my talk; it is common, plain, every-day talk."

The Society for Propagating Christian Knowledge was impressed by Occom's dedication to his missionary work enough to consider him for a wider missionary undertaking among either the Cherokee or Oneida nations. On November 12, 1756, the society commissioners recommended that the Reverend Wheelock and the Reverend Pomeroy prepare Occom to be ordained as a minister, since he was reported "to be a person of virtuous life and useful as a preacher to the Indians." Three years later, Occom passed a series of written and oral examinations, and, on August 29, 1759, was appointed a Presbyterian preacher and missionary to the Native American community. For a time he remained at Montauk as teacher and preacher, but the New York Correspondents of the Scotch Missionary Society soon decided Occom was an ideal candidate to bring the gospel to the Oneida nation of New York.

In the autumn of 1760, Occom accepted the invitation from the Scotch Missionary Society to go to New York. He and his brother-in-law, David Fowler, with the financial support of both the missionary society and local congregations, set out on horseback for Oneida on June 10, 1761. The journey took them about a month, and much of that summer Occom and Fowler lived among the Oneida and preached the gospel. Before he returned to Connecticut, Occom received a wampum belt from the Oneida nation as a token of their new friendship. His two successive visits to Oneida between 1762-1763 further strengthened their relationship. At first Occom hoped to use Oneida as a mission station to reach the tribes further to the west, but warfare between the the British and the Ottawa tribe during Pontiac's Rebellion of 1764 temporarily frustrated his plans; he returned to Mohegan and resumed missionary work among the Pequot-Mohegan, Narragansett, Niantic and Montauk villages.

At this time the Mohegan people were involved in a major ongoing land dispute with the Connecticut Colony. The dispute contributed to a split in the tribe between opposing factions led by two competing claimants to the Mohegan sachemship. The legal case for the colony, which lasted sixty years in all, went back to September 28, 1640, when Sachem Uncas allegedly conveyed to the English his right to all tribal lands, but reserved "only for his own use, certain ground which was then planted, and in that kind improved by him." These were the tribe's planting and hunting grounds, which originally comprised over 20,000 acres. According to the English, Sachem Uncas confirmed the agreement by a conveyance of the tribe's lands to Major John Mason on August 15, 1659 making him trustee. Mason, who was friendly to the Mohegans and trusted by them, surrendered the lands to the Connecticut Colony on March 14, 1660, for reasons which the court summary of the 1763-1764 land dispute do not specify. In the lawsuit, the English also claimed that Uncas had empowered the Connecticut Court to use the Mohegan lands for new towns and plantations in a renewed covenant between the colony and the tribe in 1681. This agreement the English said was to hold perpetually, through the lifetimes of Uncas' "son, grandson, and their posterity, and all their people, and that it might remain inviolable forever."

But the Mohegans claimed the English had not been given access to any tribal lands in 1640, because Uncas had granted the Connecticut settlers only a right of preemption to Mohegan lands, which meant that in the event that he was defeated by his tribal enemies the English would have rights to it. The tribe maintained that John Mason as the legal trustee of the tribe had conferred this right of preemption to the Connecticut Colony in 1660 and had not in fact passed the lands to them. The right of preemption had been again reaffirmed by Uncas in 1681. The Mohegans held that both the Mason heirs and the colony were merely the trustees of the Mohegan tribe, and the Masons' role had been primarily to advise the tribe against unwise land sales.

The Connecticut Colony challenged the Mohegan assertion that the English were merely trustees, pointing out that Major Mason had returned a tract of Mohegan tribal lands to Sachem Uncas in 1671, which came to be known as the "sequestered lands," and if Mason had been simply a trustee, the colony argued, then he should have restored all the lands to the tribe. If on the other hand, the land belonged to Connecticut the colony said he had no authority to return any part of it to the Mohegans. The Mohegans in turn claimed that the aging Major Mason, who died in 1672, had feared that the tribe might have its right to the lands challenged after his death, and so had entailed the "sequestered lands" to the tribe.

After Mason's death, his two sons, Samuel and Daniel, contended against the colony for the trusteeship which they claimed had been conferred on them by Oweneco, Uncas' son. The Mohegans directly petitioned Queen Anne for the tribal lands through their advocate Nicholas Hallam, and the Queen issued a commission in July, 1704 to bring the "Mohegan Land Case" to trial in Connecticut. When the colony failed to appear before the commissioners out of protest, the commission delivered a decision in favor of the Mohegans stating:

> It is therefore considered and determined by the said Court of our said Lady the Queen, that the said Oweneco Uncas and the Mohegan Indians, shall be immediately put into possession of all their Planting Grounds lying between New London and Norwich, containing eight Miles in Length and four Miles in Breadth [upwards of 20,000 acres] the westerly End whereof lies upon Connecticut River; and also one other large Tract of Hunting Land, between the Bounds of Norwich and Haddam; and also that the said Oweneco and the Mohegan Indians, be restored to the Improvement of their Planting Ground, called Massapeage, within New London aforesaid; and also that the said Oweneco Uncas recover his just Cost and Charges.

In 1706, the Connecticut Colony successfully appealed to the Queen for a commission of review, which was to present its findings to Governor Cornbury and the New York Council. In the end, however, the colony again failed to appear before the commission on behalf of the landholders effected by the lawsuit.

Not content to let the issue go, in 1718 the General Court of Connecticut appointed commissioners to reexamine all claims within the "sequestered lands." Connecticut was a self-governing colony with its own corporate charter and it sought to circumvent the decision of the Queen's commission of 1704. After several years of deliberation the comissioners believed they had reached a final settlement after they granted the Mohegans about five thousand acres, of the 20,000 in question, and allowed the English claimants to take the remaining 15,000. According to the stipulations of this settlement,

> The said Eastern Part of the Mohegan Lands [5,000 acres] not then disposed by the Committee, they determined and concluded that the same should forever belong to the Mohegan Indians, from Time to Time, and from Generation to Generation, so long as there should be any of the Mohegan Indians found, or known alive; and when the whole Nation, or stock of said Indians were extinct, and none of them be found (and never before) the said Eastern Part, which was then settled upon the Indians, should forever belong to the Town of New London, as their full free and indefeazable Estate in Fee. And if the said Indians, and all of them, should be gone, and not known of, and supposed to be extinct, then the said Town might enter upon said Land, and improve the same; But if after such Entry, the said Nation did come, and should desire Entry into said Land, the same should be allowed them, and such Indian or Indians should hold said Land, as in and by this Settlement was expressed.

In 1723, the Connecticut Colony approved Captain Mason's grandson's request to reside among the Mohegan tribe as their trustee. Sixteen years passed before the Mason heirs attempted to overturn the decision of 1721. In 1737 they obtained a new commission which had its findings reviewed by the Colony and Council of New York and the Governor and Assistants of the Colony of Rhode Island. These two colonies decided against the Mohegans, but the verdict was soon set aside due to the commissioners' "irregularity in the mode of proceedings." A new commission involving the colonial councils of New York and New Jersey was convened in 1742, which reversed the decision on the Mohegan claim made thirty-eight years earlier during the reign of Queen Anne, and sided with the colony, and found the Mohegans were entitled only to the

5,000 acres. After such a lengthy dispute, the Connecticut Colony considered the Mason heirs to be agitators, and the Mohegan Land Controversy to be a major test case for all the colonies. In his "Summary of the Case of the Respondents the Landholders", William DeGrey writes, "this is the case not only of the Colony of Connecticut, who are in truth no ways interested in the contest, but of the 800 landholders, and not them only, but of all the landholders of America, who are liable upon the principle contended for by the Apellants, to be brought to England to defend themselves against pretended Indian titles." Over the next two decades the Masons did not attempt to appeal the decision of the last commission, and in the interim the Connecticut Colony had "long since erected townships and villages, to the extent of many miles" on the disputed 15,000 acres taken by the colony in 1721.

When Samson Occom returned to Mohegan village in 1764, the ✓ tribe was awaiting the decision on another appeal, wherein the Masons "applied to many of the respondents, the possessors of the land, offering to give them quitclaims for the trifling equivalent of a shilling an acre." Undoubtedly Occom realized that if the appeal went against the Mohegans their future in south coastal New England would be jeopardized. Occom openly criticized the claims of the Connecticut Colony, and had the Mohegans sign a petition addressed to King George III, in which the tribe listed "many complaints." In the letter to his Majesty Occom suggested that if the verdict was favorable to the Mohegans, the tribe wanted to be placed under the immediate protection of the English Crown. Furthermore, in exchange for this protection the Mohegans offered to surrender the lands in question to the King, promising to pay an annual quit rent to his Majesty and heirs.

The officials in the Connecticut colonial government labeled the Mohegans' petition to King George III the "Notable Bribe." Occom's English neighbors accused him of encouraging the Mohegan tribe to quarrel with the Connecticut Colony. In towns near the lands in question, just the mention of the Mason family or Occom aroused suspicion and anger. Occom as a member of the tribal council was involved out of concern for the tribe's future, but the Masons, the colonists believed, were involved in the lawsuit for their own personal gain. In a letter to Richard Jackson dated February 23, 1765, Thomas Fitch of Norwalk, Connecticut, accused the Masons of pretending to act for the Mohegans while " prosecuting their own avaritious and sinister views."

The Board of Missionary Correspondents in the Colony of Connecticut arranged a meeting with Occom at the house of Reverend Williams of Lebanon on March 12, 1765. The board members criticized Occom's involvement in the land dispute, even though, as a member of the Mohegan tribal council, he had every right to advise his people. Occom was forced, in effect, to choose between his missionary work and the concerns of the Mohegans, and so he chose to apologize for his participation in the "Mohegan Land Case," saying, "as a member of the Mohegan tribe and, for many years, one of their council, it was very imprudent in me, and offensive to the Public that I should so far engage as of late I have done, in the Mason Controversy [Mohegan Land Case]; which has injured my ministerial character, hurt my usefulness, and brought dishonor upon Mr. Wheelock's School [Moor's Indian Charity School] and the correspondents. For this imprudent, rash and offensive conduct of mine, I am heartily sorry and beg forgiveness of God — of this honorable Board of Correspondents, of whom I ought to have asked further advice - and of the Public; determining that I will not for the future act in that affair unless called thereto and obliged by lawful authority." We can only guess how difficult it was for Occom to apologize for views which he continued to hold. The event had a major impact on Occom, since from this time on his relations with the whites grows increasingly fractured.

Later in 1765, Occom accompanied the Reverend Whitaker of Norwich, Connecticut, on a speaking tour in the British Isles. The first Native American pastor to preach in England, Occom spent the next three years there, preaching over 300 sermons, and collecting about twelve thousand pounds for Native American missionary work. However, on his return to Connecticut Occom found he was still resented for his involvement in the ongoing "Mohegan Land Case," and despite his success at raising money in England for missionary work, some local ministers had chosen to distance themselves from him. The Mohegan preacher also felt that while he was away in England, Wheelock had neglected Occom's family, who had been entrusted to his care. The rift between the two men widened when Wheelock diverted Native American mission money collected in England to found Dartmouth College. Occom thought it fraudulent to use funds raised to educate Native Americans at Moor's Indian Charity School for the education of whites at Dartmouth. Disenchanted by this mistreatment, Occom believed he had been used by his colonial sponsors to raise money for their selfish designs. He became even further discouraged when the Boston Board, under whose jurisdiction he preached, refused to give him support. No doubt, this series of disappointments went far in reshaping Occom's later perspective that the Native American was a "despised creature" in Colonial America. When the final decision on the "Mohegan Land Case" upheld the claims of the Connecticut Colony it only reinforced his view. Occom writes: "The grand controversy which has subsisted between the Colony of Connecticut and the Mohegan Indians above seventy years, is finally decided in favor of the colony. I am afraid the poor Indians will never stand a good chance with the English in their land controversies, because they are very poor, they have no money. Money is almighty now-a-days, and the Indians have no learning, no cunning: the English have all."

It appears that Occom became persona non grata among the English. When the Sachem Ben Uncas died in the spring of 1769, Occom attended the funeral as missionary to the Mohegan tribe. His behavior at the funeral reveals his displeasure over the presence of William Hillhouse, who in the company of two other Englishmen, was sent to the tribal funeral by the governor of Connecticut. Hillhouse writes:

> We attended the Funeral of Benjamin Uncas, late sachem of Mohegan. The Reverend Mr. Jewett preached a sermon on the Creation to a large [company] of people, both English and Indians of Mohegans and neighboring tribes, who were assembled together. The tribes generally met [for the] oration, but before divine service was over, Sampson Occom withdrew and went off, and was soon followed by others of the tribe, so that for want of their help and assistance to carry the corpse . . . rendered it almost impossible to bury at their usual Burying place, at Norwich. Therefore, by and with the consent and agreement of the sachem's family, the remains was interred at Mohegan on their own land. The temper of a number of Indians is worked up, to the highest pitch of jealousy, and distrust of the government and also of any dependance on them, Either for advice, protection, regulation, [or] friendship. It seems Mr. Mason, and his party, are continually [plying] them, with their

secret negotiations, councils . . . but what their particular plans are, does not transpire. Its said that some petition is on [underfoot]. One thing more I beg leave to add, it is said that Sampsom Occom, . . . and a number of their leading men in their Councils, & Intrigues against the Government are not Mohegans, but only interlopers, introduced by marriage or some other ways.

Occom probably walked out of the funeral as a gesture of protest against the presence of the English, showing his displeasure at their hypocrisy in being there. In 1774, the English were still questioning Occom's right to call himself a Mohegan tribesman, even though his grandfather, Tomockham, and his father, Joshua Ockham, had been members of the Mohegan tribe. Both Joshua Ockham and his son Samson served as tribal councilors to the Mohegan sachem, Ben Uncas. Samson Occom's mother, Sarah, although not Mohegan, was a Pequot tribeswoman from Groton, Connecticut, and the Mohegans had been members of the Pequot confederacy when the English first settled in Pequot country.

After Ben Uncas' death a tribal faction at Mohegan blamed Occom for the tribe's deteriorating relations with the Connecticut Colony. John Tantaquidgeon, Noah Uncas, Moses Mazzeon, Abimelech Uncas and other Mohegan tribesmen, wrote a letter to the colonial government in 1774 describing Occom as a troublemaker who is "determined to have the ordering of all Indian concerns." His critics in the tribe said that he challenged the authority of the Connecticut General Court, saying, "let the Assembly do what they please, he will break it all to pieces in spite of them!"

Apparently Occom now considered picking up the missionary effort of ten years before in New York Colony, and leading the remaining Christianized tribes of south coastal New England to Oneida. Possibly he was inspired by the Biblical story of the Hebrews' exodus out of Egypt, to lead his people out of the aftermath of the land case in Connecticut. The immediate goal was to acquire better lands outside of the jurisdiction of the Connecticut Colony, but Occom also wanted to widen his missionary work to include the Oneidas. He believed the Six Nations of the Iroquois, which included the Oneida, would be more receptive to Christian missions if a Native American Christian community lived among them. On March 13, 1773, a general gathering of tribespeople from the seven "Indian towns" of Charlestown, Groton, Stonington,

Niantic, Farmington and Montauk met at Mohegan. They decided to send one representative from each of the seven towns to meet with the leaders of the Oneida nation. A rumor of impending war among the eastern Great Lakes tribes restricted travel, so that only two of the representatives, Joseph Johnson (Occom's son-in-law) and Elijah Wampy, met with the Oneidas at Johnson Hall, New York, on October 27, 1773. There the Oneidas promised a land gift of ten square miles to the seven "Indian towns."

In January, 1774, Joseph Johnson made another trip to Oneida, where tribal leaders promised an increase in acreage, and the Oneidas officially adopted the seven "Indian towns." That summer Occom travelled to Oneida country to strengthen relations with the tribe, and soon after the Oneida formally transferred the promised land gift to the seven "Indian towns."

The next spring, some of the younger men from the seven towns went to Oneida to build homes and clear land for planting, to prepare for the exodus to come. But the migration was interrupted by the American Revolutionary War (1775-1783). Because the Six Nations were caught up in the struggle between England and the American patriots, it was unsafe for the Connecticut tribesmen to remain at Oneida. They abandoned their new homes for the duration of the conflict. Once the war was ended, the exodus was underway again. In 1783, Occom accompanied an Algonkian tribal group from the seven towns as far as Albany, leaving others in the group to guide them the rest of the way to Oneida. He returned to Mohegan where he appealed to the remaining residents of the seven towns to move to Oneida. In the autumn of 1785 Occom set out again for Oneida, returning twice to Mohegan during the next four years, to convince tribespeople to move to Brothertown, the name the Connecticut tribespeople from the "Indian towns" gave to their new homeland in New York. In time, the New England tribes that settled at Oneida came to be known as the "Brothertown Indians." They chose Samson Occom to be their minister. For the next five years, Occom tirelessly served as preacher to the Brothertown congregation and as a circuit pastor to neighboring rural whites, who saw few ministers in upstate New York. It was at Brothertown in 1792, that this Moses from Mohegan died and was buried at the age of 69. The Bible text that was read at Occom's funeral was from Job 33:12-13, which reads "Behold, in this you are not right. I will answer you. God is greater than man. Why do you contend against him, saying, 'He will answer none of my words'?" Perhaps, the choice of this Bible text was a final word to his critics.

Toward the close of the American Revolution, the Oneidas widened their invitation to the New England tribes, and asked the Mahicans to join them on their lands in New York State. The Oneida and "Brothertown Indians" granted the Mahicans a six-square-mile tract of land, and Mahican families still living in Stockbridge, Massachusetts, moved to Oneida between 1783-1789, naming their new village New Stockbridge, in memory of their ancestral home in the Berkshires. The "Stockbridge Indians" remained among the Oneida and "Brothertown Indians" until the early 19th century, when they moved further west among the Miami tribe on the White River in present-day Indiana. After several more relocations they settled down in Shawano County, Wisconsin, where the United States government granted them a permanent tract of land in 1856. Today it is known as the Stockbridge-Munsee Reservation.

While the Brothertown and Stockbridge tribal groups moved west, others of the Pequot-Mohegan, Narragansett, Niantic, Mashpee and Abenaki chose to remain in their ancestral homeland of New England. In most cases, these tribal nations were reduced to poverty, and often faced intolerance and isolation from their white neighbors. The United States began to grant citizenship to Native Americans in 1887, but it was another thirty-seven years before citizenship was conferred on all "United States born" Native Americans. Before this, denied the right to vote, they were a voiceless minority and apparently somewhat of an oddity to their "American" neighbors. Lucy Larcom, a textile worker of European ancestry in early 19th century Lowell, recalled the Penobscots' summertime visits to her area. "Sometime every summer," she writes condescendingly, "a fleet of canoes would glide noiselessly up the river, and a company of Penobscot Indians would land at a green point almost in sight from our windows. Their strange endeavors to combine civilization with savagery were a great source of amusement to us; men and women clad alike in loose gowns, stove-pipe hats, and moccasons; grotesque relics of aboriginal forest-life. The sight of these uncouth looking red men made the romance fade entirely out of the Indian stories we had heard. Still their wigwam camp was a show we would not willingly have missed."

Appendix: 1
Table Of Algonkian Confederated Tribal Nations

Abenaki
Arosaguntacook, Casco, Kennebec, Norridgewock, Ossipee, Passamaquoddy, Pejepscot, Penobscot, Pequaket, Saco, Wawenock

Massachusett
Agawam (Springfield, Ma.), Nahant, Nashoba, Nashua, Neponset, Norwottuck, Pocumtuck, Punkapoag, Quabaug, Saugus, Shawmut, Wachusett, Wessagusset, Winnisemit

Narragansett
Cowweset, Eastern Niantic, Manisses, Montauk, Pawtuxet, Shawomet, Wabaquasset, Wunnashowatuckoog

Pennacook
Agawam (Ipswich, Ma.), Agamenticus, Cocheco, Coos, Nameskeag, Nashua, Naticook, Naumkeag, Newichewannock, Ossipee, Pawtucket, Pemigewasset, Pentucket, Pequaket, Piscataqua, Saco, Souhegan, Squawkheag (Sokoki), Wamesit, Winnipesaukee

Pequot
Mohegan, Montauk, Podunck, Quinebaug, Quinnipiac, Shinecook, Tunxis, Wangunk, Western Niantic, Wunnashowatuckoog, Wusquowhannanawkit

Pocumtuck
Agawam (Springfield, Ma.), Norwottuck, Podunck, Squawkheag, Tunxis, Wangunk

Wampanoag
Capawick, Manamet, Mashpee, Matachee, Monomoy, Munponset, Nauset, Nemasket, Nobsquasset, Patuxet, Pocasset, Pokanoket, Sakonnet, Shawmut, Tommokomoth

Appendix: 2
Glossary Of Tribal Names

Most of the information in this Algonkian glossary of tribal names was compiled from John C. Huden's *Indian Place Names of New England,* (Museum of the American Indian, Heye Foundation,1962). Huden's book is presently the most reliable source on the meaning of Algonkian tribal and place names in New England. An equally noteworthy source is Fannie H. Eckstorm's, *Indian Place Names of the Penobscot Valley and Maine Coast,* (University of Maine at Orono, Maine, 1974).

Abenaki: A northern Algonkian tribal confederation situated in the Kennebec and Penobscot river valleys. The name translates "dawn people," or "easterners."

Agawam: This name was given to two different tribes, one in present-day Ipswich and one in Springfield, Massachusetts. The word means "lowland" or "overflowed by water."

Capawick: One of the two Algonkian names for present-day Martha's Vineyard, the other being *Nope.* Capawick means "enclosed harbor" or "place of refuge."

Casco: A shortened version of the Abenaki word *aucocisco.* It may refer to the *kasqu* or "blue heron."

Cocheco: A tribal name associated with both the Piscataqua and Newichewannock people of coastal New Hampshire. The word translates "place of the rapid current."

Coos: The name of this Abenaki tribe is preserved in the place name of Coos County, New Hampshire. The word translates "place of the pine trees."

Cowweset: A member tribe of the Narragansett confederation. The name translates "at the pine tree place."

Kennebec: An Abenaki tribe that lived in the lower Kennebec Valley. "Kennebec" means "long level water without rapids" or "long quiet water."

Mahican: An Algonkian confederation situated in the Hudson River Valley and western New England. The name means "wolf people."

Maliseet: Sometimes spelled "Malecite," the word means "broken talkers" or "barely understandable speech." The tribal name was given to them by their neighbors the Mic Mac, who spoke a different Algonkian dialect, and therefore had difficulty understanding the Maliseet.

Manamet: A small tribe that participated in the Wampanoag confederation. The word means "where they carry burdens upon their backs" or "a place of portage."

Mashpee: The name of a Wampanoag tribe living on Cape Cod. Mashpee translates "land near the great cove or pond."

Massachusett: An Algonkian tribal confederation centered along the shores of Massachusetts Bay. The name translates "at the great hill place," a reference to the nearby Blue Hills.

Mic Mac: This tribal nation is generally associated with their homeland of Nova Scotia, but during the late 16th and early 17th centuries they expanded into eastern Maine. The Mic Mac fought sporadic wars with the coastal tribes of eastern New England. Their name means "allies."

Missiasik: An Abenaki tribe that lives at the northern end of Lake Champlain in Vermont and Quebec. Their tribal name translates as either "grassy meadow" or "at the flint."

Mohegan: A tribe situated in eastern Connecticut. "Mohegan" is similar in both sound and meaning to the word "Mahican," another tribe, and refers to the wolf.

Monomoy: A tribal group that lived on outer Cape Cod. The Algonkian word signifies "deep black" or "mire."

Montauk: A tribe that lived on outer Long Island. The name means "at the fort" or " fort place high land."

Nameskeag: The name of a Pennacook tribe that lived in the area of present-day Manchester, New Hampshire. "Nameskeag" and its anglicized version, "Amoskeag," translate "fishing place."

Narragansett: An Algonkian tribal confederation centered along the western shore of Narragansett Bay in present-day Rhode Island. The name means "at the small narrow point."

Nashoba: A small tribe that lived in the areas of present-day Concord and Littleton, Massachusetts. The tribal name translates "between the waters or rivers," which may refer to their hunting and planting grounds between the Concord and Nashua rivers.

Nashua: A Nipmuck tribe that participated in the Pennacook confederation. Their main village was called Washacum and was located on the Nashua River in present-day Sterling, Massachusetts. The tribal name translates "where the river divides."

Naticook: A tribe that lived near present-day Merrimack, New Hampshire. The name means "at the place where the river flows downward." The Naticooks were part of the Pennacook confederation.

Naumkeag: The tribal people living at present-day Salem, Massachusetts gave this name to the harbor area. The word means either "fishing place" or "eel place."

Nauset: A Wampanoag tribe that lived on outer Cape Cod. The name means "at the place between," which refers to their location between Cape Cod Bay and the Atlantic Ocean.

Nemasket: Like the Algonkian words "Nameskeag" and "Naumkeag," the word "Nemasket" translates as "fishing place." The Nemasket people fished at Assawompsett Pond in present-day Middleboro, Massachusetts.

Neponset: The name of a tribe and river in present-day Massachusetts. The word is derived from the Algonkian *nepun* meaning "early summer."

Newichewannock: One of the two tribes belonging to the Cocheco people, who lived in the Piscataqua River area of present-day New Hampshire. The name translates "at the place between two strong currents."

Niantic: The tribal allegiance of this people was split between the Narragansetts and the Pequots. The name means "point of land on the tidal estuary."

Nipmuck: A group of inland tribes that were originally centered in present-day Worcester County, Massachusetts. The name translates "people of the fresh water places."

Nobsquasset: This Wampanoag tribe lived on Cape Cod. The name means "at the rock ledge cliff."

Norridgewock: An Abenaki tribe that lived along the upper Kennebec River. The name means "where the swift water descends."

Norwottuck: This tribe lived along the Connecticut River in present-day Massachusetts. The name translates "far from us." As members of the Massachusett confederation, they were a great distance from the center of the confederation which was at Massachusetts Bay.

Ossipee: A tribe closely associated with the Pennacook and Saco nations. The name is probably an anglicized version of *Coossipee* meaning "pine tree water place." Another meaning sometimes given is "water on the other side."

Passamaquoddy: The St. Croix River area of eastern Maine is the ancestral homeland of this tribe, which are for the most part a coastal people. The name translates "place of abundance of pollock."

Patuxet: The Algonkian tribesman Squanto, who befriended the Plymouth colonists, was a member of this tribe. The Patuxet had hunting and planting grounds in the area of present-day Plymouth, Massachusetts. The tribal name translates "at the little falls."

Paugasset: A member tribe in the Wappinger confederation of present-day western Connecticut. The name means "where the river widens."

Pawtucket: One of two Pennacook tribal seats along the lower Merrimac River at present-day Lowell, Massachusetts. The name means "at the falls in the river." Pawtucket was a popular fishing place for the Pennacook people.

Pawtuxet: A member tribe of the Narragansett nation. The tribal name is similar to the words "Patuxet" and "Pawtucket," which translate "at the falls." Socanoket was the sagamore of the Pawtuxet tribe.

Pejepscot: A coastal Abenaki village that was in the lower Kennebec Valley. These people may have belonged to the Wawenock tribe. The name means "extended long rapids."

Pemigewasset: The name of a tribe and river in present-day New Hampshire, the word translates as "extensive rapids."

Pennacook: One of the two Abenaki tribal confederacies of northern New England, the name means "at the foot hills," or "at the bottom of the hills." The name refers to the Pennacooks' hilly ancestral lands of present-day southern New Hampshire.

Penobscot: The name of an Abenaki tribe in Maine, the word means "at the descending rocks," or "at the extended ledges."

Pentucket: A tribe that lived along the lower Merrimac River near present-day Haverhill, Massachusetts. The name translates "at the twisting river."

Pequaket: An Abenaki tribe associated with the Pennacook confederation of present-day New Hampshire. The word means "broken land."

Pequannock: A tribe situated in present-day southwestern Connecticut, the word means "battlefield" or "slaughter place."

Pequot: A powerful tribal confederation centered along the Mystic River in present-day eastern Connecticut. The word translates "destroyers."

Pocasset: A member of the Wampanoag nation. The name is similar to the word "Paugasset," which means "where the stream widens."

Pocumtuck: An Algonkian confederation that occupied the Connecticut Valley in present-day Massachusetts. The word refers to "a narrow swift current" in this river.

Podunk: The Dutch called these people the "Nawaas." They lived along the lower Connecticut River south of present-day Hartford. The tribal name means "where you sink in mire."

Pokanoket: The ancestral homeland of the Wampanoag sachem Massasoit. The name translates "at or near the cleared lands."

Punkapoag: A tribe that lived in present-day eastern Massachusetts. The word means "shallow fresh water pond."

Quabaug: A Nipmuck tribe that lived in the area of present day Brookfield, Massachusetts. The name is derived from *m'squ boag* meaning "red pond." It probably refers to a spawning area for salmon, which the Algonkians called "red fish."

Quinebaug: A Nipmuck tribe that formerly occupied the area of present-day northeastern Connecticut. The name means "long pond."

Quinnipiac: A tribe that lived near present-day New Haven, Connecticut. Their name comes from the Algonkian word *quinnuppinuk* or "where we change our route."

Saco: An Abenaki tribe that lived along the Saco River in southern Maine. The tribal name means "flowing out" or "outlet," and refers to the mouth of the Saco River.

Sakonnet: A Wampanoag tribe that lived along the western shore of present-day Buzzard's Bay. In Algonkian the name means "abode of the black goose."

Saugus: A Massachusett tribe that lived near present-day Saugus, Massachusetts. Like the Algonkian word "Saco," this name also translates "outlet."

Shawmut: A Massachusett tribe that participated in the Wampanoag confederation, the Shawmuts lived where the city of Boston stands today. Their name means either "he goes there by water," "at the neck," or, possibly a "spring of water."

Sokoki: An Abenaki name for a tribe that lived southwest of the Penobscot and Kennebec. "Sokoki" is derived from the Abenaki *Sokoakiak* a person from the "south country."

Souhegan: A Sokoki tribe that lived in the Monadnock region of present-day southwestern New Hampshire. "Souhegan" means "southwest," or is possibly an anglicized version of the tribal name Squawkheag. According to the Reverend John Eliot, many of the Souhegans gathered at Pawtucket during the annual fishing season.

Squawkheag: A Sokoki village near present-day Northfield Massachusetts. The name means "watching to spear fish."

Tommokomoth: A Wampanoag tribe that resided on Nantucket. The allegiance of these people was divided between several sagamores on the island. The anglicized tribal name is derived from the Algonkian word "Tetaukimmo."

Tunxis: A tribe that lived near present-day Hartford, Connecticut. *Tunxis* which is also pronounced *Tunxis sepos,* means "fast flowing little stream."

Wabaquasset: A Nipmuck tribe that belonged to the Narragansett confederation. The name signifies "at the place where we make mats for house coverings."

Wachusett: Probably members of the Nashua tribe. The place name translates "hill" or "little hill place."

Wamesit: A Pennacook tribe that had their village at the point where the Concord River flows into the Merrimac. The name means "there is room for all."

Wampanoag: An Algonkian confederation made up of tribes in present-day southeastern Massachusetts. The name means "people of the dawn," "eastlanders," or possibly, "people of the wampum."

Wappinger: A tribal confederation that lived in present-day western Connecticut. The name is derived from the Munsee word *wapink* the opossum.

Wawenock: An Abenaki tribe that lived along the Maine coast just east of the lower Kennebec River. The name means "bay country" or "inlet country."

Wessagusset: This Massachusett tribe lived near present-day Weymouth, Massachusetts. The name has several possible translations: "at the small salt water cove;" "outlet;" and "place at the edge of the rocks."

Winnisemit: A Massachusett tribe that lived in the area of the present-day cities of Everett and Malden, Massachusetts. Winnisemit translates "fine spring."

Wunnashowatuckoog: A Nipmuck tribe that lived along the Blackstone River of present-day Massachusetts and Rhode Island. At different times this tribe belonged to both the Pequot and Narragansett confederations. The tribal name means "where the river forks" or "where the river splits."

Wusquowhannanawkit: A Nipmuck tribe that lived where today converge the state boundaries of Massachusett, Rhode Island and Connecticut. According to Roger Williams, this tribe participated in the Pequot confederation. The tribal name comes from the Algonkian word *wuskowhannanaukit,* which translates "pigeon countries." Apparently, they lived in an area that was frequented by flocks of passenger pigeons, and the bird was probably a tribal totem.

244

Notes

Chapter 1: The People

1. As early as 9000 B.C.: William Fowler, "Ceremonial and Domestic Products," in *Bulletin of the Massachusetts Archaeological Society* (Bronson Museum Attleboro, Massachusetts), Vol. 27, pp. 43-45.

1. The Late Archaic culture: Richard W. Wilkie and Jack Tager, *Historical Atlas of Massachusetts*, (The University of Massachusetts Press, Amherst, Massachusetts, 1991), I, pp.10-11.

2. According to the colonial: William Wood, *New Englands Prospect*, (Burt Franklin, New York, New York, reprint of 1967), I, p. 63.

3. Situated roughly east of the: Alfred A. Cave, "The Pequot Invasion of Southern New England: A Reassessment of the Evidence" in *The New England Quarterly*, (The New England Quarterly, Inc., Boston, Massachusetts, 1989), Vol. 62, No. 1, pp. 27-44.

3. In his *Historical Collections*: Daniel Gookin, "Historical Collections of the Indians in New England," in *Massachusetts Historical Collections*, (Johnson Reprint Corporation, New York, New York, reprint of 1968), I, p. 147.

4. These people and their Western: Benjamin Trumbull, *A Complete History of Connecticut*, (Arno Press, New York, New York, 1972), III, pp. 39-43.

4. Concerning this nation Gookin: Daniel Gookin, "Historical Collections of the Indians in New England, in *Massachusetts Historical Collections*, (Johnson Reprint Corporation, New York, New York, reprint of 1968), I, pp. 147.

5. During his stay his men: David B. Quinn, ed. *North American Discovery Circa 1000-1612*, (University of South Carolina Press, Columbia, South Carolina, 1971), IV, pp. 64-69.

5. According to William Wood: William Wood, *New Englands Prospect*, (Burt Franklin, New York, New York, reprint of 1967), III, p. 69

5. With their large stores: Gookin, "Historical Collections of the Indians in New England," in *Massachusetts Historical Collections, I, p. 152.*

5. A stipulation of the treaty: William Bradford, *Of Plymouth Plantation*, ed. S.E. Morison (Printed by Alfred A. Knopf, 1976), XII, p. 437.

7. Nauset sagamores held leadership: Charles Willoughby, *Antiquities of the New England Indians with Notes on the Ancient Cultures of the Adjacent Territory*, (Published by AMS Press Inc., New York, New York for Peabody Museum of Archaeology and Ethnology, Harvard University, Cambridge, Massachusetts, 1973), pp. 277-278.

7. Also, under the Wampanoags': Gookin, "Historical Collections of the Indians in New England" in *Massachusetts Historical Collections*, I, p. 148.

9. One of their favorite haunts: George Tilton, *History of Rehoboth, Massachusetts*, (Published by Author, 1918), II, p. 62.

9. On *Nauticon* or Nantucket: The original pronunciation of Nantucket in the Wampanoag dialect was *Nauticon*, which means "far out in the water." See Paul Whitten, "Nantuckets Last Indian," in the *Yankee Magazine*, (Yankee, Dublin, New Hampshire), November, 1961 edition, p. 148

10. Gookin claims that the Wampanoags: Gookin, "Historical Collections of the Indians in New England" in *Massachusetts Historical Collections*, I, p. 148.

10. Some of the older men: Daniel Gookin, "Historical Collections of the Indians of New England," in *Massachusetts Historical Collections*, (Johnson Reprint Corporation, New York, reprint of 1968), I, p. 148.

11. Among the more noteable: Samuel Drake, *The Book of the Indians*, (Antiquarian Bookstore, 56 Cornhill, Boston, Massachusetts, 1841), III, pp. 42-53.

13. One tribal seat, located: Daniel Gookin, "Historical Collections of the Indians in New England," in *Massachusetts Historical Collections*, (Johnson Reprint Corporation, New York, New York, 1968), I. p. 186.

13. With their famous sachem: Eva Speare, *Indians of New Hampshire*, (Courier Printing Company, Littleton, New Hampshire).

15. Even though tribal representation: Bruce G. Trigger, ed. *Handbook of North American Indians*, 15 vols. (Smithsonian Institution, Washington, D.C., 1978), Vol. 15, pp. 148-159.

15. According to William Wood: Wood, *New Englands Prospect*, II, p. 67.

16. Samuel de Champlain reported: W.L. Grant, *Voyages of Samuel De Champlain*, (Barnes and Noble Inc., New York, New York, reprint of 1967), II, p. 151.

16. In 1664, the Mohawks sent: Allen W. Trelease, *Indian Affairs in Colonial New York: The Seventeenth Century*, (Kennikat Press, Port Washington, New York, 1960), V, pp. 128-130.

16. Alternately it may signify: Eva Speare, *Indians of New Hampshire*, (Courier Printing Company, Littleton, New Hampshire), IV, p. 20, X, p. 51.

16. However, the center of the Abenaki: Bruce G. Trigger, *Handbook of North American Indians*, 15 vols. (Smithsonian Institution, Washington, D.C., 1978), Vol. 15, pp. 137-147.

17. This tribe, like the other northern: James Sullivan, "History of the Penobscot Indians" in *Massachusetts Historical Collections*, (Johnson Reprint Corporation, New York, New York, reprint of 1968), IX, pp. 207-210.

17. The fact that an Abenaki: William Teg, *Almuchicoitt*, (The Christopher Publishing House, Boston, Massachusetts, 1950), II, pp. 46-66.

18. The majority of the Abenaki: James Sullivan, *History of the District of Maine*, (I. Thomas and E.T. Andrews, Boston, Massachusetts, 1795), V, p. 97.

18. Further back in Vermont: John C. Huden, *Archaeology in Vermont*, (Charles E. Tuttle Company, Rutland, Vermont, 1971), pp. 41-43.

18. Abenaki tribes in the White: Eva Speare, *Indians of New Hampshire*, X, p. 51.

18. No doubt this name: Robert E. Cahill, *New England's Mountain Madness*, (Chandler-Smith Publishing House, Inc., Peabody, Massachusetts, 1989), pp. 3-10.

18. According to the late 18th: Sullivan, *History of the District of Maine*, IV, p. 75.

20. Before the plague thinned: Rose A. Palmer, *The North American Indians*, ed. Charles G. Abbot (Smithsonian Institution Series, Inc., New York, New York, 1929), IX, p. 296.

21. Captain John Josselyn, who was: John Josselyn, *An Account of Two Voyages to New England During the Years 1638, 1663*, (Boston: William Veazie, 1865), pp. 106-108.

23. Springtime usually brought war: Rose A. Palmer, *The North American Indians*, ed. Charles G. Abbot (Smithsonian Institution Series, Inc., New York, New York, 1929), IV, p. 99.

23. Concerning the nature of: Gookin, "Historical Collections of the Indians in New England" in *Massachusetts Historical Collections*, I, p. 162.

24. According to William Wood's: William Wood, *New Englands Prospect*, I, p. 66.

24. Mohawk warriors taken prisoner: Josselyn, *An Account of Two Voyages to New England, Made During the Years 1638, 1663*, p. 114.

24. Wood also relates a story: Wood, *New Englands Prospect*, I, p. 66.

24. Another battle related to: Mary A. Proctor, *The Indians of the Winnipesaukee and Pemigewasset Valleys*, (Towne and Robie Publishers, Franklin, New Hampshire, 1930), II, pp. 18-19.

26. For instance, when the Mohegans: David Pulsifer, *Records of the Colony of New Plymouth*, (Boston: From the Press of William White, 1859), I, pp. 10-11.

26. Again, in 1657, the Narragansetts: Nathaniel B. Shurtleff, *Records of Massachusetts*, 5 vols. (Press of William White, Boston, Massachusetts, 1853), IV, pp. 436-437.

26. This tribal name reflects: William Hubbard, *History of the Indian Wars in New England*, 2 vols. (Kraus Reprint Company, New York, New York, 1969), I, p. 37.

27. Gookin, who was familiar with: Gookin, "Historical Collections of the Indians in New England" in *Massachusetts Historical Collections*, I, p. 193.

27. A semblance of the one-time: Gookin, "Historical Collections of the Indians in New England" in *Massachusetts Historical Collections*, I, pp. 192-193.

28. The Reverend Fiske, in his: Nathan Fiske, "An Historical Account of the Settlement of Brookfield" in *Massachusetts Historical Collections*, (Johnson Reprint Corporation, New York, New York, reprint of 1968), I, p. 259.

28. Whether the Nipmucks were a: Willoughby, *Antiquities of the New England Indians with Notes on the Ancient Cultures of the Adjacent Territory*, IV, p. 277.

28. Another tribal group that: "Summary of the Case of the Respondents the Landholders, in the Mohegan Case vs. Governor and Colony of Connecticut and Others" in *Connecticut Archives,* Vol. II.

28. Contrary to popular belief: Hubbard, *History of the Indian Wars in New England,* II, p. 38.

29. The English-Mohegan friendship: Francis M. Caulkins, *History of Norwich, Connecticut,* (Published by Author at the Press of Case, Lockwood and Company, Hartford, Connecticut, 1866), II,pp. 29-30.

29. However, studies in comparative: Alfred A. Cave, "The Pequot Invasion of Southern New England: A Reassessment of the Evidence" in *The New England Quarterly,* LXII, No. 1, pp. 27-44.

29. The far ranging Mahican: Reginald P. Bolton, *Indian Life of Long Ago in the City of New York,* (Crown Publishers Inc., New York, New York), I, p. 7.

30. After their arrival at the Hudson: Bruce G. Trigger, ed. *Handbook of North American Indians,* 15 vols. Smithsonian Institution, Washington, D.C., 1978), Vol. 15, pp. 198-212.

30. Other local tribes closely: Chard P. Smith, *The Housatonic,* (Rinehart and Company, New York, New York), pp. 39-41.

30. The Mahicans moved: R.A. Douglas-Lithgow, *Dictionary of American Indian Place and Proper Names in New England,* (The Salem Press Company, Salem, Massachusetts, 1909), p. 380.

30. When the Dutch arrived in: E.B. O'Callaghan, ed. *Documents Relative to the Colonial History of the State of New York,* 15 vols. (Weed, Parsons and Company, Printers, Albany, New York, 1854), II, p. 80.

30. Before the Dutch arrived: Bolton, *Indian Life of Long Ago in the City of New York,* XXXV, pp. 130-156.

30. Mohawk depredations may have: Bolton, *Indian Life of Long Ago in the City of New York,* V, pp. 26-28.

31. Though very similar from Maine: Willoughby, *Antiquities of the New England Indians with Notes on the Ancient Cultures of the Adjacent Territory,* IV, p. 276.

32. Roger Williams states that: Roger Williams, *A Key into the Language of America,* (Wayne State University Press, Detroit, Michigan, 1973), VI, pp. 127-128.

32. According to Thomas Lechford: Thomas Lechford, *Plain Dealing or News from New England,* (Johnson Reprint Corporation, New York, New York, reprint of 1969), IX, p. 49.

33. Using colonial sources, the: Bruce G. Trigger, ed. *Handbook of North American Indians,* 15 vols. (Smithsonian Institution, Washington, D.C., 1978), Vol. 15, p. 169.

33. According to more recent: Francis Jennings, *The Invasion of America,* W.W. Norton and Company Inc., New York, New York, 1976), II, p. 31.

33. The Reverend Stephen Badger, who: Stephen Badger, "Mr. Badger's Letter Concerning the Indians of Natick" in *Massachusetts Historical Collections,* (Johnson Reprint Corporation, New York, New York, reprint iof 1968), V, pp. 39-40.

33. According to the 19th century: Arthur L. Eno, *Cotton was King: A History of Lowell, Massachusetts,* (New Hampshire Publishing Company in collaboration with the Lowell Historical Society, 1976), I, p. 8.

Chapter 2: Rooted Like The Basket Trees

35. William Wood describes the Massachusett: William Wood, *New Englands Prospect,* (Burt Franklin, New York, New York, reprint of 1967), IV, p. 70. William Wood immigrated to New England in 1629, settling near Boston. Four years later he returned to England, and in 1634 his book *New Englands Prospect* was entered in the Stationer's Register in London. The author returned to New England in 1635 settling in Sandwich on Cape Cod, where he died in 1639. Wood's book is an accurate and lively description of New England's flora and fauna. Some twenty chapters are devoted to his observations of the Algonkian tribes living near Massachusetts Bay.

35. William Bradford of Plymouth Colony: Alexander Young, ed. *Chronicles of the Pilgrim Fathers of the Colony of Plymouth,* (DaCapo Press, New York, New York, reprint of 1971), XXIII, pp. 355-356. Commonly referred to as *Mourt's Relation,* William Bradford is believed to have written the first section that describes the Pilgrims' arrival and settlement of Plymouth. Edward Winslow contributed to *Mourt's Relation,* and also authored *Good Newes from New England* in 1624. Both Plymouth authors provide fascinating descriptions of the Wampanoag people.

36. William Wood experienced their: Wood, *New Englands Prospect*, VII, p. 77.

37. Such beneficial gifts the: Young, *Chronicles of the Pilgrim Fathers of the Colony of Plymouth*, XXIII, pp. 355-356.

37. In the Narragansett account: Roger Williams, *A Key into the Language of America*, (Wayne State. University Press, Detroit, Michigan, 1973), XXI, p. 197. Roger Williams was born around 1603 in London, the third of four children belonging to James and Alice Williams. Roger Williams received his B.A. in 1627, and he and his wife Mary sailed for America on the "Lyon" in 1630. For a time he served as assistant to the Reverend Skelton of Salem, Massachusetts, but his criticism of Massachusetts religious and civil authority eventually led to his removal to Plymouth Colony between 1631-1633. William's support of separation of church and state, and his assertion that the English had no right to dispose of tribal lands merely because the Algonkian people were not christian, finally led to his banishment from the Bay Colony. Fearful of arrest, Roger Williams fled to Narragansett country, where in 1636 he founded the Providence Plantation on land purchased from the Narragansett sachem Canonicus. Eager to introduce Christianity to the Narragansett tribes, Roger Williams learned the language. In 1643 he published *A Key into the Language of America*, an invaluable work on the language and customs of the Narragansett people.

38. The Passamaquoddy consider: Charles G. Leland, *Algonquin Legends*, (Dover Publications, Inc., New York, New York, 1992), p. 18. This publication is an excellent source on the oral traditions of the Penobscot, Passamaquoddy and Mic Mac. Leland gathered most of the stories directly from tribal narrators in 1882.

38. The Cohas tribe of New: William Adams, *Indian Legends in Verse*, (W.B. Ranney Company, Concord, New Hampshire, 1922), pp. 91-94.

38. William Wood mentions a dog: Wood, *New Englands Prospect*, XIX, p. 105.

39. The Wampanoags and Narragansetts: Williams, *A Key into the Language of America*, XXI, p. 193.

39. If an accident befell any: Williams, *A Key into the Language of America*, XXI, p. 189.

39. The northern Algonkian tribes: John Josselyn, *An Account of Two Voyages to New England, Made During the Years 1638, 1663*, (Boston: William Veazie, 1865), pp. 103-104. A considerable part of Josselyn's work focuses on native plants and animals in New England. However, he does give some detailed observations on the hunting and gathering lifestyle of the northern Algonkian tribes in colonial New Hampshire and Maine.

40. Burdock leaf, well pounded: Samson Occom, *Ten Indian Remedies from Manuscript Notes on Herbs and Roots*, (Printed at Christmas by Edward Connery Lathem, 1954). Samson Occom (1723-1792) was a Mohegan tribesman, who served as both a schoolmaster and Christian missionary to the Montauk and Shinecook tribes on Long Island.

41. In Occom's *An Account*: Samson Occom, "An Account of the Montauk Indians on Long Island" in *Massachusetts Historical Collections*, (Johnson Reprint Corporation, New York, New York, 1968), X, p. 109.

41. One of the most famous: Thomas Morton, *New England Canaan*, (Burt Franklin, New York, New York, reprint of 1967), IX, pp. 150-151. Thomas Morton was born in England around 1580. As a young man he studied law in London. In 1621 he married a prosperous widow. He is rumored to have mistreated his wife, and may have even murdered a business associate. During the spring of 1642, he arrived in New England, setting up the fur trading post of "Merry Mount" at present-day Quincy, Massachusetts. His relaxed trade with the local tribes, which may have involved guns and ammunition, coupled with his fondness for merriment, resulted in his arrest by Miles Standish in 1628. He was tried at Plymouth, and susequently deported to England. The following year Morton returned to Merrymount, only to be exiled again. After serving a short jail term in England, Thomas Morton teamed up with Sir Ferdinando Gorges, who in an attempt to undermine Puritan power in the Bay Colony, was seeking to get the Massachusetts colonial charter revoked. Thomas Morton immigrated to the Massachusetts Bay Colony in 1643, despite a warning to stay out of the colony. After being imprisoned for a year by the Massachusetts authorities, he relocated to Maine in search of a more tolerant environment. Morton published New England Canaan in 1637, as a promotional publication to attract English colonists to New England.

42. The powwow, while reciting sacred: Thomas Lechford, *Plain Dealing or News from New England*, (Johnson Reprint Corporation, New York, New York, reprint of 1969), IX, p. 118. Little is

known about Thomas Lechford, except for the years 1638-1641, when he was a resident of Massachusetts Bay Colony. During his brief stay in the colony he practiced law. After his return to England he published *Plain Dealing or News from New England* in 1642.

42. While he chanted to Hobbamock: Young, ed. *Chronicles of the Pilgrim Fathers of the Colony of Plymouth*, XXIII, pp. 356-357.

42. The Wampanoags assumed that: Young, ed. *Chronicles of the Pilgrim Fathers of the Colony of Plymouth*, XXIII, pp. 358-359.

42. Roger Williams defines the word: Williams, *A Key into the Language of America*, XXI, p. 191.

43. Archaeologists and relic hunters: William S. Fowler, "Ceremonial and Domestic Products," in *Bulletin of the Massachusetts Archaeological Society* (Bronson Museum, Attleboro, Massachusetts), Vol. XXVII, pp. 43-45.

45. One Narragansett tribesman, trying: Williams, *A Key into the Language of America*, XXI, p. 191.

46. About this latter force Roger: Williams, *A Key into the Language of America*, XXI, p. 190.

46. "They imagined a great number": Occom, "An Account of the Montauk Indians on Long Island," in *Massachusetts Historical Collections*, X, p. 108.

47. To console the bereaved, friends": Williams, *A Key into the Language of America*, XXXII, pp. 247-250.

47. Involving their mortuary ceremonies: Williams, A Key into the Language of America, XXXII, p. 248-249.

47. Samson Occom states that before: Occom, "An Account of the Montauk Indians on Long Island," in *Massachusetts Historical Collections*, X, p. 109.

47. According to Roger Williams,: Williams, *A Key into the Language of America*, XXXII, p. 249.

47. In such cases where the man: Young, ed. *Chronicles of the Pilgrim Fathers of the Colony of Plymouth*, XXIII, p. 363.

48. During their wanderings on: William Bradford and Edward Winslow, *Mourt's Relation*, (Garret Press, Inc., New York, New York, reprint of 1969), p. 49.

48. Those burial plots that were: Young, ed. *Chronicles of the Pilgrim Fathers of the Colony of Plymouth*, XXIII, p.363.

48. Edward Winslow relates that: Young, ed. *Chronicles of the Pilgrim Fathers of the Colony of Plymouth*, XXI, p. 341.

49. According to Thomas Cooper: Thomas Cooper, "Traditions and Customs of the Indians of Martha's Vineyard," in *Massachusetts Historical Collections*, (Johnson Reprint Corporation, New York, New York, reprint of 1968), I, p. 140.

49. For example, in establishing: Nathaniel B. Shurtleff, ed. *Records of the Colony of Plymouth*, 12 vols.(Press of William White, Boston, Massachusetts 1855-1861), II, p. 21.

49. Again, involving the concerns of: Shurtleff, ed. *Records of the Colony of Plymouth*, 12 vols., II, p. 130.

50. The viewpoint of the English: Young, *Chronicles of the Pilgrim Fathers of the Colony of Plymouth*, XVII, p. 265.

50. The English sometimes recognized: Shurtleff, ed. *Records of the Colony of Plymouth*, 12 vols. II, p. 131.

52. Metacom (King Philip) seems to have: Samuel G. Drake, *The Book of the Indians*, (Antiquarian Bookstore, 56 Cornhill, Boston, Massachusetts, 1841), II, pp. 15-16.

52. About this, Roger Williams says,: Williams, *A Key into the Language of America*, XXII, p. 202.

53. While Passaconaway presided over: Morton, *New England Canaan*, pp. 154-155. Thomas Morton devotes considerable space to the marriage of Passaconaway's daughter to the sagamore of the Saugus tribe. The author states: "the sachem or sagamore of Saugus made choice, when he came to man's estate, of a Lady of noble discent, Daughter to Passaconaway, this Lady the younge sachem with the consent and good liking of her father marries, and takes for his wife. Great entertainment he and his received. The solemnity being ended, Passaconaway causes a selected number of his men to waite upon his daughter home into those parts that did properly belong to her husband, where the attendants had entertainment, the solemnity being ended, the attendants were gratified." This marriage ended when Passaconaway's daughter decided to visit her father. She was escorted to her native land by several Saugus warriors, who returned to Saugus after reaching their destination.

After being at Pawtucket for awhile, her father sent word to Saugus that she desired to return to her husband, but the sagamore of Saugus demanded that Passaconaway appoint several Pawtucket tribesmen as escorts to see her home. Infuriated by his son-in-law's obstinance, Passaconaway's daughter remained at Pawtucket until she remarried to Numphow, sagamore of Wamesit.

54. In cases where the oldest son: Daniel Gookin, "Historical Collections of the Indians in New England, in *Massachusetts Historical Collections*, (Johnson Reprint Corporation, New York, New York, reprint of 1968), I, p. 154. Daniel Gookin spent much of his childhood in County Cork, Ireland. A Puritan, he lived in Virginia for thirteen years, before moving to Massachusetts Bay Colony in 1643. Besides his appointment to several Massachusetts court offices, he served as superintendent of the Praying Indians in the colony in 1656, and again from 1661 to his death in 1687. Gookin wrote "Historical Collections of the Indians in New England" in 1674, but it was not published until 1792. Gookin's familiarity with the Reverend John Eliot's missionary work among the Praying Indians makes him an excellent historical source on the tribal groups in the Bay Colony.

54. The position of overseer was: Wood, *New Englands Prospect*, X, pp. 89-90.

55. Roger Williams sometimes attended: Williams, *A Key into the Language of America*, XXI, p. 192.

55. "Their sachems have not their": Gookin, "Historical Collections of the Indians in New England," in *Massachusetts Historical Collections*, I, p. 154.

55. When Obbatinewat, sagamore of: Young, *Chronicles of the Pilgrim Fathers of the Colony of Plymouth*, XIV, p. 225.

55. Edward Winslow relates how his: Young, *Chronicles of the Pilgrim Fathers of the Colony of Plymouth*, XX, p. 316.

56. Among the New England Algonkians: Solon B. Colby, *Colby's Indian History: Antiquities of the New Hampshire Indians and their Neighbors*, (Walkers Pond Press, Center Conway, New Hampshire, 1975), VII, p. 84. According to Colby, the northern Algonkian use of the word "bashaba" has been confused by both historians and poets. The notion that it is a title has come from a misunderstanding of an Abenaki idiom. When speaking English, says Colby, the Algonkians often prefixed the definite article to anything that was the best, or the greatest of its kind. Hence, the supposed title "The Bashaba" more accurately translates "Bashaba the Great", the personal name of an Abenaki chieftan. However, James Rosier, in his book titled *A True Relation of the Most Prosperous Voyage Made this Present Year 1605*, points out that the Abenaki not only called their own leaders bashabas, but also considered the English sea captain, George Waymouth, to be a bashaba over his crewmen. The application of the term bashaba to men of authority in both cultures strongly suggests that it is an Abenaki title, and not a personal name.

56. Among the Mohegans these: "Language of the Mohegans," in *Massachusetts Historical Collections*, (Johnson Reprint Corporation, New York, New York, reprint of 1968), IX, p. 99.

56. Any person acquiring the sachemship: Williams, *A Key into the Language of America*, p. 165. In his "A Key into the Language of America," Roger Williams relates an interesting side note concerning the "Sachim," a little bird about the size of a swallow, to which the Narragansett gave that name, because of its sachem or kingly courage in attacking larger birds such as crows and hawks. To the Algonkians this bird symbolized the courage expected of sachems. The bird referred to is undoubtedly the "Tyrannus tyrannus," that the English colonists appropriately named the "Kingbird."

56. In 1638 Sachem Passaconaway had: John Wheelwright, *Writings and Mercurius Americanus 1645*, (Burt Franklin, New York, New York), pp. 143-148.

57. Winslow later recalled: Young, ed. *Chronicles of the Pilgrim Fathers of the Colony of Plymouth*, XI, p 210.

57. Edward Johnson, who may have: Edward Johnson, *Wonder-Working Providence of Sions Saviour in New England*, (Barnes and Noble, Inc., New York, New York, 1959), VI, pp. 161-163.

58. The pnieses stood by thanking: Young, ed. *Chronicles of the Pilgrim Fathers of the Colony of Plymouth*, XXIII, p. 362.

58. Under the Wampanoag code of: Young, ed. *Chronicles of the Pilgrim Fathers of the Colony of Plymouth*, XXIII, p. 364.

59. If he was found guilty: Williams, *A Key into the Language of America*, XXII, p. 203.

59. The Abenaki told Captain Levett: Charles H. Levermore, *Forerunners and Competitors of the Pilgrims and Puritans*, 2 vols. (Published for the New England Society of Brooklyn, New York, 1912), II, p. 627.

59. A number of French sailors: Morton, *New England Canaan*, IX, pp. 150-151.

60. For this reason, many of: William S. Fowler, "Ceremonial and Domestic Products," in *Bulletin of the Massachusetts Archaeological Society*, Vol. XXVII, pp. 43-45.

62. Each Algonkian child between: Young, *Chronicles of the Pilgrim Fathers of the Colony of Plymouth*, (Charles C. Little and James Brown, Boston, Massachusetts, 1844), XXIII, p. 364.

63. William Wood observed women who: Wood, *New Englands Prospect*, XX, pp. 105-110.

63. Gookin notes, "Their food is": Gookin, "Historical Collections of the Indians in New England" in *Massachusetts Historical Collections*, I, pp. 150-151.

64. Josselyn writes how they made: Josselyn, *An Account of Two Voyages to New England During the Years 1638, 1663*, p. 111.

64. Roger Williams observed that: Williams, *A Key into the Language of America*, XXIII, p. 206.

64. Thomas Lechford noted that the: Lechford, *Plain Dealing or News from New England*, IX, p. 118.

64. Conbitant, sagamore of the Pocasset: Young, ed. *Chronicles of the Pilgrim Fathers of the Colony of Plymouth*, XX, p. 325.

64. Because the squa-sachem's family was: Williams, *A Key into the Language of America*, VI, p. 123.

64. Thomas Morton was so impressed: Morton, *New England Canaan*, VIII, pp. 148-149.

65. James Sullivan, who wrote the: James Sullivan, *History of the District of Maine*, (I. Thomas and E.T. Andrews, Boston, Massachusetts, 1795), V, p. 106. James Sullivan, the son of John and Margery Sullivan, was born in 1744. He spent his childhood in present-day Berwick, Maine. After studying under his father, who was a teacher, James became a student in the law office of his brother. Shortly after his marriage, he and wife moved to Limerick, Maine. In 1776 he was appointed a justice of the Massachusetts supreme court, which led him two years later to move to Groton, Massachusetts. After his political defeat in a race for the Massachusetts governorship in 1796, he won office in 1807. Sullivan authored books on history, business investment and real estate titles. His *History of the District of Maine* includes some cursory observations of the Abenaki tribes.

65. However, among the Algonkian tribes: Richard W. Wilkie and Jack Tager, *Historical Atlas of Massachusetts*, (The University of Massachusetts Press, Amherst, Massachusetts, 1991), II, p. 12. The first two chapters provide an excellent overview of Precontact and Historic Algonkian demography in the area of present-day Massachusetts.

65. Twice a year, generally in: Morton, *New England Canaan*, XVIII, p. 172.

67. "They have other devices to kill": Wood, *New Englands Prospect*, XV, p. 99.

67. In the meantime, the deer: Williams, *A Key into the Language of America*, XXVII, p. 226.

68. The name of the Pennacook sachem: Colby, *Colby's Indian History: Antiquities of the New Hampshire Indians and their Neighbors*, VII, p. 83.

69. "Their weapons were bows and": Gookin, "Historical Collections of the Indians in New England," in *Massachusetts Historical Collections*, I, p. 152.

69. And William Wood observes: Wood, *New Englands Prospect*, XV, pp. 99-100.

69. Roger Williams, who traversed many: Williams, *A Key into the Language of America*, XI, p. 147.

69. One of the most famous trails: Rowland E. Robinson, *Vermont A Study in Independence*, AMS Press Inc., New York, New York, reprint of 1973), I, pp. 10-11.

70. The Narragansett people called the: Williams, *A Key into the Language of America*, XII, pp. 155-156.

70. Some of these dugouts: Gookin, "Historical Collections of the Indians of New England," in *Massachusetts Historical Collections*, I, pp. 152-153.

71. "Salvages that live by the seaside,": Morton, *New England Canaan*, XII, pp. 157-159.

71. The Narragansetts traded with tribes: William S. Fowler, "Ostungo Effigy Ceramic Pipes," in *Bulletin of the Massachusetts Archaeological Society* (Bronson Museum, Attleboro, Massachusetts), Vol. XXXV, pp. 28-31.

71. "The Indians bring downe all": Williams, *A Key into the Language of America*, XXIV, p. 210.

72. "They take a great pride in": Morton, *New England Canaan*, IV, p. 197.

73. The New England Algonkians built: William S. Fowler, "Abodes of Four Aboriginal Periods," in *Bulletin of the Massachusetts Archaeological Society* (Bronson Museum, Attleboro, Massachusetts), Vol. XXXIV, pp. 19-20.

73. In the autumn of 1620,: Young, *Chronicles of the Pilgrim Fathers of the Colony of Plymouth*, XI, pp. 144-145.

74. Roger Williams, who noted this: Williams, *A Key into the Language of America*, VI, p. 117.

74. Roger Williams recalled, "I once": Williams, *A Key into the Language of America.*, VI, p. 128.

74. In Mary Rowlandson's account of: Mary Rowlandson, *The Narrative of the Captivity and Restoration of Mrs. Mary Rowlandson*, 30th ed. (Meriden Gravure Co., Meriden,Connecticut, 1953), p. 47. Mary Rowlandson was born Mary White about 1637 in Somerset, England. Her father, John White, immigrated to Salem, Massachusetts in 1638, and the rest of the White family followed during the next year. Fifteen years later the White family moved to Lancaster, Massachusetts, where daughter Mary married Joseph Rowlandson, the town's minister. During King Philip's War(1675-1676), Mary and her three children were taken prisoner. Mary and two of her children were ransomed or released, the youngest child dying in captivity. In1677 the Rowlandsons moved to Wethersfield, Connecticut, where husband Joseph died the following year. The date of Mary Rowlandson's death is uncertain, but she was probably still living when her captivity narrative was published in 1682. The book is a significant work for historians and cultural anthropologists. Besides relating first hand accounts of King Philip and other Algonkian leaders, the book contains descriptions of Algonkian tribal conditions during the conflict.

75. In 1621, when the Pilgrims: William Bradford and Edward Winslow, *Mourt's Relation*, (Garret Press Inc., New York, New York, reprint of 1969), IV, p. 128.

75. William Wood writes,: Wood, *New Englands Prospect*, XIII, pp. 94-95.

75. Roger Williams states: Williams, *A Key into the Language of America*, XXIX, p. 237.

76. In 1621, either the Narragansetts: William Bradford, *Of Plymouth Plantation*, (Alfred A. Knopf, New York, New York, 1976), XII, p. 96.

76. "He that is a Messenger,": Williams, *A Key into the Language of America*, VIII, p. 138.

77. During her captivity in King Philip's War,: Rowlandson, *The Narrative of the Captivity and Restoration of Mrs. Mary Rowlandson*, pp. 18-19.

77. Recognizing this characteristic in their: Wood, *New Englands Prospect*, XVIII, p.103.

79. The Wampanoag language, according: Young, *Chronicles of the Pilgrim Fathers of the Colony of Plymouth*, XXIII, pp. 366-367.

79. "Every Countrey," William Wood points: Wood, *New Englands Prospect*, XVIII, p.103.

80. According to his observations: Gookin, "Historical Collections of the Indians in New England," in *Massachusetts Historical Collections*, I, p. 149.

80. Thomas Hutchinson elaborates on: Thomas Hutchinson, *The History of the Colony and Province of Massachusetts Bay*, 2 vols. (Kraus Reprint Co., New York, New York, reprint of 1970), I, p. 402.

80. There were three main dialectic: Willoughby, *Antiquities of the New England Indians with Notes on the Ancient Cultures of the Adjacent Territory*, IV, p. 276.

82. "Their Goales be a mile long": Wood, *New Englands Prospect*, XIV, pp. 96-97.

82. The indigenous people of New England: Willoughby, *Antiquities of the New England Indians with Notes on the Ancient Cultures of the Adjacent Territory*, II, pp. 110-111.

83. William Wood writes that the: Wood, *New Englands Prospect*, XIV, p. 96.

83. They gambled off their wampum: Young, *Chronicles of the Pilgrim Fathers of the Colony of Plymouth*, XIX, p. 307.

84. Recipients begged dancers for: Williams, *A Key into the Language of America*, XXVIII, p. 231.

85. The Massachusett tribal nation: Wood, *New Englands Prospect*, p. 115.

85. The Abenaki gave the moon: *The Wabanakis of Maine and the Maritimes*, (Maine Indian Program of the New England Regional Office of the American Friends Service Committee, Bath, Maine, 1989), D-25. Like their Abenaki neighbors, the Mic Mac of Nova Scotia continue to apply seasonal names to the months of the year. This Mic Mac custom was first reported by the Jesuit missionary Father Biard who wrote how in January the Mic Mac hunted seals. From February to mid March they hunted beaver, otter, moose, bear and caribou. Between March and the end of April the spawning season brings a swarm of both

fresh and salt water fish, along with "the great search through the islets for [goose] eggs." Throughout the summer months food is in abundance. By September the Mic Mac were gathered at their fishing places to tap the annual eel migration, followed in October and November by the second hunt for caribou and beaver In December the Mic Mac sought out the tomcod, which spawns beneath the ice. See Bruce G. Trigger, *Handbook of North American Indians*, 15 vols., (Smithsonian Institution, Washington, D.C., 1978), XV, pp. 110-111.

86. Edward Winslow writes: Young, *Chronicles of the Pilgrim Fathers of the Colony of Plymouth*, XXIII, p. 367.

86. It was told by Thomas Cooper,: Thomas Cooper, "Traditions and Customs of the Indians of Martha's Vineyard" in *Massachusetts Historical Collections*, (Johnson Reprint Corporation, New York, New York, reprint of 1968), I, pp. 139-140.

87. Another Wampanoag account that: R.A. Douglas-Lithgow, *Nantucket: A History*, (G.P. Putnam's Sons, New York and London, 1914), II, pp. 17-18.

87. Like his Wampanoag equivalent: Charles G. Leland, *Algonquin Legends*, (Dover Publications, Inc., New York, New York, 1992), p. 28, pp. 114-119.

87. Turner describes the story in: Charles Turner, "A Description of Natardin or Catardin Mountain," in *Massachusetts Historical Collections*, (Johnson Reprint Corporation, New York, New York, reprint of 1968), VIII, pp. 112-116.

88. Another Abenaki tradition involving: Samuel Drake ed., *Indian Captivities*, (Antiquarian Bookstore 56 Cornhill, Boston, Massachusetts, 1839), pp. 112-116. Besides his editorial work in *Indian Captivities*, Drake published *The Book of the Indians* in 1841. The latter work is an exhaustive secondary source on the history of the Algonkian tribes during the Colonial period in New England.

89. Narragansett folklore also tells of: Williams, *A Key into the Language of America*, XV, p. 164. Like the Algonkian culture hero Wetucks, Iroquoian society speaks similarly of Hiawatha,who is said to have been instrumental in encouraging the five Iroquoian tribes to form their intertribal confederation. According to their traditions Hiawatha also introduced agriculture, the arts and medicine to the Five Nations.

89. Mount Watatic, a sizeable hill: D. Hamilton Hurd, *History of Middlesex County, Massachusetts*, 3 vols. (J.W. Lewis and Co., Philadelphia, 1890), I, p. 306.

89. The story of Chief Chocorua: Adams, *Indian Legends in Verse*, pp. 33-36.

Chapter 3: Appearence Of The "Walking Islands"

91. "Though Virginia be not above": Young, *Chronicles of the Pilgrim Fathers of the Colony of Plymouth*, XXIV, pp. 368-369.

91. "They took the first ship they": Wood, *New Englands Prospect*, IX, p. 87.

92. Most of the North American coastline: Lawrence C. Wroth, The *Voyages of Giovanni da Verrazzano 1524-1528*, (Published for the Pierpont Morgan Library, Yale University Press, New Haven and London, 1970), IX, pp. 137-143. The Algonkian name for Block Island was "Munisses" or Manisses." Both the Narragansett and Niantic people frequented this island off the Rhode Island coast.

94. In 1602, Bartholomew Gosnold: Henry S. Burrage, *Early English and French Voyages Chiefly from Hakluyt*, (Barnes and Noble, Inc., New York, New York, reprint of 1959), pp. 329-340. In this section of Burrage's compilation of explorer narratives is John Brereton's account of the Gosnold expedition to the New England coast in 1602. Most sources agree that John Brereton was an Episcopal rector, who through aquaintance with the Gosnold family was inspired to accompany the explorer to coastal New England in 1602 aboard the "Concord." Brereton recounted the voyage of 1602 in *A Briefe and True Relation of the Discoverie of the North Part of Virginia* published the same year.

95. Archer relates that one day: Gabriel Archer, "Gosnold's Settlement at Cuttyhunk" in *Old South Leaflets* 25 vols. (Burt Franklin, New York, New York), V, pp. 405-415. Gabriel Archer was a member of the crew in the Gosnold expedition to New England in 1602, and he too wrote a short narrative concerning their brief stay on Cuttyhunk Island.

253

96. In the year following Gosnold's: Burrage, *Early English and French Voyages Chiefly from Hakluyt*, pp. 346-352. Burrage's compilation also contains an account of Martin Pring's summer voyage of 1603 along the New England coast.

97. On board his ship he entertained: Burrage, *Early English and French Voyages Chiefly from Hakluyt*, p. 380, p. 392. In Burrage's collection of explorer narratives is the account of Captain George Waymouth's discoveries along the Maine coast in 1605.

97. He ordered two unsuspecting: James Rosier, *A True Relation of the Most Prosperous Voyage Made this Present Year 1605*, (March of the America Facsimile Series,University Microfilms, Inc., 1966), p. 22. James Rosier accompanied Captain Waymouth in his voyage to the Maine coast in 1605. Born in England in 1575, he took his M.A. at Cambridge in 1596. He converted to the Catholic faith in 1602, and he may have accompanied Waymouth on this voyage looking to establish a Catholic colony in Maine. The account contains observations on the Abenaki people.

98. Rosier states the names: Rosier, *A True Relation of the Most Prosperous Voyage Made this Present Year 1605*, p. 37. Sir Ferdinando Gorges claims that one of the tribesman Waymouth abducted while along the Maine coast was Squanto, but Gorges must have been confused here, for Squanto was taken captive during a later voyage made by Captain Hunt. James Rosier, who's account is the most reliable source concerning the Waymouth expedition, states that the names of the kidnapped tribesmen were Tahanedo (Nahanda), Amoret, Skicowaroes (Sketwarroes), Maneddo and Sassacomoit. There is no mention of Squanto.

98. In the spring of 1619, Captain: Charles Levermore, *Forerunners and Competitors of the Pilgrims and Puritans*, 2 vols. (Published for the New England Society of Brooklyn,New York, 1912), II, pp. 579-580. Captain Dermer attests to returning Squanto to his homeland in present-day southeastern Massachusetts in1619.

99. "The savages," Champlain writes,: W. L. Grant, *Voyages of Samuel De Champlain*, (Barnes and Noble Inc. New York, New York, reprint of 1967), V, p. 50. Between 1604 -1607 Champlain participated in a series of French expeditions along the New England coastline from Maine to Cape Cod. His account of these expeditions provide some fascinating glimpses of the Algonkian coastal tribes.

100. The Agawams, knowing the coast: Grant, *Voyages of Samuel De Champlain*, VII, p. 65.

100. "After cutting down," he observes,": Grant, *Voyages of Samuel De Champlain*, VII, p. 66.

100. Once the Nausets understood DeMonts': Grant, *Voyages of Samuel De Champlain*,VIII, p. 71.

102. "Some of the land was already": Grant, *Voyages of Samuel De Champlain*, XIII, p. 92.

102. "They make trenches in the sand": Grant, *Voyages of Samuel De Champlain*, XIV, p. 95.

105. "We withdrew," Champlain gloatingly": Grant, *Voyages of Samuel De Champlain*, XV, p. 106.

105. In the published accounts of their: Rosier, *A True Relation of the Most Prosperous Voyage Made this Present Year 1605*, p. 13.

105. Champlain describes the mourning: Grant, *Voyages of Samuel De Champlain*, XVI, pp. 108-109.

108. The Kennebecs also exhibited an: Henry O. Thayer, *The Sagadahoc Colony*, (Published by Benjamin Blom, Inc., reprint of 1971), VI, pp. 200-204. Thayer's work is a concise account of the development and subsequent demise of the Sagadahoc Colony in Maine.

109. The Abenaki, according to a letter: Thayer, *The Sagadahoc Colony*, p. 88

109. The Sagadahoc enterprise became: Henry S. Burrage, *Early English and French Voyages Chiefly from Hakluyt*, pp. 397-419. An equally detailed account of the Sagadahoc Colony is found in Burrage's compilation of early European voyages to New England.

109. In reality, these people had more: George P. Winship, *Sailors Narratives of Voyages along the New England Coast 1524-1624*, (Burt Franklin, New York, New York), pp. 179-192. Winship's collection of sailor narratives contains an account of Henry Hudson's exploits along the New England coast in 1609.

111. Frequently, the fathers invited: Levermore, 2 vols. *Forerunners and Competitors of the Pilgrims and Puritans*, II, pp. 458-459. Levermore's compilation of narratives on early European exploration along the New England coast, contains an informative account of the French explorations between 1610-1613. Father Biard, who participated in some of the expeditions, wrote about his encounters with the Mic Mac, Maliseet and Abenaki peoples.

112. "Learn our language quickly,": Levermore, 2 vols. *Forerunners and Competitors of the Pilgrims and Puritans*, II, p. 463.

113. Coming into Father Masse's lodge: Levermore, 2 vols. *Forerunners and Competitors of the Pilgrims and Puritans*, II, pp. 481-482.

114. Originally when the Abenaki on: Levermore, 2 vols. *Forerunners and Competitors of the Pilgrims and Puritans*, II, pp. 489-490.

114. In 1619, a group of Recollect fathers: Edna Kenton, *Jesuit Relations*, Vanguard Press, 1954), Introd., pp xxviii-xxx.

115. Harlow was unable to locate: Levermore, 2 vols. *Forerunners and Competitors of the Pilgrims and Puritans*, II, pp. 650-652. The island that Captain Harlow attempted to locate off Cape Cod was either Nantucket, Martha's Vineyard or Noman's Land.

116. "The next I can remember by name": John Smith, 2 vols., *Travels and Works of Captain John Smith*, (Burt Franklin, New York, New York), II, p. 192.

117. Beyond Cape Cod was the: Levermore, 2 vols. *Forerunners and Competitors of the Pilgrims and Puritans*, II, p. 654, pp. 675-676.

117. Captain Smith later wrote of Hunt,: Levermore, 2 vols. *Forerunners and Competitors of the Pilgrims and Puritans*, II, p. 572.

118. "I met with Epinow," Dermer states,: Winship, *Sailors Narratives of Voyages along the New England Coast 1524-1624*, pp. 254-255. According to William Bradford, almost all of Captain Dermer's crew were massacred by a band of Capawick warriors. See William Bradford, *Bradford's History of Plymouth Plantation*, ed.William T. Davis (Barnes and Noble, Inc., 1959), pp. 113-114.

119. Algonkians prized the white man's: William S. Fowler, "Metal Cutouts of the Northeast," in *Bulletin of the Massachusetts Archaeological Society* (Bronson Museum, Attleboro, Massachusetts), Vol. XXXIV, pp. 24-30.

119. Ceramic skills were also greatly: William S. Fowler, "Ceremonial and Domestic Products," in *Bulletin of the Massachusetts Archaeological Society* (Bronson Museum, Attleboro, Massachusetts), Vol, XXVII, pp. 51-61.

119. Samoset, a northern Algonkian: Young, *Chronicles of the Pilgrim Fathers of the Colony of Plymouth*, X, pp. 182-184.

120. "English clothes are so strange": Williams, *A Key into the Language of America*, XX, p. 187.

120. In some tribal villages certain: Williams, *A Key into the Language of America*, VI, p. 122.

121. "Their disease was the Plague,": Winship, *Sailors Narratives of Voyages along the New England Coast 1524-1624*, p. 251.

121. The elder tribal people who survived: Daniel Gookin, "Historical Collections of the Indians in New England," in *Massachusetts Historical Collections*, I, p. 148.

121. It spread from the coast: John White, *The Planters Plea*, (Printed by William Iones, 1630), IV, p. 25. John White (1575-1648) served as rector of Trinity Church in Dorchester, England for forty years. A strong supporter of English colonization in America, White envisioned the Massachusetts Bay Colony as a refuge for harried nonconformist Puritans. Even though the Reverend White never visited New England, he was instrumental in securing a patent and the necessary supplies to ensure the colony's continuation. In 1630 he published *The Planters Plea* wherein he promoted Massachusetts Bay Colony by advocating overseas colonization.

121. Among the Massachusett nation: Morton, *New England Canaan*, III, pp. 132-133.

122. Edward Winslow, travelling along the: Young, *Chronicles of the Pilgrim Fathers of the Colony of Plymouth*, XI, p. 206.

122. Later on, when the Puritans began: White, *The Planters Plea*, IV, p. 25.

122. Edward Johnson, the Puritan historian: Edward Johnson, *Wonder Working Providence of Sions Saviour in New England*, (Barnes and Noble Inc., New York, New York, 1959),I, p. 80.

122. In 1634, the Podunk, Tunxis, Agawam: William Bradford, *Of Plymouth Plantation*, ed. S.E. Morison (Printed by Alfred A. Knopf, 1976), XXV, pp. 270-271.

123. That same year the Narragansetts,: John Winthrop, *Winthrop's Journal 1630-1649*, 2 vols. (Barnes and Noble, New York, New York, 1946), Vol. I, p. 118.

123. In 1759, the Reverend Stephen Badger: Stephen Badger, "Mr. Badger's Letter Concerning the Indians of Natick," in *Massachusetts Historical Collections*, (Johnson Reprint Corporation, New York, New York, reprint of 1968), V, p. 41. Stephen Badger (1726-1803) acquired his B.A. from Harvard in 1747, and his M.A. in 1750. Between 1753-1797 he served as both minister and mission-

ary to the "Natick Indians," and some local whites who worshipped with them. As the 18th century "Natick Indian" population continued to decline chiefly from illness, a faction of whites proposed to have the meetinghouse relocated. Reverend Badger earned the faction's scorn by opposing the plan. Due to the American Revolution Badger's missionary funds from England were cut off. At times he found himself in dispute with the town over his missionary salary. Stephen Badger's parish was finally broken up in 1797, when the town of Natick succeeded in having the location of the meetinghouse moved. Badger's writings on the "Natick Indians" provide an analysis of the gradual disintegration of this Native American community.

123. Narragansett hunting parties, taking: Morton, *New England Canaan*, XIV, p. 162.

124. In this ceremony, as Thomas Cooper: Thomas Cooper, "Traditions and Customs of the Indians of Martha's Vineyard," in *Massachusetts Historical Collections*, I, p. 140.

125. In this legend, the Abenaki: Charles G. Leland, *Algonquin Legends*, (Dover Publications, Inc., New York, New York, 1992), pp. 127-130.

Chapter 4: "The English Are No Sachems"

127. According to William Bradford: Alexander Young, *Chronicles of the Pilgrim Fathers of the Colony of Plymouth*, (Charles C. Little and James Brown, Boston, 1844), IX, pp. 155-158

128. Bradford describes Massasoit: Young, *Chronicles of the Pilgrim Fathers of the Colony of Plymouth*,X, p. 194.

132. "They begane to see that Squanto": William Bradford, *Bradford's History of Plymouth Plantation*, ed. William T. Davis (Barnes and Noble, Inc., New York, New York, 1959), p. 128.

135. Plymouth Colony, having survived its: Bradford, *Bradford's History of Plymouth Plantation*, ed. William T. Davis, p. 293.

135. However, growth put pressure on the: Bradford, *Bradford's History of Plymouth Plantation*, ed. William T. Davis, p. 293.

136. In 1623 a group of English merchants: Alexander Young, *Chronicles of the First Planters of the Colony of Massachusetts Bay 1623-1636*, (DaCapo Press, New York, New York,1970).

136. At the same time, Sir Ferdinando: Jeremy Belknap, *The History of New Hampshire*, 2 vols. (Johnson Reprint Corporation, New York, New York, 1970), I, pp. 1-96.

137. Throughout the 1630s, emigration: David Cressy, *Coming Over: Migration and Communication Between England and New England in the Seventeenth Century*, (Cambridge University Press, New York, New York, 1987), p. 70.

138. In 1635, some residents of Cambridge: J. Hammond Trumbull, *The Public Records of the Colony of Connecticut*, (Johnson Reprint Corporation, New York, New York, 1968).

138. By the following spring, a number: George L. Clark, *A History of Connecticut*, (G. P. Putnam's Sons, New York, New York, 1914), II, pp. 12-13.

138. During this same period Roger Williams: John Bartlett, ed. *Colonial Records of Rhode Island*, 10 vols.(AMS Press, New York, New York, reprint of 1968), I, pp. 45-46.

139. While the Connecticut and Rhode Island: Isabel M. Calder, *The New Haven Colony*, (Archon Press, reprint of 1970), XI, p. 252.

139. The Pequots demanded tribute: Bradford, *Bradford's History of Plymouth Plantation*, ed. William T. Davis p. 300.

140. The Pequots tried to compensate: Lion Gardener, *Gardener's Pequot Warres*, (Kraus Reprint Corporation, New York, New York, 1969), p. 9. Born in England in 1599, Lion Gardener sought his fortune in the Netherlands. While working in the Low Countries as "Engineer and Master of Works of Fortification" several men employed in the interests of the Connecticut patentees convinced Gardener to emigrate to New England. The promoters for Connecticut hoped that Gardener would assist the English colonists in Connecticut by constructing fortifications. Upon his acceptance of the offer, Lion Gardener and his wife Mary set sail from the Netherlands to England, and from there to Boston, where under the supervision of John Winthrop, Jr. he relocated to the mouth of the Connecticut River. There he directed the building of the fort at Saybrook. The assistance that was promised from Boston did not come, and Gardener soon found himself poorly equipped for the subsequent Pequot War, which proved to be both brief and bloody. Before his death on Long Island in

1663, Gardener wrote "Leift Lion Gardener His Relation of the Pequot Warres," one of four contemporary narratives about this conflict. Unlike the other accounts, Gardener's work was never published until the 19th century. No doubt, men such as Captain John Mason and John Winthrop, Jr., who benefited from the war, had little interest in an account that partly blamed the English for provoking Pequot hostility. Gardener's account presents a more personal dimension to the war.

140. The Pequots were aware the: "Letters of Roger Williams to Winthrop" in *Old South Leaflets* 25 vols. (Burt Franklin, New York, New York, III, pp. 1-20.

140. Sassacus had nearly convinced the: Edward Johnson, *Wonder-Working Providence of Sions Saviour in New England*, ed. J.F. Jameson (Barnes and Noble, Inc., New York, New York, 1959), VI, pp. 161-164. Edward Johnson (1599-1672) came to New England on the "Arbella" in the company of John Winthrop. Throughout most of his life he served the interests of the Massachusetts Bay Colony as captain of the Charlestown militia, town clerk of Woburn, deputy of the General Court and Puritan historian. Johnson's literary style is in fact a classic expression of the Puritan view that history reveals God to be the ultimate authority in all earthly events.

141. As Gardener's men brought the: Gardener, *Gardener's Pequot Warres*, pp. 15-16.

141. Gardener and the rest of his: Gardener, *Gardener's Pequot Warres*, pp. 15-16.

141. Captain Gardener posted a: Gardener, *Gardener's Pequot Warres*, p. 19.

142. Having terrorized the English, the: Trumbull, ed. *The Public Records of the Colony of Connecticut*, I, pp. 9-10.

143. That night, the sentinels reported: John Mason, "A Brief History of the Pequot War" in *Massachusetts Historical Collections*, (Johnson Reprint Corporation, New York, New York, reprint of 1968), VIII, pp. 135-138. John Mason (1600-1672) emigrated from England to Massachusetts Bay Colony in 1633. Before his arrival in New England, Captain Mason trained as a soldier under Sir Thomas Fairfax during a period of conflict in the Netherlands. After two years in Massachusetts Mason became one of the founders of Windsor, Connecticut. When war broke out between the Pequots and the Connecticut colonists, the colony called upon Mason's military experience as a soldier to lead an expedition against the Pequots. After a devestating assault on the fort at Mystic Mason became a celebrated war hero, and in time his military rank was changed to major. Besides his involvement in Connecticut military affairs, Mason held political office in the colony. Toward the end of his life he became a resident of Norwich,Connecticut. John Mason's "A Brief History of the Pequot War" is considered to be the most reliable of the four contemporary accounts of the conflict.

143. Mason writes: "There being two": Mason, "A Brief History of the Pequot War" in *Massachusetts Historical Collections*, VIII, pp. 138-140.

144. The rest of the English forces: Mason, "A Brief History of the Pequot War" in *Massachusetts Historical Collections*, VIII, pp. 141-144.

144. In the end, when the sachem: Gardener, *Gardener's Pequot Warres*, p. 22.

145. Four years later, John Winthrop's son: Nathaniel B. Shurtleff, ed. *Records of Massachusetts*, 5 vols. (Press of William White, Boston, Massachusetts, 1853), II, p. 71.

145. According to the Connecticut: Kevin McBride, "Mashantucket Pequot Ethnohistory Project" in *Rooted Like the Ash Trees: New England Indians and the Land*, (Eagle Wing Press, Inc., Naugatuck, Connecticut, 1987), pp. 24-27. In this article Kevin McBride documents the history of the Pequot people after their defeat in 1637.

145. According to Edward Johnson, the: Johnson, *Wonder-Working Providence of Sions Saviour in New England*, VI, p. 170.

145. Several days after the battle: Gardener, *Gardener's Pequot Warres*, pp. 21-22.

145. Forty armed men were immediately: John Winthrop, *Winthrop's Journal 1630-1649*, 2 vols. (Barnes and Noble, Inc. New York, New York, reprint of 1959), II, p. 75.

145. They agreed to the following terms: Shurtleff, ed. *Records of Massachusetts*, II, p.55.

146. Because of its central location: John Eliot, "Eliot's Brief Narrative of July 20, 1670" in *Old South Leaflets* 25 vols. (Burt Franklin, New York, New York), I, pp. 3-8.

147. He requested that the commissioners: Henry Bowden and James P. Ronda, ed. *John Eliot's Indian Dialogues: A Study in Cultural Interaction*, (Greenwood Press, Westport,Connecticut, 1990), p. 60. In his preface to this rare volume, first printed in 1671, John Eliot admits to his readers that the dialogues are not historical accounts of discussions between Praying Indians and unconverted tribes-

men. However, in no way does this diminish the value of the dialogues, for the basic themes of these imaginary conversations were derived from Eliot's real life missionary encounters with local tribesmen. The dialogues reveal both varied and recurring Algonkian responses to the Puritan missionary appeal.

147. The court sessions handled altercations: Shurtleff, *Records of Massachusetts*, II, p. 55.

147. In 1656, Daniel Gookin was appointed: Gookin, "Historical Collections of the Indians in New England," in *Massachusetts Historical Collections*, I, pp. 168-196.

147. It was Eliot's conviction that his: John Eliot, "Eliot's Brief Narrative of July 20, 1670" in *Old South Leaflets*, I, pp.3-8.

148. In 1654, the Massachusetts court: Shurtleff, *Records of Massachusetts*, III, pp. 365-366.

148. It was only a matter of time: Gookin, "Historical Collections of the Indians in New England," in *Massachusetts Historical Collections*, V, p. 50.

149. According to Daniel Gookin this: Gookin, "Historical Collections of the Indians in New England," in *Massachusetts Historical Collections*, X, p. 111.

149. The Jesuits were fairly successful: Cotton Mather, *Magnalia Christi Americana*, 2 vols. (Russell and Russell, New York, New York, 1852), II, p. 643. Cotton Mather, eldest child of Increase Mather, was born in Boston on February 12, 1663. A graduate of Harvard College, he lived out his life in the Bay Colony. One of the most voluminous colonial authors, Cotton Mather completed 445 printed works in his lifetime. His work *Magnalia Christi Americana*, an ecclesiastical history of the New England settlements, was published in 1702. Cotton Mather shared the pulpit of Old North Church with his father Increase, and was in general agreement with him on allowing the Massachusetts authorities to deal with the Salem witchcraft controversy of 1692. Cotton Mather was married three times and had eleven children. No stranger to personal loss, his second wife Elizabeth and three of his children died from a measle epidemic in November, 1713. He died in 1728, and is buried in the family tomb at Copps' Hill, Boston.

149. As a captive of the Abenaki at: Mather, *Magnalia Christi Americana*, II, p. 635.

149. On one occasion during his: John Williams, *Redeemed Captive Returning to Zion*, (Books for Librarian Press, Freeport, New York, reprint of 1970), pp. 9-92. The Reverend John Williams (1664-1729) became the Congregational minister of Deerfield, Massachusetts in 1686. During his first year at Deerfield he married Eunice Mather, a relative of Cotton Mather. Tragedy struck the Williams family on February 29, 1704 when a band of Canadian French and their "Indian allies" attacked the frontier town. Among the many casualties were two of Reverend Williams' sons who died during the attack, and his wife who perished later during the exhaustive trek north to Canada. Williams remained a captive of the French until 1706. His daughter Eunice, who was also taken captive, married an Iroquoian tribesman and converted to Catholicism, and despite subsequent visits to Deerfield chose to live in Canada. After settling down again in Deerfield, Reverend Williams married Abigail Bissell, who bore him five children. In 1707 he published an account of his captivity. The work has literary merit as both a jeremiad and an example of Puritan historiography. Like the narrative authored by Mary Rowlandson, the Williams account quickly became a popular captivity narrative. A second edition of *The Redeemed Captive Returning to Zion* was published in 1728, a year before Reverend Williams' death.

150. For this reason Gookin described: Gookin, *Historical Collections of the Indians in New England*, (Towtaid, 1970), X, p. 108.

150. Wannalancit told of his decision: Gookin, "Historical Collections of the Indians in New England" in *Massachusetts Historical Collections*, I, p. 187.

150. The Reverend John Eliot told the: Bowden and Ronda, ed. *John Eliot's Indian Dialogues: A Study in Cultural Interaction*, p. 88.

150. To further limit the influence of the: Shurtleff, *Records of Massachusetts*, II, p. 177.

151. Kinsman hesitates to become a: Bowden and Ronda, ed. *John Eliot's Indian Dialogues: A Study in Cultural Interaction*, p. 89.

152. Their political and social customs: Robert J. Naeher, "Dialogue in the Wilderness: John Eliot and the Indian Exploration of Puritanism as a Source of Meaning, Comfort and Ethnic Survival" in *The New England Quarterly*, (The New England Quarterly, Inc., Boston, Massachusetts, 1989), LXII, No. 3, pp. 352-353.

152. Roger Williams tells how an: Williams, *A Key into the Language of America*, XXI, pp. 198-199.

152. Wampanoag and Narragansett creation: Josselyn, *An Account of Two Voyages to New England, Made During the Years 1638, 1663*, (Boston: William Veazie, 1865), p. 105.

152. Where the tribal customs had been: Henry W. Bowden, *American Indians and Christian Missions: Studies in Cultural Conflict*, (The University of Chicago Press, Chicago, Illinois,1981), IV, pp. 96-133. Bowden's work presents an excellent comparative study of French and English Christian missions to the Algonkian and Iroquoian peoples of the Northeast.

154. Catholic missionary efforts toward the: Calvin Martin, "The European Impact on the Culture of a Northeastern Algonquian Tribe: An Ecological Interpretation" in *The William and Mary Quarterly*, (Williamsburg, Virginia), XXX, pp. 3-26.

154. "One thing I cannot here omit,": Samuel Penhallow, *The History of the Wars of New England with the Eastern Indians*, (Kraus Reprint Corporation, New York, New York, reprint of 1969), p. 85. Samuel Penhallow immigrated from England to Massachusetts Bay Colony in 1686, and shortly thereafter moved to Portsmouth, New Hampshire. His marriage to Mary Cutt, the daughter of New Hampshire Colony's president, introduced Penhallow to provincial politics. During his political career he served New Hampshire as a justice of the peace, speaker of the General Assembly, provincial treasurer and chief justice of the Supreme Court. In 1726 he published his *History of the Wars of New England with the Eastern Indians*, a detailed narrative of events concerning Queen Anne's War (1703-1713) and Lovewell's War (1722-1726).

155. By 1670, some Algonkian tribes in: Shurtleff, *Records of Massachusetts*, IV, pp. 512-513.

155. The Massachusetts court based its: Gookin, "Historical Collections of the Indians in New England" in the *Massachusetts Historical Collections*, I, p. 179.

156. The Massachusetts court tried to: Shurtleff, *Records of Massachusetts*, I, pp. 293-294.

156. To make sure the fences were: Trumbull, *The Public Records of the Colony of Connecticut*, III,pp. 42-43.

156. English swine herds would: Williams, *A Key into the Language of America*, XIX, p. 182.

156. And sometimes they butchered the: Gookin, *Historical Collections of the Indians in New England*, II, p. 19.

157. The English plantations in Rhode: Bartlett, *Colonial Records of Rhode Island*, I, pp. 412-413.

157. Similarly, the Connecticut Colony: Trumbull, *The Public Records of the Colony of Connecticut*, I, p. 18.

157. The Rhode Island settlements "ordered": Bartlett, *Colonial Records of Rhode Island*, I, p. 117.

158. Connecticut Colony held the: Trumbull, *The Public Records of the Colony of Connecticut*, I, pp. 303-304.

158. A Wampanoag tribesman named: Nathaniel B. Shurtleff, *Records of the Colony of New Plymouth*, (From the Press of William White, 1855), IV, p. 112.

158. In another case, Plymouth: Shurtleff, *Records of the Colony of New Plymouth*, IV, p. 22.

158. A few years after this incident: Shurtleff, *Records of the Colony of New Plymouth*, IV, p. 167.

159. The Massachusetts court ordered: Shurtleff, *Records of Massachusetts*, I, p. 297.

159. In another court case that: Shurtleff, *Records of the Colony of New Plymouth*, III, p. 138.

159. On another occasion, five: Shurtleff, *Records of the Colony of New Plymouth.*, IV, p. 51.

159. In 1658, Plymouth authorities: Shurtleff, *Records of the Colony of New Plymouth.*, III, pp. 133-134.

160. In Rhode Island, an imprisoned: Bartlett, *Colonial Records of Rhode Island*, II, p. 509.

160. In 1669, the Connecticut Colony: Trumbull, *The Public Records of the Colony of Connecticut*, II, p. 117.

161. Miantonomo gathered about a thousand: William Hubbard, *History of the Indian Wars in New England*, 2 vols. (Kraus Reprint Company, New York, New York, 1969), I, pp. 39-43. William Hubbard served as the Congregational minister in Ipswich, Massachusetts from 1658 -1702. A proponent of moderation in the Bay Colony, Hubbard opposed the witchcraft trials supported by Increase and Cotton Mather. His *A Narrative of the Troubles with the Indians* was published a year after King Philip's War ended. A popular narrative of the war in colonial times, historians still consider Hubbard's work to be a reliable source. William Hubbard died in 1704 at the age of 83.

162. In August, 1645, both sides agreed: Bradford, *Of Plymouth Plantation*, ed. Samuel Morrison, XII, p. 437.

164. Soon afterwards, Sequasson: Trumbull, *The Public Records of the Colony of Connecticut*, I, pp. 303 - 306.

165. The Massachusetts magistrates informed: Shurtleff, *Records of Massachusetts*, IV, p. 437.

166. When the Wabaquasset Nipmucks: Shurtleff, *Records of Massachusetts*, IV, p. 378, p. 386.

167. Similarly, the Pennacook tribal: Solon B. Colby, *Colby's Indian History: Antiquities of the New Hampshire Indians and their Neighbors*, (Walker's Pond Press, Center Conway, New Hampshire, 1975), VII, pp. 86-87. Colby's publication is a curious collection of history, archaeology, legends and colonial folktales on the Algonkian tribes of colonial New Hampshire. Particular emphasis is placed on the Abenaki, Pennacook and Sokoki tribal groups.

168. The Narragansett chieftans declared: Gardener, *Gardener's Pequot Warres*, pp. 25-26.

Chapter 5: "As High As The Sun Is Above The Earth"

169. The Mohawk War (1664-1671) began: E. M. Ruttenber, *History of the Indian Tribes of the Hudson's River*, (Kennikat Press, Port Washington, New York, reprint of 1971), VI, pp. 120-157.

169. The Pocumtuck nation on the: Richard I. Melvoin, *New England Outpost: War and Society in Colonial Deerfield*, (W.W. Norton and Company, New York, New York, 1989), I, pp. 43-45. In his focused study of the New England frontier outpost of Deerfield, Massachusetts, Melvoin presents some intriguing insights on the role of the Mohawks in both the Mohawk War and King Philip's War.

170. The delay was to their advantage,: E. B. O'Callaghan, ed. *Documents Relative to the Colonial History of the State of New York*, 15 vols. (Weed, Parsons and Company, Printers, Albany, New York, 1854), III, pp. 67-68.

170. Each of these warriors had a gun: Gookin, *Historical Collections of the Indians in New England*, (Towtaid, 1970), p. 37.

170. Their imprisonment created a stir: Gookin, *Historical Collections of the Indians in New England*, pp. 38-39.

171. In fact, the Mohawks destroyed: John C. Huden, *Archaeology in Vermont*, (Charles E. Tuttle Company, Rutland, Vermont), p. 43.

171. Ten years after this conflict: Shurtleff, ed. *Records of Massachusetts*, V, p. 320.

171. They also pointed out that the: Gookin, "Historical Collections of the Indians in New England" in *Massachusetts Historical Collections*, I, p. 165.

172. Some of the native people in the: Gookin, "Historical Collections of the Indians in New England" in *Massachusetts Historical Collections*, I, p. 162.

172. In 1669, the Abenaki, Pennacook and Sokoki: John Eliot, "Eliot's Brief Narrative of July 20, 1670" in *Old South Leaflets*, I, pp. 3-8.

172. This was the last campaign: Gookin, "Historical Collections of the Indians in New England" in *Massachusetts Historical Collections*, I, pp. 166-167.

173. The English found Alexander and: Hubbard, *History of the Indian Wars in New England*, I, pp. 50-51.

174. In April, 1671, King Philip was: Hubbard, *History of the Indian Wars in New England.*, I, pp. 54-55.

174. The condescending manner of the: Allan Forbes, *Other Indian Events of New England*, (Walton Advertising and Printing Company, Boston, Massachusetts, 1941), pp. 47-48.

174. Many Algonkian tribesmen were: Charles Lincoln, ed. *Narratives of the Indian Wars*, (Barnes and Noble, Inc., New York, New York, reprint of 1966), p. 59.

176. To curtail the Wampanoags from: Sydney V. James, *Colonial Rhode Island*, (Charles Scribner's Sons, New York, New York, 1975), V, pp 75-93.

176. Tobias and Mattashunnamo: Mather, *Magnalia Christi Americana*, II, pp.559-560.

176. About this same time Peter Nunnuit: Thomas Church, *The History of the Great Indian War of 1675 and 1676 Commonly Called King Philip's War, also the Old French and Indian Wars, from 1689 to 1704*, Notes and Appendix by Samuel Drake, (H. Dayton, New York, New York), p. 27. Thomas Church (1673-1748), was the first of fourteen children born to the popular Captain Benjamin Church, an officer in the Plymouth militia during King Philip's War. He based his work from memoranda kept by his father. Published in 1712, "Entertaining Passages Relating to Philip's War" not only chronicles Captain Benjamin Church's military exploits against King Philip, but also includes his "Expedition More Lately Made Against the Common Enemy, and Indian Rebels in the Eastern Parts

of New England." Thomas Church's writing style is dramatic with its scenes of military marches in pursuit of Philip's warriors, hand-to- hand combat and face-to-face encounters with several famous Algonkian leaders. The book became an instant best seller.

177. King Philip sent no response: David Pulsifer, ed. *Records of the Colony of Plymouth*, 12 vols. (Press of William White, Boston, Massachusetts 1855-1861), X, pp. 362-365.

177. In the spring of 1675,: Church, *The History of the Great Indian War of 1675 and 1676 Commonly Called King Philip's War, also the Old French and Indian Wars, from 1689 to 1704*, Notes and Appendix by Samuel Drake, pp. 20-26.

178. A week before hostilities: Lincoln, ed. *Narratives f the Indian Wars*, pp. 7-17.

178. On June 25, the Wampanoags: Pulsifer, *Records of the Colony of Plymouth*, pp. 362-365.

179. These warriors "possessed themselves": Church, *The History of the Great Indian War of 1675 and 1676 Commonly Called King Philip's War, also the Old French and Indian Wars, from 1689 to 1704*, Notes and Appendix by Samuel Drake, pp. 43-44.

179. Earlier, before any hostilities began: Lincoln, ed. *Narratives of the Indian Wars*, pp. 12-13.

179. The Narragansetts were ordered to: Hubbard, *History of the Indian Wars in New England*, I, pp. 76-77.

180. Most of these women and children: Lincoln, *Narratives of the Indian Wars*, p. 30.

181. The Nipmucks had promised to: Hubbard, *History of the Indian Wars in New England*, I, pp. 98-101.

182. Hubbard described this disaster as the: Hubbard, *History of the Indian Wars in New England*, I, pp. 113-119.

182. Treat marched from Westfield: Mather, *Magnalia Christi Americana*, II, pp. 565-566.

183. The Massachusetts Governor and: Colby, *Colby's Indian History: Antiquities of the New Hampshire Indians and their Neighbors*, VIII, pp. 95-98.

184. First of all, they claimed,: Douglas Leach, ed. *A Rhode Islander Reports on King Philip's War: The Second William Harris Letter of August, 1676*, (Roger Williams Press, East Providence, Rhode Island, 1963), pp. 23-26.

185. If this was insufficient evidence,: Trumbull,ed. *The Public Records of the Colony of Connecticut*, II, pp. 355-356.

185. Though the Narragansetts delivered: Leach, ed. *A Rhode Islander Reports on King Philip's War: The Second William Harris Letter of August, 1676*, p. 27.

185. Captains Mosely, Johnson, Mason and: Hubbard, *History of the Indian Wars in New England*, I, pp. 135-139.

186. William Harris later writes: Leach, *A Rhode Islander Reports on King Philip's War: The Second William Harris Letter of August, 1676*, pp. 37-39.

186. Just before they entered Nipmuck: Hubbard, *History of the Indian Wars in New England*, I, pp. 155-165.

187. As Pierce led his forces down: Hubbard, *History of the Indian Wars in New England*, I, pp. 173-178.

187. "It was sufficient matter of rejoicing": Hubbard, *History of the Indian Wars in New England*, I, pp. 183.

188. Due to their increasingly desperate: Rowlandson, *The Narrative of the Captivity and Restoration of Mrs. Mary Rowlandson*, p. 68.

188. On May 18, 1676, Captain Holyoke: Hubbard, *History of the Indian Wars in New England*, I, pp. 230-231.

189. According to a suspect account: Mather, *Magnalia Christi Americana*, II, p. 573.

189. The Mohawks pursued them across: Lincoln, ed. *Narratives of the Indian Wars*, p. 97.

190. Rowlandson writes, they "were": Rowlandson, *The Narrative of the Captivity and Restoration of Mrs. Mary Rowlandson*, p. 42.

190. William Harris describes the sudden: Leach, *A Rhode Islander Reports on King Philip's War: The Second William Harris Letter of August, 1676*, p. 75.

191. On the night of his: Thomas Church, *The History of the Great Indian War of 1675 and 1676 Commonly Called King Philip's War, also the Old French and Indian Wars, from 1689 to 1704*, Notes and Appendix by Samuel Drake, pp. 141-142.

192. Over two thousand English: Gary B. Nash, *Red, White and Black: The Peoples of Early America*, (Prentice-Hall, Inc., Englewood Cliffs, New Jersey, 1974), p. 126.

192. In September, 1677, a mixed band: Melvoin, *New England Outpost: War and Society in Colonial Deerfield*, pp. 124-128.

193. In fact, according to Edward Rawson: Shurtleff, *Records of Massachusetts*, V, p. 126.

193. At the Philips garrison the Philips: Drake, *The Book of the Indians*, VIII, p. 103.

194. The initial response of the English to: Jeremy Belknap, *History of New Hampshire*, 2 vols. (Johnson Reprint Corporation, New York, New York, 1970), I, pp. 71-73.

194. Major General Denison, commander: Belknap, *History of New Hampshire*, I, pp. 73-77.

195. In September, an expedition of two: Belknap, *History of New Hampshire*, I, pp. 74-77.

195. Mogg claimed a hundred tribesmen: Belknap, *History of New Hampshire*, I, pp. 77-79.

195. Since Mogg was surety for the: Belknap, *History of New Hampshire*, I, pp. 78-79.

196. Two of those who fled reported: Belknap, *History of New Hampshire*, I, p. 80.

196. And so it proved true, for between: Pulsifer, *Records of the Colony of Plymouth*, X, p. 390.

196. Fifty English soldiers and ten Natick: Belknap, *History of New Hampshire*, I, p. 81.

197. The Massachusetts colonial government: Belknap, *History of New Hampshire*,.I, p. 82.

197. In the spring of 1678, Major Shapleigh: Belknap, *History of New Hampshire*, I, pp. 82-83.

197. As the decade drew to a close: O'Callaghan, *Documents Relative to the Colonial History of the State of New York*, IX, p. 795.

198. The Mohawks handed a wampum: Shurtleff, *Records of Massachusetts*, V, pp. 319-320.

198. "The Indians called Christians feigning": Leach, *A Rhode Islander Reports on King Philip's War: The Second William Harris Letter of August, 1676*, p. 67.

199. On their arrival in the harbor some: Allan Forbes, *Other Indian Events of New England*, (Walton Advertising and Printing Company, Boston, Massachusetts, 1941), pp. 57-64.

199. The Massachusetts Court "ordered": Shurtleff, *Records of Massachusetts*, V, p. 64. Most of the Praying Indian residents of Hassanamesit and Wamesit were never interned at Deer Island. This was because the lives of these Praying Indians were disrupted by King Philip's War. Hassanamesit was overrun by Algonkian forces allied with King Philip in November, 1675. Two hundred residents were led off by these warriors, and some later chose to take up the cause of the Wampanoag sachem. Likewise, to the north the Wamesits were forced to abandon their village due to harassment from their English neighbors. Most of the Wamesits retreated into northern New England, where they joined up with their sachem Wannalancit.

199. Despite the order of the Court: Shurtleff, *Records of Massachusetts*, V, p. 64.

199. During the following year after: George M. Bodge, *Soldiers in King Philip's War*, (Genealogical Publishing Company, Baltimore, Maryland, 1967), XVII, pp. 403-404.

200. In all, the Natick "Praying Indians": Bodge, *Soldiers in King Philip's War*, XVII, p. 404.

200. As the declining "Praying Indian": Daniel Mandell, "To Live More Like My Christian English Neighbors: Natick Indians in the Eighteenth Century" in *The William and Mary Quarterly*, (Published by the Institute of Early American History and Culture, Williamsburg, Virginia, 1991), Vol. XLVIII, p. 564.

200. Fifteen years later, the"Praying Indian": *Acts and Resolves of the Province of Massachusetts Bay 1715-1716*, (Wright and Potter Printing Company, State Printers, Boston, Massachusetts, 1892), IX, p. 402.

201. By 1680, some forty families had: Samuel A. Green, *Groton Historical Series*, 5 vols. (University Press, Cambridge, Massachusetts, 1890), II, pp. 125-136.

201. Most of Dunstable's former residents: Elias Nason, *A History of the Town of Dunstable, Massachusetts*, (Alfred Mudge and Sons, Boston, Massachusetts, 1792), II.

201. Among the coastal New Hampshire: Belknap, *History of New Hampshire*, V, p. 145.

203. Consequently, in the spring of 1688,: Belknap, *History of New Hampshire*, I, pp. 124-125.

204. Some were willing to settle along: Samuel Penhallow, *The History of the Wars of New England with the Eastern Indians*, (Kraus Reprint Corporation, New York, New York), p. 17.

204. Penhallow admits some of these: Penhallow, *The History of the Wars of New England with the Eastern Indians*, p. 15.

205. A letter from Richard Waldron dated: Nathaniel Bouton, ed. *State Papers of New Hampshire*, 10 vols. (John B. Clarke, State Printer, Manchester, New Hampshire, 1868), II, pp. 50-51. Fear of the local northern Algonkian tribes in some frontier towns was practically non-existent just prior to the outbreak of King William's War. Dover, New Hampshire was such an example. Squaws were often allowed to apply "at each garrison house for liberty to sleep in them: this was done in time of peace, and they were readily admitted into Waldron's, Heard's, the elder Coffin's, and Otis's at their own request, they were shown how to open the doors and gates, in case they wished to leave the house in the night." It was these very squaws, who opened the gates to the warriors in the assault of June 28, 1689. See *New Hampshire State Papers*, II, p. 49.

206. A minority of soldiers that defended: Penhallow, *The History of the Wars of New England with the Eastern Indians*, p. 26.

206. Captain Henchman wrote to the council: "Captain Thomas Henchman's Pennacook Spies" in *Massachusetts Archives*, Vol. 107, p. 139.

206. Ironically the council had sent a: Bouton, ed. *State Papers of New Hampshire*, II, p. 49. There were those in New England, who derided the Pennacooks' competency as spies. Reflecting on this ridicule in his letter to the Governor's Council in Boston, Captain Henchman states, "Sir I was very loth to trouble you and expose myself to the censure and derision of some of the confident people, that would pretend to make sport with what I send down by Captain Tom (alias Thomas Ukqucakussennum)." One can assume that the council was more attentive to Pennacook observations concerning the French and their northern Algonkian allies after the attack on Dover.

207. The attacks on the Piscataqua: Belknap, *History of New Hampshire*, I, pp. 144-145.

208. Church consented to their "being": Church, *The History of the Great Indian war of 1675 and 1676 Commonly Called King Philip's War, also the Old French and Indian Wars, from 1689 to 1704*, pp. 177-206.

209. On July 23, 1689, the residents: "Dunstable Petition of July 23, 1689" in *Massachusetts Archives*, Vol. 107, p. 230.

209. A petition from Groton in 1694: "Groton Petition of 1694" in *Massachusetts Archives*, Vol. 113, p. 89.

209. Even the more secure settlement of: "Chelmsford Petition" in *Massachusetts Archives*, Vol. 70, p. 358.

210. Some English captives enroute to: Samuel Drake, ed. *Indian Captivities*, (Boston: Antiquarian Bookstore and Institute, 56 Cornhill, Boston, Massachusetts, 1839), p. 61. Drake's work is an informative compilation of some well known and not so well known New England captivity stories from both King Philip's War and the French and Indian Wars.

210. "I have heard of two specimens of an: Belknap, *History of New Hampshire*, II, p. 67.

211. Quintin Stockwell and other captives: Drake, ed. *Indian Captivities*, p. 62.

211. Likewise, when the young John Gyles: Drake, ed. *Indian Captivities*, p. 81.

211. "A captive among the Indians": Drake, ed. *Indian Captivities*, p. 78.

212. During the dance the tribespeople: Drake, ed. *Indian Captivities*, p. 84.

212. Silas and Timothy Rice of Westborough,: Charles Hudson, *History of the Town of Marlborough*, (Press of T.R. Marvin and Son, 42 Congress St., 1862), IV, pp. 105-106.

212. Oughtsorongaughton returned to: Kristina Nilson Allen, *On the Beaten Path: Westborough, Massachusetts*, (Published by Westborough Civic Club and Westborough Historical Society, 1984), pp. 12-14.

213. Gyles who was an unadopted tribal: Drake, ed. *Indian Captivities*, pp. 96-97.

213. Sachems from the Penobscot,: Penhallow, *The History of the Wars of New England with the Eastern Indians*, p. 16.

214. According to Penhallow, by 1705: Penhallow, *The History of the Wars of New England with the Eastern Indians*, pp. 38-39.

214. One of the more devestating raids: Williams, *Redeemed Captive Returning to Zion*, p. 14.

214. To further secure these towns the: Charles J. Hoadly, *The Public Records of the Colony of Connecticut*, 15 vols. (Johnson Reprint Corporation, New York, New York, 1968), Vol. VI, pp. 464-465.

215. On July 13, 1713, delegates from the: Penhallow, *The History of the Wars of New England with the Eastern Indians*, pp. 77-82.

215. In August, 1717, the English and Abenaki: Penhallow, *The History of the Wars of New England with the Eastern Indians*, pp. 83-86.

216. While the English denied the charge: Penhallow, *The History of the Wars of New England with the Eastern Indians*, pp. 116-117.

216. Towards the close of Queen Anne's War: Penhallow, *The History of the Wars of New England with the Eastern Indians*, pp. 49-50, p. 67.

217. At this time, the Norridgewock tribe: O'Callaghan, *Documents Relative to the Colonial History of the State of New York*, IX, pp. 937-938.

217. Before leaving, Baker ordered his: Penhallow, *The History of the Wars of New England with the Eastern Indians*, p. 88.

217. "The charge of the war was by this": Penhallow, *The History of the Wars of New England with the Eastern Indians*, p. 48.

218. On his fourth expedition he and: Penhallow, *The History of the Wars of New England with the Eastern Indians*, pp. 109-113.

218. When they returned to the English: Penhallow, *The History of the Wars of New England with the Eastern Indians*, p. 115.

219. Nontheless, Penhallow says that: Penhallow, *The History of the Wars of New England with the Eastern Indians*, p. 124.

220. He writes: "In the latter part of": Drake, ed. *Indian Captivities*, pp. 90-91. One of the most fascinating captivity stories edited by Samuel Drake is that of John Gyles, who was taken prisoner by the Maliseet during King William's War. Gyles was released from his nearly six years of captivity in 1698, but he did not publish his captivity narrative until 1736. A popular narrative written in the literary tradition of captivity genre, Gyles' account contains some first hand observations of his Maliseet captors.

221. The family of John Fitch was taken: Drake ed. *Indian Captivities*, pp. 139-140.

221. English residents from the neighboring: D. Hamilton Hurd, *History of Middlesex County, Massachusetts*, 3 vols. (J.W. Lewis and Co., Philadelphia, 1890), I, pp. 307-308.

222. In September, 1759 Major Robert Rogers: Belknap, *History of New Hampshire*, I, pp. 319-320.

222. On October 16, 1780, three hundred: Ivah Dunklee, *The Burning of Royalton By the Indians*, (George H. Ellis Company, Printers, Boston, Massachusetts, 1906), pp.9-36.

223. Sixty years later the Penobscot tribe: O'Callaghan, *Documents Relative to the Colonial History of the State of New York*, VII, p. 582.

223. In fact, the Plymouth Court passed: Pulsifer, *Records of the Colony of New Plymouth in New England 1623-1682*, Part III, p. 254.

223. Between 1767 and 1802, the Mashpee: "Report of a Committee on the State of the Indians in Mashpee and Parts Adjacent in1767" in *Massachusetts Historical Collections*, (Johnson Reprint Corporation, New York, New York, reprint of 1968), III, pp. 12-17.

223. The combined Algonkian population: "The Number of Indians in Connecticut," in *Massachusetts Historical Collections*, (Johnson Reprint Corporation, New York, New York, 1968), Vol. III, pp. 117-119.

223. According to a census taken in 1754,: "Slaves in Massachusetts, 1754" in *Massachusetts Historical Collections*, (Johnson Reprint Corporation, New York, New York, 1968), Vol. III, pp. 95-97.

223. The Mohegans complained that two: Trumbull, *The Public Records of the Colony of Connecticut*, V, pp.420-421.

224. Soon afterwards, two Niantic men: Trumbull, *The Public Records of the Colony of Connecticut*, V, p. 518.

224. At the Quinnipiac reservation in: Richard G. Carlson, "The Quinnipiac Reservation: Land and Tribal Identity" in *Rooted Like the Ash Trees: New England Indians and the Land*, (Eagle Wing Press, Inc., Naugatuck, Connecticut, 1987), pp. 46-47.

Chapter 6: "The Mohegan Lands Should Forever Belong To The Mohegan Indians"

225. A sixteen year old Mohegan youth: William De Loss Love, *Samson Occom and the Christian Indians of New England*, (The Pilgrim Press, Boston, Massachusetts, 1899). De Loss Love's biography of Samson Occom is an invaluable source on the Mohegan pastor's missionary work among the Pequot-Mohegan and Montauk people of 18th century Connecticut and Long Island.

225. His eye condition prevented him: James A. Levernier and Douglas R. Wilmes, *American Writers Before 1800: A Biographical and Critical Dictionary*, (Greenwood Press, Westport, Connecticut, 1983), pp. 1098-1101.

226. He served as a schoolmaster and: Eleazar Wheelock, "Wheelock's Narrative (1762)" in *Old South Leaflets* 25 vols. (Burt Franklin, New York, New York), I, pp. 1-20.

226. Here, in 1751, Occom married: Dumas Malone, *Dictionary of American Biography*, (Charles Scribner's Sons, New York, New York, 1933), pp. 614-615.

226. "Now you see what difference": Samson Occom, *Samson Occom's Diary*, 3 vols. (Dartmouth College, Hanover, New Hampshire), I, p. 91.

227. In the sermon he emphasizes the: Samson Occom, *A Sermon Preached at the Execution of Moses Paul*, (Bennington: Printed for William Watson, 1780), pp. 2-15.

229. When the colony failed to: "Summary of the Case of the Respondents the Landholders, in the Mohegan Case vs. Governor and Colony of Connecticut and Others" in *Connecticut Archives*, Vol. II, p. 334.

231. In his "Summary of the Case of the": "Summary of the Case of the Respondents the Landholders, in the Mohegan Case vs. Governor and Colony of Connecticut and Others" in *Connecticut Archives*, Vol. II, p. 334.

231. The officials in the Connecticut: Henry Babcock, "Henry Babcock to William Pitkin" in *Collections of the Connecticut Historical Society*, (Published by the Connecticut Historical Society, Hartford, Connecticut, 1921), XIX, pp. 160-161.

231. In a letter to Richard Jackson dated: Thomas Fitch, "Thomas Fitch to Richard Jackson" in *Collections of the Connecticut Historical Society*,(Published by the Connecticut Historical Society, Hartford, Connecticut, 1921), XIX, pp. 273-276.

232. Occom was forced, in effect,: De Loss Love, *Samson Occom and the Christian Indians of New England*, IV.

232. Later in 1765, Occom accompanied: Allan Forbes, *Some Indian Events of New England*, (Walton Advertising and Printing Company, Boston, Massachusetts, 1934), pp. 48-58.

233. Hillhouse writes: "We attended the": "Mohegan Indian Disaffection Towards Connecticut Government Shown at the Funeral of Benjamin Uncas," in *Connecticut Archives*, Vol. II, p. 286.

234. In 1774, the English were still: "Samson Occom's Right to Be a Mohegan Indian is Questioned in 1774," in *Connecticut Archives*, Vol. II, 315.

234. John Tantaquidgeon, Noah Uncas,: "Occom Manages Affairs of the Tribe Especially the Distribution of Rents, October, 1774," in *Connecticut Archives*, Vol. II, p. 314.

235. For the next five years, Occom: Bowden, Henry W., *American Indians and Christian Missions: Studies in Cultural Conflict, (*The University of Chicago Press, Chicago, Illinois, 1981), p. 145.

236. Towards the close of the American: Kenneth Mynter, "Leaving New England: The Stockbridge Indians" in *Rooted Like the Ash Trees: New England Indians and the Land*, (Eagle Wing Press, Inc., Naugatuck, Connecticut, 1987), pp. 51-53.

236. The Oneida and "Brothertown Indians": "Mr. Kirkland's Answer to Queries, Respecting Indians," in *Massachusetts Historical Collections*, (Johnson Reprint Corporation, New York, New York, reprint of 1968), IV, pp. 67-74.

236. After several more relocations they: Bruce G. Trigger, *Handbook of North American Indians*, 15 vols. (Smithsonian Institution, Washington, D.C., 1978), XV, pp. 198-112.

236. "Sometime every summer," she writes: Lucy Larcom, *A New England Girlhood; Outlined from Memory,* (Boston: Houghton Mifflin, 1889), VIII, p. 165.

Glossary Of Tribal Names

Informative sources on the study of New England Algonkian tribal and place names are:

John C. Huden, *Indian Place Names of New England*, (Museum of the American Indian, Heye Foundation, 1962).

Fannie Hardy Eckstorm, *Indian Place Names of the Penobscot Valley and Maine Coast*, (University of Maine at Orono, Maine, 1974).

Lincoln N. Kinnicutt, *Indian Names of Places in Worcester County, Massachusetts*, (The Commonwealth Press, Worcester, Massachusetts, 1905).

R.A. Douglas-Lithgow, *Dictionary of American Indian Place and Proper Names in New England*, (The Salem Press Company, Salem, Massachusetts, 1909).

Carl Masthay, "New England Indian Place Names" in *Rooted Like the Ash Trees: New England Indians and the Land*, (Eagle Wing Press, Inc.,Naugatuck, Connecticut, 1987).

Bibliography

PRIMARY SOURCES

Bartlett, John.*Colonial Records of Rhode Island*. New York: AMS Press, 1968.

Bouton, Nathaniel. *State Papers of New Hampshire*.Boston: 1792.

Bowden, Henry W. and Ronda, James P. *John Eliot's Indian Dialogues: A Study in Cultural Interaction*. Westport, Connecticut: Greenwood Press, 1980.

Bradford, William. *Of Plymouth Plantation*. New York: Alfred A. Knopf, 1976.

Bradford, William, and Winslow, Edward. *Mourt's Relation*. New York: Garret Press, 1969.

Burrage, Henry. *Early English and French Voyages Chiefly from Hakluyt*. New York: Barnes and Noble,1959.

Church, Thomas. *The History of the Great Indian War of 1675 and 1676 Commonly Called King Philip's War, also the Old French and Indian Wars, from 1689 to 1704*. ed. Samuel Drake. New York: H. Dayton, [n.d.]

Drake, Samuel. ed. *Indian Captivities*. Boston: Antiquarian Bookstore and Institute,1839.

Gardener, Lion. *Gardener's Pequot Warres*. New York: Kraus Reprint, 1969.

Gookin, Daniel. *Historical Collections of the Indians in New England*. New York: Johnson Reprint, 1968.

Grant, W.L. *Voyages of Samuel De Champlain*. New York: Barnes and Noble,1967.

Hubbard, William. *History of the Indian Wars in New England*. New York: Kraus Reprint,1969.

Jameson, Franklin. *Narratives of New Netherlands 1609-1664*. New York: Barnes and Noble,1959.

Johnson, Edward. *Wonder-Working Providence of Sions Saviour in New England*. New York: Barnes and Noble, 1959.

Josselyn, John. *An Account of Two Voyages to New England, Made During the Years 1638, 1663*. Boston: William Veazie,1865.

Leach, Douglas. *A Rhode Islander Reports on King Philip's War: The.Second William Harris Letter of August, 1676*. East Providence, Rhode Island: Roger Williams Press, 1963.

Lechford, Thomas. *Plain Dealing or News from New England*. New York: Johnson Reprint, 1969.

Levermore, Charles. *Forerunners and Competitors of the Pilgrims and Puritans*. New York: The New England Society of Brooklyn, 1912.

Lincoln, Charles. *Narratives of the Indian Wars*. New York: Barnes and Noble, 1966.

Mather, Cotton. *Magnalia Christi Americana*. New York: Russell and Russell, 1852.

Morton, Thomas. *New England Canaan*. New York: Burt Franklin, 1967.

Occom, Samson. *A Sermon Preached at the Execution of Moses Paul*. Bennington, Vermont: William Watson, 1780.

Occom, Samson. *Samson Occom's Diary*. Hanover, New Hampshire: Dartmouth College, [n.d.].

Occom, Samson. *Ten Indian Remedies from Manuscript Notes on Herbs and Roots*. Edward Connery Lathem, 1954.

O'Callaghan, E.B. *Documents Relative to the Colonial History of the State of New York*. Albany, New York: Weed, Parsons, 1854.

Penhallow, Samuel. *The History of the Wars of New England with the Eastern Indians*. New York: Kraus Reprint,1969.

Rosier, James. *A True Relation of the Most Prosperous Voyage Made this Present Year 1605*. March of the America Facsimile Series, University Microfilms: 1966.

Rowlandson, Mary. *The History of the Captivity and Restoration of Mrs.Mary Rowlandson*. Meriden, Connecticut: Meriden Gravure,1953.

Shurtleff, Nathaniel. *Records of the Colony of Plymouth*. Boston: William White,1853.

Shurtleff, Nathaniel. *Records of Massachusetts*. Boston: William White, 1853.

Smith, John. *Travels and Works of Captain John Smith*. New York: Burt Franklin, [n.d.].

Steele, Zadock. *Burning of Royalton By the Indians*. Montpelier, Vermont: E. P. Walton, 1818.

Trumbull, J. *The Public Records of the Colony of Connecticut*. New York: Johnson Reprint, 1968.

Wheelwright, John. *Writings and Mercurius Americanus 1645*. New York: Burt Franklin, [n.d.].

White, John. *The Planters Plea*. William Iones, 1630.

Williams, John. *Redeemed Captive Returning to Zion*. Freeport, New York: Books for Libraries Press, 1970.

Williams, Roger. *A Key into the Language of America.* Detroit: Wayne State University, 1973.

Winship, George. *Sailors Narratives of Voyages along the New England Coast 1524-1624.* New York: Burt Franklin, [n.d.].

Winthrop, John. *Winthrop's Journal.* New York: Barnes and Noble, 1959.

Wood, William. *New Englands Prospect.* New York: Burt Franklin, 1967.

Wroth, Lawrence. *The Voyages of Giovanni da Verrazzano 1524-1528.* New Haven: Yale University Press, 1970.

Young, Alexander. *Chronicles of the First Planters of the Colony of Massachusetts Bay 1623-1636.* New York: DaCapo, 1970.

Young, Alexander. *Chronicles of the Pilgrim Fathers of the Colony of Plymouth.* New York: DaCapo, 1971.

SECONDARY SOURCES

Adams, Nathaniel. *Annals of Portsmouth.* Norris,1825.

Adams, William. *Indian Legends in Verse.* Concord, New Hampshire: W.B. Ranney, 1922.

Allen, Kristina Nilson. *On the Beaten Path: Westborough, Massachusetts.* Westborough, Massachusetts: Westborough Civic Club and Westborough Historical Society, 1984.

Bacon, Oliver. *A History of Natick.* Boston: Darmell and Moore,1856.

Belknap, Jeremy. *History of New Hampshire.* New York: Johnson Reprint, 1970.

Bell, Charles. *History of Exeter, New Hampshire.* 1818.

Bodge, George M. *Soldiers in King Philip's War.* Baltimore: Genealogical Publishing, 1967.

Bolton, Reginald. *Indian Life of Long ago in the City of New York.* Crown Publishers, [n.d.].

Bowden, Henry W. *American Indians and Christian Missions: Studies in Cultural Conflict.* Chicago: University of Chicago Press, 1981.

Cahill, Robert E. *New England's Mountain Madness.* Peabody, Massachusetts: Chandler-Smith Publishing House, 1989.

Calder, Isabel. *The New Haven Colony.* Archon Press, 1970.

Carlson, Richard G. *Rooted Like the Ash Trees: New England Indians and the Land.* Naugatuck, Connecticut: Eagle Wing Press, 1987.

Caulkins, Francis. *History of Norwich, Connecticut.* Hartford, Connecticut: Lockwood, 1866.

Chase, George. *History of Haverhill, Massachusetts.* 1861.

Clark, Charles. *The Eastern Frontier.* New York: Alfred A. Knopf, 1970.

Clark, George L. *A History of Connecticut.* New York: G.P. Putnam's Sons, 1914.

Colby, Solon B. *Colby's Indian History: Antiquities of the New Hampshire Indians and their Neighbors.* Center Conway, New Hampshire: Walker's Pond Press, 1975.

Cressy, David. *Coming Over: Migration and Communication Between England and New England in the Seventeenth Century.* New York: Cambridge University Press, 1987.

DeForest, John. *History of the Indians of Connecticut.* Hartford: William James Hammersley, 1852.

De Loss Love, W. *Samson Occom and the Christian Indians of New England.* Boston: Pilgrim Press, 1899.

Drake, Samuel G. *The Book of the Indians.* Boston: Antiquarian Bookstore, 1841.

Douglas-Lithgow, R.A. *Dictionary of American Indian Place and Proper Names in New England.* Salem, Massachusetts: Salem Press, 1909.

Douglas-Lithgow, R.A. *Nantucket: A History.* New York: Knickerbocker Press, 1914.

Dow, Joseph. *History of the Town of Hampton, New Hampshire,* [Salem, New Hampshire ?]: Salem Printing Co., 1893.

Dunklee, Ivah. *Burning of Royalton, Vermont By Indians.* Boston: George E. Ellis Co., 1906.

Eckstorm, Fannie Hardy. *Indian Place Names of the Penobscot Valley and Maine Coast.* Orono, Maine: University of Maine Press, 1974.

Forbes, Allan. *Other Indian Events of New England.* Boston: Walton Advertising and Printing, 1941.

Forbes, Allan. *Some Indian Events of New England.* Boston: Walton Advertising and Printing, 1934.

Gage, Thomas. *History of Rowley, Massachusetts.* Boston: Ferdinand Andrews, 1840.

Gille, Frank H. *Encyclopedia of Massachusetts.* New York: Somerset, 1984.

Green, Samuel, *Groton Historical Series.* University Press, Cambridge, Massachusetts 1890)

Griffin, S.G. *A History of the Town of Keene.* Keene, New Hampshire: Sentinel Printing Co., 1904.

Hazen, Henry. *History of Billerica, Massachusetts.* A. Williams Co., 1883.

Hodge, Frederick. *Handbook of American Indians.* New York: Rowman and Litchfield, 1965.

Huden, John C. *Archaeology in Vermont.* Rutland, Vermont: Charles E. Tuttle, 1971.

Huden, John C. *Indian Place Names of New England.* Museum of the American Indian, Heye Foundation, 1962.

Hudson, Charles. *History of the Town of Marlborough, Massachusetts.*Marlborough, Massachusetts: T.R. Marvin & Son, 1862.

Hurd, D. Hamilton. *History of Middlesex County, Massachusetts.* Philadelphia: J.W. Lewis, 1890.

Hutchinson, Thomas, *The History of the Colony and Province of Massachusetts Bay.* New York: Kraus Reprint, 1970.

James, Sydney. *Colonial Rhode Island.* New York: Charles Scribner's Sons, 1975.

Jennings, Francis. *The Invasion of America.* New York: W.W. Norton, 1976.

Kenton, Edna. *Jesuit Relations.* Vanguard Press, 1954.

Kinnicutt, Lincoln N. *Indian Names of Places in Worcester County, Massachusetts.* Worcester, Massachusetts: Commonwealth Press, 1905.

Leach, Douglas. *Flintlock and Tomahawk.* New York: MacMillan, 1959.

Leitch, Barbara. *A Concise Dictionary of Indian Tribes of North America.*Algonac, Michigan: Reference Publications, 1979.

Leland, Charles. *Algonquin Legends.* New York: Dover, 1992.

Levernier, James A. and Wilmes, Douglas R. *American Writers Before1800: A Biographical and Critical Dictionary.* Westport, Connecticut: Greenwood Press, 1983.

Malone, Dumas. *Dictionary of American Biography.* New York: Scribner's Sons, 1933.

Marvin, Abijah. *History of the Town of Lancaster, Massachusetts.* 1879.

Melvoin, Richard I. *New England Outpost: War and Society in Colonial Deerfield.* New York: W.W. Norton, 1989.

Merrill, Joseph. *History of Amesbury, Massachusetts.* Haverhill, Massachusetts: Franklin Stiles, 1850.

Molloy, Anne. *Wampum.* New York: Hasting House, 1977.

Nash, Gary. *Red, White and Black: The Peoples of Early America.* Englewood Cliffs, New Jersey: Prentice-Hall, 1974.

Nason, Elias. *History of the Town of Dunstable, Massachusetts.* Boston: Alfred Midge & Sons, 1877.

Palmer, Rose. *The North American Indians.* New York: Smithsonian Institution,1929.

Parsons, Langdon. *History of the Town of Rye, New Hampshire.* Rumford Printing Co., 1905.

Proctor, Mary. *The Indians of the Winnipesaukee and Pemigewasset Valleys.* Franklin, New Hampshire: Towne and Robie, 1930.

Quinn, David. *North American Discovery Circa 1000-1612.* Columbia, South Carolina: University of South Carolina Press, 1971.

Rivard, Jean-Jacques. *A Handbook of Indian Artifacts from Southern New England.* Attleboro, Massachusetts: Massachusetts Archaeological Society, 1976.

Russell, Howard S. *Indian New England Before the Mayflower.* Hanover, New Hampshire: University Press of New England, 1980.

Ruttenber, E.M. *History of the Indian Tribes of the Hudson's River.* Port Washington, New York: Kennikat Press, 1971.

Safford, Marion. *The Story of Colonial Lancaster.* Rutland, Vermont: Tuttle, 1937.

Scales, John. *History of Dover, New Hampshire.* 1923.

Simmons, William S. *Spirit of the New England Tribes: Indian History and Folklore 1620-1984.* Hanover, New Hampshire: University Press of New England, 1986.

Sullivan, James. *History of the District of Maine.* Boston: Thomas and Andrews, 1795.

Teg, William. *Almuchicoitt.* Boston: Christopher, 1950.

Thayer, Henry. *The Sagadahoc Colony.* Benjamin Blom, 1971.

The Wabanakis of Maine and the Maritimes. Bath, Maine: Prepared for and published by the Maine Indian Program of the New England Regional Office of the American Friends Service Committee, 1989.

Tilton, George. *History of Rehoboth, Massachusetts.* 1918.

Trelease, Allen. *Indian Affairs in Colonial New York: The Seventeenth Century.* Port Washington, New York: Kennikat, 1960.

Trigger, Bruce G. *Handbook of the North American Indian.* Washington, D.C.: Smithsonian Institution, 1978.
Trumbull, Benjamin. *A Complete History of Connecticut.* New York: Arno Press, 1972.
Vexler, Robert I. and Swindler, William F. *Chronology and Documentary Handbook of the State of Vermont.* Dobbs Ferry, New York: Oceana Publications, 1979.
Waters, William. *History of Chelmsford, Massachusetts.* Lowell, Massachusetts: Courier Printing, 1917.
Weeks, Alvin G. *Massasoit of the Wampanoags.* 1920.
Wilkie, Richard W. and Tager, Jack. *Historical Atlas of Massachusetts.* Amherst, Massachusetts: University of Massachusetts, 1991.
Willoughby, Charles. *Antiquities of the New England Indians with Notes on the Ancient Cultures of the Adjacent Territory.* New York: AMS Press Inc. for Peabody Museum of Archaeology and Ethnology, Harvard University, 1973.

Index

Cape Cod, 8-9, 73, 87, 93, 95, 98, 100-102, 109, 115-118, 127, 158, 176, 187, 223
Cape Cod Bay, 8, 100, 102, 127
Cape Elizabeth, Me., 207
Cape Neddick, Me., 200
Captives, 59-60, 211-212
Carolinas, 79, 107
Carrabasset, Me., 81
Casco Bay, 93, 137
Cascos, see Tribes
Caughnawaga, 172
Champlain, Samuel de, 16, 40, 56, 98-105
Champlain, Lake, 16
Champlain Valley, 32
Charles River, 10, 137, 153, 199
Charlestown, Ma., 136, 156
Charlestown, N.H., 222
Charlestown, R.I., 223, 234
Chauquaqock (Swords-men), 120
Chawmun, see Matachees
Checkatabutt, 11, 133, 156
Checktabutt, Josiah, 11, 25, 172
Checkesuwand, 45
Chelmsford, Ma., 138, 183-184, 187, 200-201, 206, 209, 216
Chementicook, Me., 80
Chemquassabamticook, Lake, 78
Chepachet, R.I., 81
Chesapeake Bay, 107
Chesuncook, Me., 80
Chilmark, Ma., 86
Chinquapin, 82
Chipmunk, 82
Chocorua, 89
Chunkey, 82, see also Algonkians
Church, Captain Benjamin, 84, 176-180, 191, 207-208, 216, 220
Coatuit Brook, 8
Cockaponset, R.I., 81

Coddington, William, 138
Cohasset, Ma., 78, 81, 116
Conbitant, 8, 53, 64, 76, 130-132
Concord, Ma., 11, 136
Concord, N.H., 13, 24, 183
Concord River, 13, 124, 137, see also Musketaquid
Coneconam, 83-84, 115, 125, 135
Connecticut, 78, 80-81
Connecticut Colony, 138-139, 142, 144-145, 152, 156-158, 160, 164, 185, 218, 224, 230-233
Connecticut River, 13, 16, 26, 28-29, 32, 69, 75, 110, 122, 136, 138-139, 141-142, 165, 181-182, 217
Contoocook, N.H., 80
Contuit Pond, 8
Cooper, Lieutenant, 182
Cooper, Thomas, 49, 86, 124
Coos, see Tribes
Coos County, N.H., 15
Cotton, John, 148
Cowassuck, 217
Cowwesets, see Tribes
Crow, 89
Crown Point, N.Y., 222
Cummaquids, see Matachees
Cupheags, see Tribes
Cushman, Robert, 50
Cutshamequin, 11, 57, 141, 145-146, 163
Cuttyhunk Island, 95-96

– D –
Damaris Cove, Me., 219
Danbury, Ct., 214
Dartmouth College, 232
Dartmouth, Ma., 179
"Dauphine," 93
Davenport, John, 139

Davenport, Rev. James, 225
Davies, Captain Robert, 107-109
Dedham, Ma., 185, 198
Deer, 67
Deer Island, 199
Deerfield, Ma., 13, 77, 138, 149, 181-182, 188, 192, 200, 206, 211, 214
DeForest, John, 145
DeGrey, William, 231
DeLaet, John, 110
DeMonts, Pierre Du Gua, 98-102, 106, 110
Denison, Captain, 187
Derby, Ct., 30
Dermer, Captain, 98, 118, 120-121
Dominion of New England, 203, 208
Dorchester, Ma., 136, 138
Dover, N.H., 136, 138, 194, 196, 200-201, 205-206, 214, 219
Druillettes, Father Gabriel, 115
Dudley, Governor, 213, 215
Dummer, Governor William, 215
Dummerston, Vt., 221
Dummer's War, see Lovewell's War
Dunstable, Ma., 137, 200-201, 206, 209, 214-216, 218, 220
Durham (Oyster River), N.H., 194, 200-201, 207
Durkee, Adan, 222
Dustin, Hannah, 149
Duxbury, Ma., 136, 173

– E –
Eastern Indians, 15, see also Tarrantines
Eastham, Ma., 127, 158, 173
Eaton, Theophilus, 139
Edwards, Rev. Jonathan, 225

Eliot, Rev. John, 79-80,
120, 146-148, 150-151,
153, 172-173, 183
Elizabeth Islands, 9, 95
Endicott, Captain John,
140-141, 156
Epenow, 116, 118, 125
Esopus, *see* Tribes
Essex County, Ma., 220
Ewanghos, 163
Exeter, N.H., 137-138, 194,
200-201, 214

– F –

Falmouth (Casco), Me.,
196-197, 201, 207,
213, 216, 219
Farmington, Ct., 214, 223-
224, 235
Fiske, Rev., 28
Fitch, James, 148
Fitch, John, 221
Fitch, Thomas, 231
Five Nations, *see* Iroquois
Flesche, Josse, 110
Fort Amsterdam, 169
Fowler, David, 227
Fowler, Mary, 226
Francis I, King of France,
92
French and Indian War
(1754-1763), 221
French and Indian Wars,
20, 31, 60, 70, 84, 115,
201-222

– G –

Gardener, Captain Lion,
141-142
Gay Head, Ma., 86
George III, King of
England, 231
Georgetown, Me., 215
Gibbons, Edward, 57
"Gift of God", 107
Gilbert du Thet, Father
114
Glooskap, 38, 87, 125
Gongequa, 13

Gookin, Daniel, 3-5, 10, 27,
55, 62-63, 69, 74, 80,
121, 147, 149-150,
154, 170, 183-184, 199
Gorges, Sir Ferdinando,
97-98, 116-117, 136
Gosnold, Bartholomew, 94-
96, 119
Governor and Council for
New England, 98, 136
Grafton, Ma., 147
Granby, Ct., 42
Great Lakes, 91-92
Great Swamp Fight, 186
Greenland, N.H. 220
Green Mountains, 30, 32
Griffin, Owen, 84
Groton, Ct., 145, 223-225,
234
Groton, Ma., 28, 80, 137,
187, 200-201, 207,
209, 214-215, 221
Guilford, Ct., 139
Gullona, *see* Thunderbird
Gyles, John, 36, 59, 84,
211-213, 220

– H –

Hackensacks, *see* Tribes
Hadarawansett, 13
Hadley, Ma., 138, 200
"Half Moon," 109
Halifax, Ma., 173
Halifax, Vt., 221
Hallam, Nicholas, 229
Hall, Henry, 224
Hall, Mary, 33
Hammonasset, Ct., 81
Hampton, N.H., 137-138,
194, 200
Hanover, N.H., 222
Harlow, Captain Edward,
115, 117
Harmon, Captain, 217
Harris, William, 186, 190,
198
Hartford, Ct., 13, 138-139,
142, 144, 161-162,
164, 168, 196, 200,
214
Harvey, William, 158

Hassanamissit, *see* Tribes
Hatfield, Ma., 138, 181-
182, 189, 192-193, 200
Hathorne, Captain
William, 192, 195
Haverhill, Ma., 138, 200,
207, 220
Hebron, Ct., 225
Henchmen, Captain
Thomas, 206
Herbal remedies, 40
Hiacoomes, 62
Higginson, John, 57
Hillhouse, William, 233
Hilton, Colonel, 216
Hinsdale, N.H., 221
Historic Period, 1, 71, 75,
119
Hobson, Captain, 116
Hobbamock
(Hobbamoqui), 39-
40, 42, 124
Hobbamock (Wampanoag
pniese), 48, 55-56, 83-
84, 130-134
Hobbamock Point, Me., 40
Holyoke, Captain, 188
Honabetha, 100
Hoosic River, 189
Hope, Mount (Montaup), 8
Hopkins, Stephen, 129-130
Horton, Lieutenant
Richard, 222
Housatonic River, 30, 81,
214
House, Colonel John, 222
Housetonucks, *see* Tribes
Hubbard, William, 26-29,
182, 187-188
Hubbub, 83, *see also*
Algonkians
Hudson, Henry, 109-110
Hudson River, 23, 29-30,
91, 110, 169
Hunt, Captain Thomas,
117-118
Hunting, Captain, 199
Hutchinson, Captain, 181
Hutchinson, Thomas, 80

273

275

Pemigewassets, *see* Tribes
Pendleton, Major, 197
Penetic, 114, *see also* Mount
   Desert Island
Penhallow, Samuel, 31,
   154, 204, 213-214,
   217, 219-220
Pennacook, 13, 32, 80,
   149, 183-184, 221
Pennacooks, *see* Tribes
Penobscot River, 16-17, 31,
   80, 88, 99, 109, 116,
   121, 201
Penobscots, *see* Tribes
Pentuckets, *see* Tribes
Pequakets, *see* Tribes
Pequannocks, *see* Tribes
Pequots, *see* Tribes
Pequot War, 4, 26, 139-
   145,155
Peskeompscut, 188
Pessacus, 163
Pettaquamscott, 186
Philips, Major, 193
Pierce, Captain, 187
Pike, Captain, 207
Pilgrims, 75-76, 98, 117-
   119, 124, 127-128,
   131-135
Pipsissewa, 82
Piscataqua River, 15, 31,
   56, 80, 136-138, 192,
   200
Piscataquas, *see* Tribes
Pistapaug, 81
Piumbukhuo, 151
Plague, *see* Smallpox
Plymouth Colony, 1, 7, 10,
   32, 50, 76, 105, 119,
   127-136, 148, 158-160,
   168, 173-174, 176-179,
   182, 185, 187-188,
   190, 207, 223
Plymouth Company, 107,
   136
Plymouth, England, 97
Plymouth, Ma., 8, 57, 66,
   76, 79, 124, 128, 192,
   see also Patuxet
Pnieses, 40, 48, 55, 132,
   191

Pocapawmet, *see* Tribes
Pocassets, *see* Tribes
Pocumtuck, 13
Pocumtucks, *see* Tribes
Podunks, *see* Tribes
Pohkenonpamitt, 159
Pokanokets, *see* Tribes
Pomeroy, Rev. Benjamin,
   225, 227
Pomham, 163
Ponagansett, R.I., 81
Popham, George, 107-109
Port Fortune, 105, *see also*
   Monomoy
Port Royal, Nova Scotia,
   101, 105-108, 110-114,
   119
Portsmouth (Little
   Harbor), N.H., 136,
   138, 196-197, 200,
   205, 207, 215, 220
Portsmouth, R.I., 138-139,
   157
Potatucks, *see* Tribes
Poutrincourt, Sieur de, 98,
   101-106, 110-113
Powhatan, 91
Powwows, 40-42, 55, 59, 84,
   134, 150, 152-153
Praying Indians, 33, 52, 67,
   123, 146-154, 160,
   170, 185, 187, 193,
   196-200
Prence, Governor, 173
Prentice, Captain, 186
Presumpscott River, 193
Princeton, Ma., 78
Pring, Martin, 70, 84, 96-
   97, 108
Providence Plantation, 7,
   187
Providence, R.I., 138-139
Provincetown, Ma., 9
Punkapoags, *see* Tribes
Puritans, 137-139, 149-151,
   160, 204
Putney, Vt., 221
Pynchon, Major John, 181-
   182, 196-198

– Q –
Quabaugs, *see* Tribes
Quabbin Reservoir, 28
Quadequina, 98, 128
Quahog, 82
Quantin, Father, 114
Quatchet, 38
Quatisicke, 76, 166-167
Quebec, 114-115, 149, 169,
   203, 211, 217, 222
Queconsicq, 107
Queen Anne's War, 213-
   215
Queens, N.Y., 30
Quenockross, 65
Quinebaugs, *see* Tribes
Quinnapin, 191
Quinnipiacs, *see* Tribes
Qunnekamuck, 84
Quonnipaug, 81

– R –
Raccoon, 82
Raliegh, Gilbert, 107-108
Ralle, Father Sebastian,
   217
Ralleau, Secretary, 106
Randolph, Vt., 222
Rawson, Edward, 193
Raynham, Ma., 122
Reading, Ma., 214
Recollect order, 114
Rehoboth, Ma., 159, 180,
   187
Repent, 159
Rhode Island, 81, 139, 154,
   157-158, 160, 176,
   178-180, 185, 190, 198
Rice, Silas, 212
Rice, Timothy, 212
Richards, Major, 196
Richardson, Captian
   Robert, 216
Richardson, Lieutenant
   James, 183-184, 197
Richmond, N.Y., 30
Ridgefield, Ct., 214
Rockaways, *see* Tribes
Rockingham, Vt., 221
Rocroft, Captain, 118
Rogers, Major Robert, 222

277